A Critique of the Methodology of
ANWAR AL-AWLAKI
and his Errors in the Fiqh of Jihād

A Critique of the Methodology of Anwar Al-'Awlaki
and his Errors in the Fiqh of Jihād

1st Edition © Jamiah Media 2011 C.E. / 1432 A.H.

ISBN: 978-0-9567281-4-2

All rights reserved. No part of this publication may be re-produced, photo-copied, scanned, stored or transmitted in any other shape or form without the prior permission of the copyright owners.

Published by:
Jamiah Media
London
Email: admin@salafimanhaj.com

In conjunction with:
Call to Islam
116 Bury Park Road
Luton LU1 1HE

Cover design & Typesetting:
Ihsaan Design
www.ihsaandesign.co.uk

Edited by Abū Fātimah Azhar Majothī

A Critique of the Methodology of
ANWAR AL-AWLAKI
and his Errors in the Fiqh of Jihād in Light of the Qur'ān, Sunnah and Classical to Contemporary Scholars of Ahl us-Sunnah

with points of benefit compiled from the works of:
Imām Abū 'Ubayd al-Qāsim ibn as-Sallām al-Azdī, 162-224 AH/774-836 CE
Imām, al-Mujtahid Ibn ul-Munāsif, 563-620 AH/1168-1223 CE
Shaykh ul-Islām Ibn Taymiyyah, 661-728 AH/1263-1328 CE
Ibn an-Nahhās (d. 814 AH/1411 CE)
Imām al-Albānī
Imām Muhammad bin Sālih al-'Uthaymīn
Shaykh 'Abdullāh bin 'AbdurRahmān al-Bassām
Al-'Allāmah, Sālih al-Fawzān
Shaykh, Dr 'Abdullāh al-Jarbū'
Shaykh Mashhūr Hasan Āl Salmān
Shaykh 'AbdulMālik ar-Ramadānī al-Jazā'irī
Shaykh, Dr Muhammad Bāzmūl
Shaykh, Dr 'AbdusSalām as-Sihaymī
Shaykh 'Abdul'Azeez bin Rayyis ar-Rayyis
Shaykh, Dr Abū Anas Hamād bin Ibrāhīm Āl 'Uthmān

By Abū Ameenah 'AbdurRahmān Sloan and 'AbdulHaq al-Ashantī

Forewords by Shaykh Muhammad al-Mālikī and Shaykh Jalāl Abualrub

Narrated 'Abdullāh Ibn 'Amr Ibn al-'Ās ﷺ:
"I heard Allāh's Messenger ﷺ saying: *"Allāh does not take away knowledge by taking it away from (the hearts of) the people, but He takes it away by the death of the scholars till when none of the (scholars) remains, people will take as their leaders ignorant people who when consulted will give their verdict without knowledge. So, they will go astray and will lead the people astray."*

- Sahīh al-Bukhārī

How many Muslims have been killed due to ignorant adventures which have angered the kuffār, who have been stronger than them in such instances, and have led to death, displacement and destruction, *la hawla wa la quwwata ilabillāh*! They also claim that such ventures are jihād when they are not jihād because the conditions of jihād have neither been met and nor have the pillars of jihād been achieved. Therefore, such ventures are not jihād rather they are transgressive actions which Allāh does not command to do.

- Al-'Allāmah Sālih al-Fawzān

CONTENTS

Foreword by Shaykh Muhammad al-Mālikī 8

Foreword by Shaykh Jālal Abualrub 13

Introductory Principles 19
    First Principle 19
    Second Principle 20
    Third Principle 20
    Fourth Principle 22
    Fifth Principle 25
    Sixth Principle 26
    Seventh Principle 33
    Eighth Principle 34
    Ninth Principle 35

Chapter 1: "Imām" Anwar bin Nāsir al-'Awlakī, His Methodological Background and Shifts 39

Chapter 2: 'Awlakī and his "Explanation" of the Book 'Constants on the Path of Jihad' by al-Qā'idah Member Yūsuf al-'Ayrī 47

Chapter 3: 'Awlakī Mocks the Da'wah of Tasfiyah and Tarbiyah, Hereby Mocking the Da'wah of Imām al-Albānī 67

Chapter 4: 'Awlakī Claims Jihād Does Not Need the Permission of A Leader 73

Chapter 5: 'Awlakī's Errors in the Fiqh of Jihād and his Opposition to the Classicial and Contemporary Scholars of Ahl us-Sunnah in Many Issues 85

Chapter 6: 'Awlakī Claims CNN and BBC Have Spread Islam Enough to Have Established the Hujjah on Humanity Today!? 93

Chapter 7: 'Awlakī's View on Leaving the Arena of Battle if the Muslims are Overwhelmed 100

Chapter 8: 'Awlakī says 'Iraq is "New Jihād Front for the Muslims"!? 106

Chapter 9: 'Awlakī Tries to make an Analogy Between the Martydom and Bravery of the Sahabah and the Contemporary Manifestation of Suicide Bombings: An Analysis 112
    The Martyrdom And Bravery of the Companions 113
    Analysis 119

Chapter 10: 'Awlakī Exhorts Others to Armed Jihad yet Does not do it Himself 137

Chapter 11: 'Awlakī Insinuates that Civilians can be Purposefully Targeted in Armed Combat 140
    Shaykh Abū Anas Hamād bin Ibrāhīm Āl 'Uthmān on the Prohibition of Transgression when Fighting 147
    The prohibition of killing women and children is muhkam and the Prophet never allowed it at all 158
    The use of manjanīq from Imām al-Mujtahid Ibn ul-Munāsif's (563-620 AH/1168-1223 AH) "Kitāb ul-Injād fī Abwāb il-Jihād" 162
    Shaykh 'AbdulMālik ar-Ramadānī al-Jazā'irī on using the hadīth in Abū Dāwud regarding the indiscriminate attack on the people of Tā'if with manjanīq 167

Chapter 12: 'Awlakī Claims that Imam Muhammad bin 'AbdulWahhāb gave his Bay'ah to the Ottoman Khalīfah in Istanbul!? 170

Chapter 13: Mockery of Usul? The "Maslahah and Mafsadah" in Fiqh of Jihād According to 'Awlakī 181

Chapter 14: 'Awlakī's Flagrant Disregard of the Covenants of Safety and Secuirity in Islam and his Praise of Major Nidal Hasan and the Fort Hood Shooting 189

Chapter 15: 'Awlakī's Praise of the Nigerian Youth Umar Farouk AbdulMutallab and the Northwest Airlines Flight 253 Attempted Plane Bombing 217

Chapter 16: 'Awlakī Insinuates that the UK and US is Dar ul-Harb and Therefore Muslims can Extract al-Fay' from These Lands, But Not Ghanīmah!!? 225

Chapter 17: Critique of Awlakī's 2011 'Fatwa' on 'The Ruling on Dispossessing the Disbeliever's Wealth in Dar ul-Harb' 238
    'Awlakīs' Tadlīs 244

Chapter 18: Conclusions Regarding Anwar al-'Awlakī 253

Jamiah Media Publications 259

بسم الله الرحمن الرحيم

FOREWORD BY
SHAYKH MUHAMMAD BIN 'ABDULLAH AL-MĀLIKĪ

[Imām of Masjid Barā' ibn Mālik in Jeddah, KSA and Student of the Muhaddith, Shaykh Muhammad 'Ali Ādam al-Ethiopī]

الحمد لله وحده، والصلاة والسلام على من لا نبي بعده ، أما بعـــد:

فقد اطلعت على دراسةٍ متأنيةٍ، مستفيضةٍ، في نقدِ وتفنيدِ منهجِ أحدِ غلاةِ الحزبيين التكفيريين في هذا العصر ألا وهو أنورُ العولقي والذي خرجَ على الناسِ بآراءَ شاذةٍ، وأفكارٍ منحرفةٍ بخصوصِ عبادةٍ عظيمةٍ تتطلبُ فقهاً جمّاً لمن أرادَ أن يخوضَ غمارَها، ويصبو إلى تثقيفِ الناسِ حيالَها، لكن في هذا الوقتِ الذي غابَ فيه أكثرُ الوعي، واندرسَ فيه أكثرُ العلمِ، واتخذَ الناسُ رؤوساً جُهَّالاً، خصوصاً الشبابُ منهم، وبالأخص الناطقين بغيرِ اللغةِ العربيةِ، إذ يحولُ هؤلاءِ الذين يَدَّعُون أنّهم دعاةٌ وهم لمّا يطلبوا العلمَ على أهلِه، أقولُ يحولُ هؤلاءِ بينَ العلمِ الذي هو النورُ الذي أنزلَهُ اللهُ للناسِ ، وكذلِكَ فهم يحولون بينه وبين الشبابَ منهم خاصةً، فيأتي مثلُ هذا الكتابِ الموسومِ بـ : [نقدِ منهجِ أنورِ العولقي وأخطاءِه في مسائلَ الجهادِ] كإغاثةٍ لهفانٍ لطُلابِ الحقِ، خصوصاً الناطقين منهم باللغةِ الانجليزيةِ، وقد جمعَ فيه مؤلفوه جمعاً

طيباً لأقوالِ عددٍ من أهلِ العلمِ في القديمِ والحديثِ في مسائلَ الجهادِ، وإني لأوصي بطباعةِ هذا الكتاب، ونشره خصوصاً بين فئةِ الشَّباب وبالأخصِ في بلادِ الغرب حيثُ لا يوجدُ علماءُ، والساحةُ خاليةٌ لمثلِ العولقي من الأدعياء للعبثِ بثوابتِ الدِّينِ، وبعقولِ المسلمينَ.

فجزى اللهُ الأخوةَ في مؤسسةِ [سلفي منهج دوت كوم]، وبالأخصِ منهم من عرفتُه بالعملِ الدءوب نُصرةً لهذا الدِّينِ؛ الأخُ عبدُالحقِ بنُ كوفي بنُ كوسي آل أشانتي، ففي كتاباتِه نَفَسٌ يُعرفُ منه الحِلمُ، والعلمُ، والصبرُ، والسبرُ، فجزاهم الله خيراً على هذا العملِ القيِّمِ، الدَّالِ على وعيٍ ناضجٍ، وعلمٍ جيدٍ، أسألُ اللهَ لهم مزيداً من التوفيقِ وصلى الله على نبينا محمدٍ، وعلى آله وصحبه أجمعين.

وكتبه
محمد بن عبدالله المالكي

[Translation]

All praise is due to Allāh alone and may prayers and peace be upon the one whom there is no prophet after him, to proceed:

I have read the detailed and extensive study critiquing and refuting the methodology of one of the fanatical partisan Takfīrīs of this era, Anwar al-'Awlakī, who has manifested his obscure views and unusual ideas to people in regards to a great act of worship which requires substantial understanding for whoever wants to delve into its midst and aspire to educate people about. However, during this time wherein much consciousness (of the dīn) is absent, and much knowledge has disappeared, people have taken ignorant people as their leaders. This is especially the case for young people, and more so for those who do not speak Arabic, as they turn to those who claim to be Du'āt [preachers] when they did not study with people of knowledge. I say: they obstruct between knowledge which is a light which Allāh revealed to the people and likewise, they particularly place themselves between knowledge and the youth.

In light of this, this book entitled *A Critique of the Methodology of Anwar al-'Awlakī and his Errors in Issues of Jihād* has come to quench the thirst of the seekers of truth, especially those who speak the English language. The authors have compiled good collections of statements from a number of scholars past and present in regards to jihād and thus I encourage this book to be published and distributed especially among the youth and more so the youth in the West wherein there are no 'Ulamā and the arena is left for the likes of al-'Awlakī to tamper with the constants of the religion and the Muslims' minds. May Allāh reward the brothers from salafimanhaj.com especially those of them whom I know work hard to aid this deen, such as the brother 'AbdulHaq bin Kofi bin Kwesi al-Ashantī, as his precious writings are known for forbearance, knowledge, patience and examination. May Allāh increase them in goodness for this valuable work which demonstrates mature awareness and good knowledge.

I ask Allāh to increase them in success and may prayers be upon our Prophet Muhammad, his family and all our companions.

Muhammad bin 'Abdullāh al-Mālikī
29 Shawwāl 1431 AH/October 8 2010 CE

FOREWORD BY SHAYKH JALĀL ABUALRUB

[Author, Translator and Ex-Afghan War Veteran]

The Khawārij said: "O Messenger of Allāh! Be just, because you have not been just!"

The Khawārij was the first sect to appear in Islām. They started their mission by disputing the decisions of the most righteous, wise and knowledgeable leader of all times, Prophet Muhammad ﷺ, the Last and Final Prophet and Messenger from Allāh. The first 'issue' they raised in their dispute with the perfect human leader, was money. They simply accused the Prophet of Allāh ﷺ, of not being fair in distributing the wealth among Muslims. Ever since, the Khawārij's slogans and methods, and their rudeness towards Muslim leaders and scholars, have not changed. If the first Khārijī was this rude and rebellious against the Prophet of Allāh ﷺ, then it is not surprising that successive Khawārij would maintain this demeanor with those who are less than the Prophet ﷺ.

The Khawārij desire power and fame and this is why they publically dispute with Muslim leaders and scholars. They also think that they, among all Muslims, have the inherit right to govern the affairs of Muslims since they are the only ones who understand jihād, aspects of war and peace, and Islām itself, so Muslims are made to believe. As for the Muslims who disagree with them, well, they simply are not Muslims. Consequently, their blood, property and honor are for the Khawārij to take, so the Khawārij take all that. This is simply the way of the Khawārij as proved by their statements and actions, as well as, the blood of Muslims that stains their hands every time a new Khārijī sect rises and mainly directs its viciousness at Muslims.

When one reads how the Prophet of Allāh ﷺ, described this deviant sect, one is amazed at different levels with regards to various aspects of the Khawārij psyche. How can anyone say, in the first sentence, "O, Messenger of Allāh," then follow it by the statement, "You haven't been just"[1]? The contradiction here is very clear and evident. This person admitted that Muhammad ﷺ, is the Messenger of Allāh, yet thought that he is incapable of being just and fair. Any way one may explain the statement of the first Khārijī, it is a terrible thing to think and say about Allāh and His Messenger ﷺ. The Khawārij still practice this evil behavior towards the Prophet's Sunnah, by often contradicting it and misinterpreting it to justify their deviation from it. Otherwise, how can a Muslim hear the Prophet's hadīth that one of the two most-wicked men is he who kills 'Ali ibn Abī Tālib,[2] his cousin, husband of his daughter, and the fourth best member of his Ummah? Yet, a Khārijī man would spend the night in prayer in preparation for the assassination of 'Ali the next morning? This person then kills 'Ali ibn Abī Tālib at dawn, while considering this action to be the best deed he has ever performed in Islām. Ignorance alone is not sufficient to describe this behavior. It is an inherit defect in the mind as well as in the methodology of the person who behaves in this dreadful manner.

How can a Muslim hear the Prophet's commandment not to kill women and children – in war, as Bukhārī and Muslim reported from 'Abdullāh ibn 'Umar, or his prohibiting directing attacks on places of worship of other religions[3], yet does exactly what the Prophet ﷺ has prohibited? How can one hear the Prophet's statement that Allāh will forbid Paradise for one who commits suicide (according to a hadīth collected by Bukhārī), yet, directs others, with great emphasis on the word 'others', to commit suicide in the name of both the religion that outlaws it and the Prophet ﷺ who prohibits it? Amazingly, those who

---

[1] Bukhārī & Muslim collected a hadīth in this meaning.
[2] *As-Silsilah as-Sahīhah*, vol.4, p.325.
[3] According to a hasan hadīth found in *At-Ta'liqat ar-Radhiyyah 'Ala ar-Raudhah an-Nadiyyah*, by Imām Siddīq Hasan Khān, with notes by Imām al-Albānī, vol. 3, p.450.

lure young Muslims into committing suicide in the name of the religion, by making this act appear to them as if it represents martyrdom itself, never commit this act themselves. They must think of themselves as being the brain, while young Muslims represent the muscle. The muscle can be replaced by another muscle, but the brain cannot be replaced, and so, they send others to their death while resting safely in their homes and mansions with their family and children.

Modern day Khawārij are not different from their ancestors. Only the methods are slightly different. For example, the Khawārij use of the word 'Jihād' to describe their actions has not changed ever since their ancestors called 'Jihād' what was ***not*** a war against the enemies of Islām, but a war against the Prophet's companions, the very generation that transferred Islām to them. This is a recurring aspect of the legacy of the Khawārij, in that they are not known by their jihād against the disbelievers, as Imām Ibn Taymiyyah stated, but by extreme acts of violence against fellow Muslims who disagree with them. Even when the Khawārij fight the disbelievers, the cause is usually unclear and the effect of their uncontrolled violence and viciousness is usually directed at Muslims, who suffer the most in the Khawārij supposed jihād. One can bring ample evidence to this fact, especially where Khawārij detonate themselves in the middle of a Muslim population to kill one or a few disbelieving soldiers, killing multitudes of Muslims in the process. As for victory, where is it? Muslims suffer far more after the Khawārij start their 'jihād' than before they start it, with no victory or end in sight, unless Allāh brings relief to the ummah in spite of the Khawārij efforts to cause mischief and bloodshed among Muslims.

The Khawārij way is a distinct methodology that has many aspects to it. As Imām Ibn Taymiyyah stated, the Khawārij are 'Qur'ānis' [followers only of what is in the Qur'ān and totally ignoring the Sunnah].[1] They have doubts about Allāh's wisdom, because they doubt the wisdom of His Prophet's Sunnah. This is clear from the conduct of

---

[1] Imām Ibn Taymiyyah, *Majmū' al-Fatāwā*, vol. 28, p. 295.

their ancestors, who disputed with every leader Muslims have had, including and starting with the Prophet of Allāh himself, the most righteous and just man ever.

Khawārij need justification for their actions to be able to recruit others for their cause and to secure more funds and popularity among the masses. Therefore, the Khawārij misinterpret the Qur'ān, and reject the parts of the Sunnah that do not agree with their deviant interpretation of the Qur'ān. They seek power, but know that Muslims will not follow them, unless they convince them that their leaders have exited from Islam since, the Khawārij assert, they do not rule by what Allāh has revealed. Their methodology is a deviation from the religion. However, they use the religion to justify their deviant behavior. One might say that today's rulers do not rule by what Allāh has revealed as they should, and therefore, what is the problem with calling them disbelievers? However, the Khawārij used the same method and slogans with the best generation to have ever been raised for mankind, the Prophet's companions, when they accused them of not ruling by what Allāh has revealed, and consequently, considered them as apostates from Islām. The Khawārij killed 'Uthmān ibn 'Affān and 'Ali ibn Abī Tālib, and tried to kill Mu'āwiyah. These three leaders ruled by what Allāh has revealed and will always be among the best, most righteous leaders mankind has ever known. Yet, the Khawārij called them disbelievers. Therefore, the defect is in the slogan and those who propagate it.

Among the characteristics of the Khawārij, is that when they propagate their ideas, they speak rapidly and aggressively, bombarding their audience with numerous statements in an effort to assert their ideas through quoting what seems to be supporting evidence that establishes their deviant methodology. This is the Khawārij way that concentrates on intimidation to scare opponents and confuse the ignorant. I often remind my audience that this is the clear manifestation of the Prophet's statement,

((الخوارج كلاب النار))

"The Khawārij are the dogs of the Hellfire."[1]

When someone approaches them, dogs bark aggressively and continually to intimidate any perceived threat. This is how the Khawārij behave in this life. In the Hereafter, they will be the dogs of the Hellfire, a punishment that befits their crimes.

The Khawārij also love to shed the blood of Muslims who do not agree with their deviations. To the Khawārij, one is a Muslim if one agrees with them, meaning, their particular sect. This is because the Khawārij have always divided into numerous sects and groups, each accusing the other Khawārij sects of being ignorant and disbelievers.

Even though it has become clear as daylight that the Khawārij accuse their opponents of exiting from Islām, the Khawārij try and seek financial and material support from Muslim masses. However, the Khawārij consider the very masses they seek their support of being disbelievers, because they do not rebel against their rulers who do not rule by what Allāh has revealed, so the Khawārij assert. What is more astounding is that many Muslims do give material and financial support to the Khawārij, even though the Khawārij generally consider them as apostates from Islām. Having gained support and funds from many ordinary uninformed Muslims, the Khawārij return the favor by committing acts of mass violence that cause tremendous mischief and cost Muslims dearly in life, security and property.

As stated, the Khawārij cause mischief and commit indiscriminate violence that touches Muslims in their lives and property. Currently they have also hijacked the true Islamic causes and the term 'Jihād', and brought no victory to Muslims, only military occupation and horrific losses and suffering. They also added a new dimension to their

---

[1] This hadīth was collected by Imāms Ahmad (18342) and at-Tirmidhī (2926); at-Tirmidhī graded it as authentic, from the Hasan grade; al-Albānī also graded it as authentic, from the *Sahih* grade, *Sahih al-Jami'*, no., 3347.

deviation from the true religion by using the word 'Salafiyyah' to describe their methodology, a methodology that is in direct contradiction to the way of the as-Salaf as-Sālih, the righteous ancestors of Muslims. The Khawārij and followers of as-Salaf are as different from each other as 'Uthmān and 'Ali are different from those who murdered them.

What does Anwar 'Awlakī have to do with all of this? I leave the answer to this important question to this critique of Anwar al-'Awlakī's methodology and errors, by my dear brothers, Abū Ameenah 'Abdur Rahmān Sloan and 'AbdulHaq al-Ashantī. I encourage everyone to read this book and to benefit from the clear evidence contained in it about a modern day Khārijī called 'Anwar al-'Awlakī. I ask Allāh to bless brothers Abū Ameenah and 'AbdulHaq, and to benefit Muslims from their knowledge. All the thanks and praises are due to Allāh, and may Allāh's peace, mercy and blessing be on His Prophet, Muhammad, and his household. May Allāh's mercy and pleasure be bestowed on Muhammad's companions and all those who follow their righteous guidance.

Jalāl Abualrub
Friday 29th April 2011 CE/26 Jumādā al-Ūlā 1432 AH
www.islamlife.com

INTRODUCTORY PRINCIPLES

Indeed, all praise is due to Allāh, we praise Him, we seek His aid, and we ask for His forgiveness. We seek refuge in Allāh from the evil of our actions and from the evil consequences of our actions. Whomever Allāh guides, there is none to misguide and whoever Allāh misguides there is none to guide. We bear witness that there is no god worthy of worship except Allāh and we bear witness that Muhammad is the servant and Messenger of Allāh.

First Principle

From the greatest features of those who preach for Allāh is calling to tawhīd in the way traversed by the Prophet ﷺ and all of the Prophets, as Allāh said:

﴿ وَلَقَدْ بَعَثْنَا فِى كُلِّ أُمَّةٍ رَّسُولاً أَنِ ٱعْبُدُواْ ٱللَّهَ وَٱجْتَنِبُواْ ٱلطَّٰغُوتَ ﴾

"And We certainly sent to every nation a Messenger, [saying], 'Worship Allāh and avoid Tāghūt.'" *{An-Nahl (16): 36}*

Allāh said to His Prophet Muhammad ﷺ:

﴿ قُلْ هَٰذِهِۦ سَبِيلِىٓ أَدْعُوٓاْ إِلَى ٱللَّهِ ﴾

"Say, 'This is my way; I invite to Allāh...'"
{Yūsuf (12): 108}

Meaning "*to tawhīd*" to singling out Allāh in worship,

Introductory Principles

﴿ قُلْ هَٰذِهِۦ سَبِيلِىٓ أَدْعُوٓاْ إِلَى ٱللَّهِ عَلَىٰ بَصِيرَةٍ أَنَا۠ وَمَنِ ٱتَّبَعَنِى وَسُبْحَٰنَ ٱللَّهِ وَمَآ أَنَا۠ مِنَ ٱلْمُشْرِكِينَ ﴾

"Say, 'This is my way; I invite to Allāh with insight, I and those who follow me. And exalted is Allāh; and I am not of those who associate others with Him.'" *{Yūsuf (12): 108}*

Thus, if you want to know a true caller from others, then look at his condition, and if he is concerned with Tawhīd, calls to Tawhīd and strives hard in that, then you will know that he is a true caller.

Second Principle

Mistakes are not all on the same level, there are errors in *ijtihād* wherein if a man makes *ijtihād* he is between one reward or two rewards. There are also errors wherein *ijtihād* within those matters are unacceptable as in the case of most of the errors in matters of belief. There are errors wherein if a man falls into them he is deemed sinful, errors wherein a man is deemed an innovator and errors wherein a man is to be deemed a disbeliever. For this reason, when you mention to some people that so and so has erred, they say *"there is no one except that he makes mistakes, and the Prophet judged that we are prone to error"* – this is correct; however errors are not all on the same level and all are taken to account based on the level of error committed.

Third Principle

The criteria for truth are that you look at a man's condition and assess: is his *da'wah* based on the Book of Allāh and the Sunnah of His Messenger ﷺ, and what the *Salaf us-Sālih* from the Sahābah, Tābi'īn and those who followed them, traversed or not? If so, then he is a caller to truth. An error with many ignorant people is that they think that the criteria of *da'wah* is that a man has a lot of followers or that those who attend his lessons and lectures are many, yet this is a huge misunderstanding. For the Prophet ﷺ stated, as reported in the Sahīh from the hadīth of Ibn 'Abbās ؓ: *"A Prophet will come on the Day of Judgement and he will have a man or two with him. Then another Prophet will come with a group of men with him, while another Prophet will come with a small group of followers. Then another Prophet will come with no followers with him whatsoever."* This is in regards to a Prophet, Allāh chose him to have this great status and yet with that he will come with no one with him; his *da'wah* is still successful without doubt because he is Prophet.

So the criteria of truth is not having many followers, rather from what the Prophet ﷺ informed of, is that, in the hadīth of Abū Hurayrah and Ibn 'Umar, and in the wording of Abū Hurayrah (as reported in Sahīh Muslim): The Messenger of Allāh ﷺ said: *"Islām began as something strange, and will return (to being) strange as it began, Tūbah is for the Ghurabā (strangers)."* Thus, the people of truth are a few yet this is not a proof of their *da'wah* being erroneous. Rather, when you read the Book of Allāh you will find that Allāh in many verses clarifies that the people of bātil are many and the people of truth are few. Allāh says,

﴿ وَلَقَدْ أَرْسَلْنَا نُوحًا وَإِبْرَٰهِيمَ وَجَعَلْنَا فِى ذُرِّيَّتِهِمَا ٱلنُّبُوَّةَ وَٱلْكِتَٰبَ فَمِنْهُم مُّهْتَدٍ وَكَثِيرٌ مِّنْهُمْ فَٰسِقُونَ ﴾

"...and among them is he who is guided, but many of them are defiantly disobedient." *{Hadīd (57): 26}*

And Allāh says,

﴿ وَإِن تُطِعْ أَكْثَرَ مَن فِى ٱلْأَرْضِ يُضِلُّوكَ عَن سَبِيلِ ٱللَّهِ إِن يَتَّبِعُونَ إِلَّا ٱلظَّنَّ وَإِنْ هُمْ إِلَّا يَخْرُصُونَ ﴾

"And if you obey most of those upon the earth, they will mislead you from the way of Allāh." *{Al-'An'ām (6): 116}*

Introductory Principles

Therefore, having many followers is neither the criteria for the truth nor is eloquence, articulacy or heroic speech. Many people see an eloquent man who is articulate, poetic and a strong speaker who *"says it as it is"* and think that he is on the truth due to that, and this is a mistake. Yes, eloquence, being articulate and bravery if used in order to support Allāh's dīn is sought-after; yet it is not the criteria for truth or *bāṭil*. This eloquence and articulacy has to be looked at to see: if it is being used to support the dīn or not. If it is being used to support Allāh's Book, the Sunnah of His Messenger ﷺ and the way of the first and foremost ones then bring this (eloquence)! But if it (such eloquence and articulacy) is being used in a way which opposes Allāh's *Shar'* then it is unacceptable.

Fourth Principle

There is a big difference between giving advice and *ghībah* (backbiting); many people do not differentiate between the two and many common people are confused about this. On the contrary, how many of those who want good have been blocked from good due to this? They say *"they are backbiting so-and-so"* and *"how can you read that when they are backbiting so-and-so?"* etc. It is therefore important for us to know that *naseehah* and *gheebah* can be interlinked and also distinguished from each other in important matters. As for the matter wherein they are connected, then this is in regards to mentioning something about a person that he dislikes, but advice is mentioning those things that a person dislikes out of giving advice and warning people from his error, as an advice to him initially and then an advice to the general public secondly.

As for *ghībah*, then it is not applied to matters related to the dīn, so if a man is mentioned for things that he dislikes without a religious benefit then this is *ghībah*. This is *ḥarām* as Allāh forbade it in His Book and so did the Messenger ﷺ as mentioned in his Sunnah. But if a clarification of a person's condition is in order to advise people and to warn them from his errors so that Allāh's creation is not misguided due to his statements then this is sought-after. Imām Ibn 'AbdulBarr stated: "The Sharī'ah has permitted speaking about a man in matters wherein there is a specific benefit such as in marriage."

As is found in the hadīth in Sahīh Muslim of Fātimah bint Qays wherein the Prophet ﷺ was asked by Fātimah about Abū Jahm and Mu'āwiyah and the Prophet said: *"As for Mu'āwiyah then he is poor and has no money, and as for Abū Jahm then his stick does not leave his side, marry Usāmah."* So pay attention: this is mentioning things about a man which he dislikes, but it is permissible as there is a benefit in mentioning that to the woman; so then what about a greater issue, such as the Ummah of Muhammad ﷺ? The error of the one who erred is to be clarified so that the error will neither be followed nor will people be misguided and oppose the *Sharī'ah* of Muhammad ibn 'Abdullāh ﷺ.

Imām Ahmad recorded in his *Musnad* (hadīth no. 21453) from the hadīth of Abū Dharr al-Ghifārī that the Prophet ﷺ advised him saying:

((وأمرني أن أقول بالحق وإن كان مرا))

"And He ordered me to say the truth even if it is bitter."

Look at the statement of the Tābi'ī Imām, Muhammad ibn Sīrīn, which is recorded in the *Muqaddimah* of Sahīh Muslim, vol.1, p.15:

إن هذا علم الدين، فانظر عمن تأخذون دينكم

This is the knowledge of your religion, so look to whom you take your religion from.

Imām Muslim also recorded in the *Muqaddimah* of his *Sahīh* (vol.1, p.15) that Muhammad ibn Sīrīn said:

لم يكونوا يسألون عن الإسناد فلما وقعت الفتنة قالوا سموا لنا رجالكم فينظر إلى أهل السنة فيؤخذ حديثهم وينظر إلى أهل البدع فلا يؤخذ حديثه

> They did not used to ask about the Isnād (chains of narration) but when the Fitnah arose they said, "Name us your men!" so they looked to Ahlus Sunnah and they took their narrations and they looked to the people of innovation and they did not take their narrations.

The Imām Abū 'Abdillāh Muhammad bin 'Abdillāh ﷺ, also well known as Ibn Abī Zamanayn, and is one of the top four most well-known scholars of the Madhhab of Imām Mālik, said:

ولم يـــزل أهل السنة يعيبون أهل الأهواء المضلة، وينهون عـــن مجالستهم، ويخوفون فتنتهم، ويخبرون بخلاقهم، ولا يرون ذلك غيبة لــــهم، ولا طعناً عليهم.

> And Ahlus Sunnah never ceases to expose the people of desires, the deviants. And they prohibit sitting with them, and fear their trials and narrate in opposition to them, and this is neither seen as backbiting them nor insulting them.[1]

Regardless of who is the speaker or caller, Ahlus Sunnah wal-Jamā'ah were firm upon this affair of exposing and criticizing the callers to falsehood and making clear this religion. Imām adh-Dhahabī ﷺ recorded in Volume 2 of his *Tadhkirat ul-Huffādh* that Imām Abū Dāwūd as-Sijistānī ﷺ said:

ابني عبد الله كذاب

> My son 'Abdullāh is a habitual liar.

---

[1] Reported in *Usūl as-Sunnah*, p. 293.

Al-Ḥāfidh Ibn Hajar al-'Asqalānī ﷺ mentioned in volume 11 of his *Tahdhīb at-Tahdhīb* under the biography of Yahya bin Abī Unaysah that Zayd ibn Abī Unaysah said about his brother:

أخي يحى يكذب وحجاج وأشعث وابن إسحاق كل هؤلاء أحب إلي من يحى.

My brother Yahya lies, and Hajjāj and Ash'ath and Ibn Ishāq, they are all more beloved to me than Yahya.

Fifth Principle

All are to be held accountable for their statements, Allāh says,

﴿مَّا يَلْفِظُ مِن قَوْلٍ إِلَّا لَدَيْهِ رَقِيبٌ عَتِيدٌ﴾

"Man does not utter any word except that with him is an observer prepared [to record]." *{Qāf (50): 18}*

This is regarding the one who speaks as no one else will be held accountable for his word; so what about if he was to speak to the masses? He speaks and addresses his words to all of them so he is accountable for his words. All of us are sought to refer to this, whether the words are in a lecture, class, "lesson", book, interview or whatever. When statements are highlighted which oppose the *Sharī'ah*, some people may say *"akhī this is a literary writer and they are vast in their speech,"* etc.[1] Yet the *Sharī'ah* does not differentiate between a literary writer, a poet, a speaker, a preacher or others! Rather, poets are censured because they say that which they do not do, Allāh says,

﴿وَٱلشُّعَرَآءُ يَتَّبِعُهُمُ ٱلْغَاوُونَ ۞ أَلَمْ تَرَ أَنَّهُمْ فِى كُلِّ وَادٍ يَهِيمُونَ ۞ وَأَنَّهُمْ يَقُولُونَ مَا لَا يَفْعَلُونَ﴾

---

[1] **Translator's note:** this is a common excuse which is made to defend Sayyid Qutb and some of his erroneous views within his *'tafsīr'*.

> "And the poets [only] the deviators follow them; do you not see that in every valley they roam and that they say what they do not do?" {Ash-Shu'arā' (26): 224-226}

Thus, everyone is accountable for their statements whether the person is a preacher, a speaker, a literary writer, a poet, a prose writer or whatever. Articulacy, literary skill, poetry or "saying it as it is" does not grant a person freedom to say whatever he likes, rather every statement that he makes he will be held accountable for. This is especially the case if many people are influenced by his words, for his sin will affect more than just him alone as is verified in Sahīh Muslim in the hadīth of Jareer ibn 'Abdillāh al-Bajalī that the Prophet said: *"Whoever starts a bad thing in Islam, and others do likewise after him, there will be written for him a burden of sin like that of those who followed him up until the Day of Judgement, without it detracting in the least from their burden."*[1]

Sixth Principle

In order to reject criticisms of people, some people say *"this speech (that you are refuting) is cut and out of context"* – this is sometimes suggested when a critique is forwarded. There are two aspects to this:

- Cutting and pasting which changes the meaning (of what was intended) and this is *dhulm* (oppression) and *kadhib* (lying) about which a person will be held accountable. And it is not permitted for anyone to follow the statement of a person about another person if it is solely based on statements which have been cut, taken out of context and have changed the meaning of what was intended by the speaker being critiqued.
- Cut statements which have further attestation and do not change the meaning.

---

[1] **Translator's note:** The hadīth is also reported by at-Tirmidhī, an-Nasā'ī and Ibn Mājah.

This is what the Imāms of Islām adhered to and you will see that if the Imāms refuted anyone they would make reference to further supporting evidences from the person's statements and then refute. If they also wanted to use as evidence Allāh's Book and the Sunnah of His Messenger ﷺ then they would use that which is relevant to what they were discussing. Furthermore, if cut speech does not change the meaning of the reality (of what was intended) then it has to be accepted. So if one wants to claim that certain speech is cut, taken out of context and has changed the meaning then he has to clarify and bring proof. Mere cutting of statements is not sufficient to refute.

Some people also say: *"your words about so-and-so are delving into his intentions"*. It can be said to this: that this is general, so if a man is refuted on account of what he said or wrote, is this deemed to be "speaking about the person's intentions" or a refutation of what the person himself manifested? How often it is heard, when a deviant person is refuted with clear speech and proofs, that this is *"speaking about his intentions"*? This is a mistake because his speech has to be looked into. If the speech criticising him is based on a statement that he said or an action that he did then it is not *"looking into a person's intentions"*.

Furthermore, the apparent and the internal are interconnected as mentioned in the *hadīth* of Nu'man ibn Bashīr ؓ in the *Sahīhayn*: that the Messenger of Allāh ﷺ said: *"There is a piece of flesh in the body, if it is sound then the whole body will be sound, but if it is corrupted then the whole body will be corrupted – indeed that piece of flesh is the heart."* Therefore, if a man said a statement and by his actions it is known that he wants something then the critique of him is based on his action – this is not considered to be speaking about a person's intentions. What is also used to divert speaking about a person who erred is to say: *"the person has served the deen"*. It can be said to this: *"Yes, the person may have served the deen; however at the same time he is also opposing the deen! And we are sought to stop him opposing the deen so that we will not be held accountable with Allāh, the Lord of the Worlds."* This is especially the case

Introductory Principles

as this is forbidding evil, and of the greatest characteristics of this Ummah of Muhammad is that it is an Ummah established on commanding the good and forbidding the evil. Allāh says,

﴿ كُنتُمْ خَيْرَ أُمَّةٍ أُخْرِجَتْ لِلنَّاسِ تَأْمُرُونَ بِٱلْمَعْرُوفِ وَتَنْهَوْنَ عَنِ ٱلْمُنكَرِ ﴾

"You are the best nation produced [as an example] for mankind. You enjoin what is right and forbid what is wrong…" *{Āli Imrān (3): 110}*

Forbidding the error of the one who makes a mistake and the one who destroys the dīn with his misguidance is a great reason for curses to be lifted from the Ummah of Muhammad ﷺ. Allāh says,

﴿ لُعِنَ ٱلَّذِينَ كَفَرُوا۟ مِنۢ بَنِىٓ إِسْرَٰٓءِيلَ عَلَىٰ لِسَانِ دَاوُۥدَ وَعِيسَى ٱبْنِ مَرْيَمَ ۚ ذَٰلِكَ بِمَا عَصَوا۟ وَّكَانُوا۟ يَعْتَدُونَ ۝ كَانُوا۟ لَا يَتَنَاهَوْنَ عَن مُّنكَرٍ فَعَلُوهُ ۚ لَبِئْسَ مَا كَانُوا۟ يَفْعَلُونَ ﴾

"Cursed were those who disbelieved among the Children of Israel by the tongue of David and of Jesus, the son of Mary. That was because they disobeyed and [habitually] transgressed. They used to not prevent one another from wrongdoing that they did. How wretched was that which they were doing." *{Al-Mā'idah (5): 78-79}*

Such forbiddance results in evil curses being lifted from the Ummah of Muhammad ﷺ. So it is wājib on the whole Ummah of Muhammad to support those who forbid the evil of doubts, innovations and misguidance. We ask Allāh, who there is no god except He, to make us from those who command the good and forbid the evil of desires and doubts.

How often is it stated when deflecting criticisms that *"the person has some good"*? Yes, the person may have some good, but we have to know that Allāh did not create evil solely, and there is not a creation except that it has some good in it. Imām Ibn ul-Qayyim G stated in his book *Shifā' al-'Alīl* that Allāh's creation are between good and that there are instances where evil is overpowered, and he mentioned this even in regards to Iblees as is found in his book *Madārij us-Sālikīn*. How many of the creation fall into disobedience due to Iblees and then make *tawbah*? How many of the creation disobey Allāh due to Iblees and then make *tawbah* and their condition after the *tawbah* becomes better than their condition before? So there is nothing from the creation of Allāh except that its good can overpower its evil.

Their statement and principle *"he has some good"* necessitates that even Iblees should not be refuted and this is *bātil* which Allāh has invalidated when He explained the misguidance of Iblees, and the Messenger of Allāh ﷺ also invalidated this by refuting the one who erred openly. A group of men came to the Prophet ﷺ as relayed in Sahīh Muslim in the *hadīth* of 'Adiyy ibn Hātim where a speaker of this group stood and spoke saying: *"Whoever obeys Allāh and the Messenger, then he is guided, and whoever disobeys the two of them, then he is misguided."* Do you find that the Messenger of Allāh ﷺ was over-courteous with him because he was with a visiting group and their representative speaker? No not at all! Rather, when the man's error was overt, the Messenger of Allāh ﷺ censured the error openly. The Messenger of Allāh said ﷺ: *"What a bad speaker you are! Instead say: 'And whoever disobeys Allāh and His Messenger'."*

As a result, Imām Abu'l-'Abbās Shaykh ul-Islām Ibn Taymiyyah mentioned in *Majmū' al-Fatāwā*, and as did Imām 'Abdul'Azīz bin Bāz ؒ, that: Whoever errs openly is to be corrected openly. It is not to be said *"Leave him and do not criticise him because he has good in him"* and the likes of such unacceptable objections. Also from such unacceptable objections are that some people say: *"His intention is good"*, in response to this it should be said: *"His intention could be good and he could desire good yet you have to know that acts of worship have to have two conditions: ikhlās, a sincere intention and (in) following of the Messenger of Allāh ﷺ."* Allāh says,

$$\lbrace \text{قُلْ هَلْ نُنَبِّئُكُم بِٱلْأَخْسَرِينَ أَعْمَالًا ۚ ٱلَّذِينَ ضَلَّ سَعْيُهُمْ فِى ٱلْحَيَوٰةِ ٱلدُّنْيَا وَهُمْ يَحْسَبُونَ أَنَّهُمْ يُحْسِنُونَ صُنْعًا} \rbrace$$

"Say, [O Muhammad], 'Shall we [believers] inform you of the greatest losers as to [their] deeds? [They are] those whose effort is lost in worldly life, while they think that they are doing well in work.'" *{al-Kahf (18): 103-104}*

Their intention is good, yet when they were in opposition to the way of the Messenger ﷺ their action was evil. Ad-Dārimī reported a *hadīth* which mentions that some people were gathered praising Allāh ten times while using stones to count the *tasbīh* and *tahlīl*. When Abdullāh ibn Mas'ūd saw them, he forbade what they were doing. One of them said: *"Yā 'AbdarRahmān, by Allāh, we did not intend except good!"* Look my brothers! His intention is good, Ibn Mas'ūd ﷺ however said: *"How many desire the good yet never gain it?"* So a good intention is not sufficient, rather it has to be accompanied by good action in line with the Prophet ﷺ. This is known in reality, because if a man wants to go to Makkah, may Allāh bless him with *Tawhīd* and the Sunnah, yet takes a route which does not lead him to Makkah, although he has good intention, will he reach Makkah? No! So along with good intention there has to be good action which is traversing the way that will lead him to Makkah.

Also there are those who say, when objecting to criticisms, that: *"you are just relying on quotes from newspapers and the media when these are not trustworthy"* – this can be refuted from a number of angles. Firstly, those people (who are being criticised) depend on newspapers in order to transmit their own statements, so you will see that they themselves will write an article and then send it to the newspapers or write out a *"fatwa"* and then send it to the newspapers. So this indicates that the person is himself happy with using newspapers and the media as a source of transmitting his statements. Secondly, most of these people (who are being criticised) are media friendly and are often on TV channels and have their articles within the papers (and now there is the web wherein everyone is able to write). So if there was a lie made against him they would not keep quiet if it was speech ascribed to him, and if he did keep quiet, he would be blamed. So if they (those being criticised) were lied against, they would clarify just as they have done when many other matters were falsely ascribed to them, thus absolving themselves from those claims. Therefore, if the newspapers, or any other medium, transmitted anything from those media friendly speakers specifically, or from others generally, and they did not negate the accusations from themselves, this indicates that such statements are affirmed from them and whoever attributes such statements to them is correct.

What is also stated in deflecting criticisms is that it is said: *"We asked so-and-so about the statements and he negate that he made such statements"* and this is what many of the Harakīs (activists) and Hizbīs (biased partisans) do. So you will see that if any of them say something which was widely distributed in the newspapers or gatherings witnessed by *thiqāt* and then their followers go and ask them, they (i.e. the Hizbīs and Harakīs) will say: *"No, this is not true I didn't say that"*. This is unacceptable. So if the person is truthful, he should stand in front of the people and denounce the speech as being false but if trustworthy witnesses were there then show that they were relating falsely. As for the person mentioning something which was then distributed in the newspapers and via other means but then in private sessions he denies that he even said such statements to his followers, this is unacceptable. The person also has to negate the accusations in front of the masses as his speech was disseminated in front of the masses. So it is not correct for a person to just negate the speech ascribed to him within private sessions with his followers. This is playing around, we ask Allāh to grant us all good health.

It will also thus be said that: *"so-and-so has other speech other than this speech"*, so you will see a person say something and then his followers will come and find other speech and say: *"he has other speech which opposes this speech so how can you ascribe what you have to him?"* It can be said to this: Allāh has taught us in His Book that whoever errs, this error is affirmed so that his error be accepted by doing what Allāh mentioned when He said:

﴿ إِلَّا ٱلَّذِينَ تَابُوا۟ وَأَصْلَحُوا۟ وَبَيَّنُوا۟ ﴾

"Except those who repent, rectify and manifest (the truth)…"
{Al-Baqarah (2): 160}

They have to have repented from the sin, rectified themselves from what they corrupted initially and manifest the truth by saying that they erred beforehand and have now retracted. Imām Ibn ul-Qayyim mentioned this in his book *Iddat us-Sābirīn*. What also has to be known is that some of them play around in the name of repentance, so you'll find someone making many errors and then say *"all what I stated before I have retracted from is……"* but there has to be a general and clear *tawbah* with an explanation, saying: *"I erred in such-and-such a matter and I repent for it"*. One cannot just come with general statements which confuse the common people. This is a matter of the deen and Allāh knows what is in the hearts, glory unto Him.

Some of them also say: *"Did you advise so-and-so before you refuted him?"* Firstly, it can be said that the condition of giving advice has no evidence. Rather, whoever errs openly is to be censured openly, as it was mentioned beforehand that the Prophet ﷺ censured a spokesman from a group of people openly and he did not take him by the hand to advise him initially and then after that refute him. Rather, the Prophet ﷺ censured him openly without giving advice. This is the first matter, the condition of giving advice has no proof for it, whoever wants to obligate people to advice a person before he can be refuted has to bring evidence for this. This advice has to be in the context of the *masālih* (benefits) and *mafāsid* (harms) because sometimes the benefit of giving advice can take precedence over refuting him initially, and sometimes the benefits in refuting the person can take precedence over the benefit of giving advice. As a result, the matter has to be looked into and the greater benefit has to take precedence. Secondly, according to what we know, there is not a man from those famous Harakīs and Takfīrīs except that he has been advised! Not once, but many times! Advised by the *'Ulamā* and students of (Islamic) knowledge; but with all this they still continue (in their ways).

Seventh Principle

If you loved a person and this person made an error which obligated his *tabdī'* (declaring him an innovator) and *tadlīl* (declaring him to be misguided) there will arrive a tribulation. So at this point one has to inquire: is the love of this person for Allāh's sake? If so then you would free yourself from this person because he made an error which obligated his misguidance. If the love was not for the sake of Allāh, or was for the sake of Allāh and then changed, and you remained with your love of him and you did not treat him in the way the *Sharī'ah* demands, then your love here is not for the sake of Allāh. So look at yourself because love for the sake of Allāh is a serious matter, as it is verified in the Two Sahīhs in the hadīth of Abū Hurayrah that the Prophet said: *"There are seven whom Allāh will shade in His (Throne's) Shade on the Day when there is no shade except His Shade..."* We ask Allāh to make us from them, along with our parents, children and wives. He said in the hadīth: *"...two men who love each other for Allāh's sake, meeting for that and parting upon that..."* So love for the sake of Allāh is a serious matter enough for one to be shaded on the Day when there will be no shade except (the Shade of the Throne of) Allāh. Bishr al-Hāfi and Imām Sufyān ath-Thawrī, as al-Bayhaqī reported in *Shu'b ul-Īmān,* stated:

Love for the sake of Allāh and hate for the sake of Allāh, is when you see a man who loves another for the sake of Allāh but then the man invents a new matter in Islām and yet the other man continues to love him, then know that the man does not love him for the sake of Allāh.

Imām Abū 'Abdir-Rahmān Muqbil bin Hādī al-Wādi'ī ﷺ said a statement which is worthy of being written in gold:

فأهل السنة ليست لديهم محاباة بخلاف المبتدعة.

So Ahlus Sunnah do not have with them (blind) love (for individuals) in opposition to the innovators.[1]

We ask Allāh to grant us love for His sake.

Eighth Principle

Of the most important things that the Salaf warned against was *talawwun* (changing colour and assuming various forms) in the dīn in regards to matters where it is not permitted to differ. As for a person having a different view in a matter where it is permitted to differ, in *fiqh* issues, then this is allowed because the Imāms of the Sunnah had different views which changed over time. Imām ash-Shāfi'ī had certain views when he was in Irāq but his views differed when he went to Egypt. Imām Ahmad also had different views, for which there are differing narrations from him numbering two or three, regarding certain issues. Yet all of this was in matters which it is permitted to differ. As for matters where it is not permitted to differ, pay attention to this, it is incorrect to use the speech of Imām ash-Shāfi'ī for example, and this is what many of the Harakīs and Takfīrīs do. If his (i.e. the Takfīrī's) statement is criticised and he moves onto a next innovation he will say:

---

[1] Muqaddimah of *Tuhafat-ush-Shābir Rabbānī*, p. 4.

What I am doing is what Imām ash-Shāfi'ī did when he changed his view when he was in Egypt and then changed his view in Irāq.

This is an error, as the *Salaf* censured assuming various views in matters wherein it is not permitted. Ibn 'AbdulBarr reported in *Jāmi' Bayān 'Ilm wa Fadlihi* that Ibrāheem an-Nakhā'ī said: *"Talawwun in the deen is disliked."* It is also reported that Hudhayfah ibn al-Yamān said, and pay attention: *"It is censured to deny what you know and to claim to know that which you deny. Beware of talawwun in the deen because the deen of Allāh is one."* He spoke the truth may Allāh be pleased with him. Assuming various positions (talawwun) in matters wherein it is not permitted to differ is not correct to hold in the Sharī'ah of Muhammad ﷺ. So know that when you see a man nearly everyday assuming various forms in matters where it is not permitted to differ, then you should be aware that he is upon misguidance resulting in him going from one innovation to another.

Ninth Principle

It is a must to differentiate between a scholar, preacher, admonisher, literary writer, student of knowledge, pious worshipper and others. It is incorrect to mix them all together (as being on the same level) otherwise we will fall into a grave calamity. It is verified in the Two Sahīhs from the hadīth of Abū Sa'īd ؓ that the Prophet ﷺ said: *"Among those who came before you was a man who killed ninety-nine men. So he asked about where he could find the most knowledgeable of the people on earth. He was told to go to a Monk (a pious worshipper), so the man asked him 'I have killed ninety-nine people, is there any tawbah for me?' The monk replied 'No'. So the man killed him too to make the number of those who had killed one hundred. He then asked again about where he could find the most knowledgeable person on the earth and was told to go to a scholar. The man said to the scholar 'I have killed a hundred people, is there any tawbah for me?' The scholar replied 'Yes, what is there between you and tawbah?*

Introductory Principles

Go to such and such a land where there are some people worshipping Allāh, go and worship with them.'" To the end of the hadīth. Pay attention brothers, when the matter became confused and mixed up and he did not differentiate between the pious worshipper and the scholar this calamity occurred. When did the pious worshipper make a mistake? When he transgressed his bounds, if he remained on what he was doing in terms of worship then his action would not be censured, but when he transgressed this and placed himself into the position of the people of knowledge he erred and his recompense was to be killed. Likewise, those admonishers that you see who give sermons, or those reciters and *du'āt* or others, when they transgress their bounds - then know for certain that they are incorrect in doing so. Thus, the people have to differentiate between the *du'āt*, admonishers and reciters and between the 'Ulamā and students of knowledge.[1] Al-Khatīb al-Baghdādī reports the hadīth:

((من أشراط الساعة أن يلتمس العلم عند الأصاغر)).

From the signs of the Hour is that knowledge will be taken from the Smaller ones.

Ibn al-Mubārak said:

الأصاغر من أهل البدع.

The smaller ones are the people of innovation.

Narrated 'Abdullāh Ibn 'Amr Ibn al-'Ās:
"I heard Allāh's Messenger saying: *"Allāh does not take away knowledge by taking it away from (the hearts of) the people, but He takes it away by the death of the scholars till when none of the*

---

[1] These introductory principles have been adapted from the nine introductions provided by our Shaykh, 'Abdul'Azīz bin Rayyis ar-Rayyis' critique of Dr 'Ā'id al-Qarnī which is available to download in audio format from www.islamancient.com and translated into English here:
http://www.salafimanhaj.com/pdf/SalafiManhaj_AlQarni.pdf.

(scholars) remains, people will take as their leaders ignorant people who when consulted will give their verdict without knowledge. So, they will go astray and will lead the people astray."¹

Abū Hurayrah narrated that the Messenger of Allāh said: *"There will come upon the people years of deceit wherein the liar will be regarded as truthful and the truthful will be considered a liar and the dishonest will be trusted and the trustworthy one will be considered dishonest and the Ruwaybidah will begin to speak!"* Then it was asked: *"What are the Ruwaybidah?"* He replied: *"The foolish insignificant man who speaks about general affairs."*²

The following narration is also important in regards to Al-Awlakī:

عن ابن مسعود قال: كيف بكم إذا لبستكم فتنة يهرم فيها الكبير ويربو فيها الصغير يتخذها الناس سنة إذا ترك منها شيء قيل: تركت السنة؟ قيل: يا أبا عبد الرحمن؟ ومتى ذلك؟ قال: إذا كثرت جهالكم وقلت علماؤكم وكثرت خطباؤكم وقلت فقهاؤكم وكثرت أمراؤكم وقلت أمناؤكم وتفقه لغير الدين والتمست الدنيا بعمل الآخرة.

From Ibn Mas'ūd who said: *"How will you be if tribulation afflicts you which the old have grown old upon and the young have been cultivated upon, and which the people have taken as Sunnah. To the extent that if these actions are not done it will be said 'the Sunnah has been left'."* It was said: *'O Abā 'AbdarRahmān, when will that be?'* Ibn Mas'ūd replied: *"If your ignoramuses are many, and your 'Ulamā are a few, and if your Khutabā' are many and your Fuqahā are a few; and if your leaders are many and your*

---

¹ Saheeh al-Bukhārī vol. 1, no. 100
² Reported by Ahmad in his Musnad, Ibn Mājah and others with a weak chain of narration, but Ahmad has another chain of narration for the hadīth, which makes the hadīth *hasan*.

trustworthy people are a few, and when you gain understanding of other than the deen and you try to attain the dunya with the action of the Hereafter."[1]

---

[1] Nu'aym bin Hammād, *Kitāb ul-Fitan*. It is also relayed in 'Ali bin Hisāmuddīn al-Muttaqī al-Hindī (d. 975 AH/1567 CE), *Kanz ul-'U'mmāl fī Sunan il-Aqwāl wa'l-Af āl* (Beirut: Mu'assat ar-Risālah, 1989 CE), p.1795. It can be accessed Online from the website of *Imām Muhammad bin Saud Islamic University* here:
http://www.imamu.edu.sa/DContent/BOOKS/arabic_ibook14/part2/home.html

CHAPTER 1

"IMAM" ANWAR BIN NASIR AL-'AWLAKI, HIS METHODOLOGICAL BACKGROUND AND SHIFTS

Anwar bin Nāsir al-'Awlakī gained popularity due to many of his audio lectures being widespread in certain Islamic bookstores; lectures such as *The Life of the Prophet* ﷺ 'set' (Makkan and Madinan periods), *Lives of the Prophets, The Hereafter* 'set', *The Life of Abu Bakr* ؓ 'set', *The Life of Umar* ؓ 'set', *Constants on the Path of Jihād, The Story of Ibn al-Akwa (aka Book of Jihād by Ibn an-Nahhās)* etc.

His earlier lectures (pre 2003) were characterised by an archetypal Ikhwānī methodology, along with sounding like a carbon-copy of Hamza Yūsuf! These lectures during this phase focused on Muslims **"putting aside differences and uniting for the greater good"** and Ikhwānī notions of **"fiqh of priorities"** and **"organized collective work of the Islamic movement"** and **"we unite on what we agree on and allow each other on matters we differ on"** and speaking on **"corrupt, dictatorial, totalitarian regimes in the Muslim world who the people resent"** along with also citing Sayyid Qutb within this. This can be seen in 'Awlakī's lectures *Lessons Learned from the Sahābah Living as a Minority* (given at a JIMAS conference [!!] during the Bank Holiday weekend of August 2002 CE in Leicester) and also in his lecture *Tolerance: The Hallmark of a Muslim* which can be heard online.[1]

Awlakī can also be seen in this video from the PBS documentary *Muhammad: Legacy of a Prophet* (2003)[2] giving a *khutbah* at a Musallah

---

[1] http://www.halaltube.com/tolerance-a-hallmark-of-a-muslim.
[2] Refer to 2:09- 3:27 of Part 5 of the documentary as it has been placed in *Youtube*.

Chapter 1

in an American Congress building at Capitol Hill (!!!?).[1] Also see him in his interview with Ray Suarez in October 2001[2] and his participation in a documentary (circa 2001/02) on Ramadān wherein 'Awlakī states "I think that in general Islām is presented in a negative way, I mean there's always this association between Islām and terrorism when that is not true at all, **I mean Islām is a religion of peace**"!?[3] In the lecture *It's a War Against Islām,* 'Awlakī's exaggeration vis-a-vis politics can be seen during that phase while he was in the US. He stated after twelve minutes into the lecture while discussing the situation of a certain American Muslim who had been imprisoned:

"...and I'm gonna repeat it again, I take it as an article of faith for myself to believe that he is innocent"!?

An article of faith?! This demonstrates an emotive side prone to reactionary outbursts at the drop of a hat. He takes a current issue and says publically that **"he takes it as an article of faith"**!? Did Allāh command him to take such an issue as an article of faith like that? 'Awlakī therefore, on account of emotions and methodology, developed into a full-blown takfīrī-jihādī which in fact was the logical progression of a dedicated adherent of the Quṭbī-Ikhwānī method. This, mixed in with the animosity that developed during the so-called US "war on terror" and the injustice and oppression that was felt by some parts of the Muslim community in America, was a recipe for disaster and contributed to 'Awlakī morphing into an al-Qā'idah supporter. The post 9/11 scenario in the US eventually culminated in 'Awlakī making Hijrah to Yemen wherein his rhetoric became more vociferous. As for this being in line with the Ikhwānī methodology, then the author of *al-'Aqabāt,* which is a manual of the Ikhwānī methodology, states (vol.2, p.596):

---

[1] http://www.youtube.com/watch?v=0dTihDNYtuY&feature=related.
[2] http://www.pbs.org/newshour/updates/religion/july-dec09/alawlaki_11-11.html.
[3] http://www.youtube.com/watch?v=3BgG2ZLm2M8.

When the Islamic movement is tested with a terrorist leader that is not religious and who arrests the du'āt, then the plan is as follows:
- lessening the conveyance of the da'wah in order to do secretly, via individual da'wah and contacts.
- apparent membership to an organization that is concerned with the spirit of education and limit their da'wah to purifying the souls.
- Linking up with organizations that teach the Qur'ān and charitable, educational foundations that work for Islam and da'wah underneath them.
- Working hard and striving vigorously in order to receive invitations to give lessons in mosques, give khutbahs or teach in schools.

The use of popular, or rather populist, audio lectures and personality cults around speakers and talks is another feature of the Ikhwānī method. The author of *al-'Aqabāt* states (vol.2, p.382):

From these means are: open sessions which includes questions asked via phone; from these means are: Islamic audios wherein the most powerful audios are chosen by people to listen to; from these means are: distributing Islamic books wherein the best books are chosen to be read in the fields of ideology, da'wah and history.

The author continues:

From these means are: **via giving general lectures with active da'wah which attracts the listeners to the lecture wherein the dā'iyah diagnoses the issues affecting the Muslims;** distributing Islamic magazines, da'wah newspapers and ideological publications amidst the youth; **lectures wherein memorable Islamic events are told such as the battle of Badr;** preparing visits, journeys and outings; anāshīds for da'wah, history and guidance;

Chapter 1

and finally from these means of da'wah are: Islamic theatrics and historical plays.

Yet also within the Ikhwānī method is apparent denial of takfīrī-jihādī operations in order to maintain a united front against Muslim governments and otherwise. Salāh as-Sāwī, one of the main Ikhwānī ideologues, stated in his book *ath-Thawābit wa'l-Mutaghayyirāt* [Constants and Variables], pp.264-265, in regards to avoiding condemnations of those who float in their ideological orbit, regardless of the extent of errors committed:

> **Not getting involved in denouncing other factions who work for Islām via knowledge-based condemnations for example under the banner of "condemning extremism and radicalisation" regardless of what operations these factions get involved in, which may appear to be contrary to moderation, good intent and maturity. If it is a necessity to comment on some crude actions that have been committed then what firstly should be condemned is state terrorism which manifests extremism and harshness, this represents an anticipated reaction to what the governments do out of their extremism and enmity against Islām and the extremism of the governments in rejecting ruling by the Sharī'ah. There is no way to resolve these repercussions and prevent the means to the extremism of the two camps however except by ruling by the Sharī'ah and establishing the Book of Allāh within the Ummah which deters extremism and austerity. Due to the absolute condemnation of these jihādi acts rivalry naturally developed among these factions and filled the arena of Islamic action with tribulations and agitation, unless there was prior co-ordination and mutual distribution of roles. Jāhiliyyah is the most careful in questioning the Islamists within these gatherings in order to get condemnation of jihādi actions which are conducted by some factions under the banner of "the war on extremism". Due to this, much pressure will be exerted and they**

will accuse them of colluding with the conspirators in these operations if they do not condemn them and openly free themselves from such actions. With this, its aims are achieved with full precision and the Islamic trends will split apart and fuel fitna between the factions from one angle and make an example out of these jihādi manifestations by punishing them, from another angle. From here comes the necessity of fully safeguarding and utterly detailing what the Islamists do within such gatherings from statements and sayings which affect any one of these factions. It is not far off to say that the interests of Islamic action may require that a team of men have to perform some jihādi efforts[1] and apparently let others bear blame.[2] It is not far off to achieve that in practice if the Islamic action reaches

---

[1] Shaykh, Dr 'AbdusSalām as-Sihaymī (Associate Professor at the *Department of Fiqh* at the *Sharī'ah College, the Islamic University of Madīnah*) says about this: **Meaning: causing devastation and bombings which they think will harm the established system.**
See 'AbdusSalām bin Sālim bin Rajā' as-Sihaymī, *Fikr ul-Irhāb wa'l-'Unf fi'l-Mamlakati'l-'Arabiyyah as-Saudiyyah: Masdaruhu, Asbābu Instishāruhu, 'Ilāj* [The Ideology of Terrorism and Violence in the Kingdom of Saudi Arabia: Its Origins, the Reasons for Its Spread and the Cure] (Cairo: Dar ul-Menhaj, 1426 AH/2005 CE), p.128.

[2] Shaykh, Dr 'AbdusSalām as-Sihaymī comments on this:
> Out of prior co-ordination and mutual distribution of roles as he mentioned before, this is placed under the principle "the ends justify the means". So in order for their true situation not to be exposed some of them will denounce the bombings and havoc that some cause, while some others will support such actions. This indicates that the Muslim Brotherhood, and those groups that were born out of it, have two wings: a political-ideological wing and also a paramilitary wing. Between the two are mutual exchanging of roles via the use of different names according to the time and circumstances of the country that they are in. This is what he mentioned in regards to not denouncing errors which contradict moderation regardless of what these groups may get involved in, which are actions which oppose the regulations of the Divine Legislation. How can he permit for them what he prohibits to others and prohibit to them what he permits to others? What is this except for playing about with the *dīn* and the minds of the followers?

See 'AbdusSalām bin Sālim bin Rajā' as-Sihaymī, *op.cit,*.p.128

Chapter 1

> a stage of consciousness wherein it is possible to at least agree on anything that is likely to help the continuation of the Islamist message within these circles without confusion or agitation.

Hence, if you glance at the innocent titles of 'Awlakī's lecture series, you would be easily forgiven for thinking that they are free from any kind of neo-Takfīrī agenda, yet upon closer scrutiny of the actual contents of these lectures it becomes self-evident that al-'Awlakī is actually a Takfīrī-Jihādī propagator who not only makes takfīr of the scholars who do not agree that Muslims should wage armed jihād during times of weakness, by referring to them as being "hypocrites", but also supports a range of takfīrī neo-Khawārij groups and thus twists the proofs in order to justify certain actions, as we will see in this study.

This brand of takfīrī-jihādī is of the subtle kind, because unlike Abdullāh Faisal,[1] who is less tactful in his takfīrī approach and thus easily exposed, al-'Awlakī exercises a rather different process when herding his unfortunate audience towards his corrupted notions of takfeer and jihād. Al-'Awlakī gains your trust through well manicured lectures which breach the perimeters of the heart, thus leaving you open for him to administer his poisonous takfīrī ideologies. As for the link from this to al-Qā'idah, then as we stated beforehand the Ikhwānī-Qutbī trend leads to such ideas, Shaykh Dr 'AbdusSalām as-Sihaymī noted that:

> **Usāmah bin Lādin was of those influenced by the ideology of Aymān adh-Dhawāhirī and Ayman adh-Dhawāhirī was of those who made the books and articles of Sayyid Qutb as a constitution for him and his follows to adhere to.**[2] **They exert**

---

[1] For a more detailed analysis of this hardcore neo-*takfīrī*:
http://www.salafimanhaj.com/ebook.php?ebook=45

[2] Shaykh, Dr 'AbdusSalām as-Sihaymī comments on this:
> **Ayman adh-Dhawāhirī himself confirmed that the books of Sayyid Qutb are the main constitution for him and his followers in the third series of his**

whatever they are able in order to implement (the ideas) of these books in a practical way. I quoted from Sayyid Qutb prior which indicated that he revived the ideology of the Khawārij during this era and he is considered the ideological founder of these concepts during this time.[1]

Indeed, Sayyid Qutb stated in *Dhilāl*, vol.4, p.122 – which is a work which 'Awlakī refers to in some of his lectures:

> "There is neither a Muslim State nor a Muslim society on the face of the earth which has the principle of interaction within it which is Allāh's Sharī'ah and Islamic fiqh."

Qutb also said in *Dhilāl*, vol.3, p.1634:

> "The Muslims today do not struggle because the Muslims do not exist; the issue of the existence of Islām is one which today needs a cure."

'Awlakī stated in part 5 of *Thawābit 'ala'd-Darb il-Jihād* [Constants on the Path of Jihād] after 31 minutes:

> "People like Sayyid Qutb, **we recognise the value of his words because he wrote them with ink and blood,** people like 'Abdullāh 'Azzām and like Shaykh Yūsuf al-'Ayrī whom we reading his book. These are people whom Allāh Subhānu wa Ta'ala gives a certain life to their words after they die, so it is as if their soul leaves their body and enters their words and it gives their words a new life."

Thus, al-'Awlakī has traversed two distinct approaches:

---

published memoirs which were printed in ash-Sharq al-Awsat newspaper in Ramadān 1422 AH.
See 'AbdusSalām bin Sālim bin Rajā' as-Sihaymī,*op.cit,*.p.176
[1] 'AbdusSalām bin Sālim bin Rajā' as-Sihaymī, *op.cit,*.p.176.

- The Ikhwānī and Quṭbī phase, characterised by his earlier lectures while in the States.
- The Takfīrī-Jihādī phase, which is his current persuasion.

He therefore jumped onto the bandwagon of the Takfīrī mavericks and Khawārij bandits and ditched the wishy-washy Ikhwānī methodology.

CHAPTER 2

'AWLAKI AND HIS "EXPLANATION" OF THE BOOK 'CONSTANTS ON THE PATH OF JIHĀD' BY AL-QA'IDAH MEMBER YUSUF AL-'AYRI

Al-'Awlakī, who utilises the archetypal approach of the Khawārij *Qa'diyyah*,[1] has 'explained' a book by a Saudi jihādī, Yūsuf al-'Ayrī (Abū Qutaybah Al-Makkī), who according to his biographer and follower 'Eesā bin Sa'd al-Awshān (and translated by "al-Barbaree" and "edited by Aboo Irsād") did not even study at school!!?[2] See the first page of the biography written by 'Eesā al-'Awshān.[1]

---

[1] Those who wage verbal warfare and verbal rebellion from the comfort zone of their armchairs or mimbars, but never really participate in the Jihād which they are obsessed with.

[2] Yūsuf bin Sālih bin Fahd al-'Ayrī, also known as Abū Qutaybah al-Makkī, born in Dammām in 1973 CE, was a representative of the group which called themselves *'al-Qā'idah in the Arabian Peninsula'* which was headed by 'Abdul'Azīz al-Muqrin. Both died after shoot-outs with the Saudi police and al-'Ayrī was killed on 31 May 2003 CE. He fought in Afghanistan against the Soviets and then returned to Saudi Arabia in the early nineties and set himself up as a *takfīrī* ideologue. He has authored many books some of which have been translated into English by the *takfīrīs* of *Tibyan Publications*. Despite the fact that they were both killed by Saudi police forces they are still oddly referred to by some as being "mujāhideen" who "died in the path of Allāh"!?

In an interview with Mshari al-Zaydi of *Sharq al-Awsat* newspaper Shaykh 'AbdulMuhsin al-'Ubaykān *(hafidhahullāh)* of Riyadh, the Shaykh was asked:

> Many of the theoretical advocates of Al Qaeda, such as Yousef Al Airy and Faris Al Showail, have been quoting the religious edicts and opinions of prominent sheikhs on issues of Takfir and Jihād, implying that they are merely repeating the beliefs of Saudi religious leaders. What is your opinion on such practices?

Shaykh 'AbdulMuhsin al-'Ubaykān *(hafidhahullāh)* answered:

Yusuf al-'Ayrī, who was one of those killed by the Saudi security forces because he was with the terrorists who had killed innocent Muslims in Saudi Arabia, wrote a letter entitled the *Global Campaign to Resist Transgression: Falsification, Treachery and Lying Claims* (this 'global campaign' was headed generally by Safar al-Hawālī), wherein al-'Ayrī says on pages 16-17:

> SubhānAllāh! The understandings have overturned, Safar just yesterday authored books wherein he clarified that the Arab Tawāghīt have the most evil impact on the Ummah and that they are the ones who have replaced the dīn of Allāh and that they are the reasons for the corruption and filth of the Ummah. Salmān had fiery tapes wherein he would warn the tāghūt governments and that all acknowledge that the most dangerous thing for the Ummah is the deception of these governments and their seeking to destroy this dīn. We do not wish to transmit what confirms this from their (i.e. Safar and Salmān) books and statements as all who know them are certain that these were their previous views. Then today comes and we see that the "Sahwa" of yesteryear has turned into "Ghaflah". For these (Safar and Salmān) and the government are in the same ditch and have become an associated enemy.
>
> Did you not tell us before that these governments are in the hand of the enemy?
>
> Did you not say to us before that the direct colonisation had ended and that the indirect colonisation of the Muslim lands was via these governments?

These new militant leaders are the product of a revival that calls for political incitement and discord. **They are willing to do anything that will serve their cause.**
Mshari al-Zaydi, *"Interview with Sheikh Abdul- Mohsen Bin Nasser Al-Obeikan"* in *Sharq al-Awsat*, 24 May 2005 CE see: http://www.asharq-e.com/news.asp?section=3&id=85.
[1] This was available online but appears to have been taken down from the site where the salafimanhaj.com team first found it in 2007.

> Did you not drill into our heads before that the worse dangers to the Ummah are these governments which implement the desires of the enemy?
> Did you not say to us before that these governments wage a war against Islam?
> Did you not make takfīr of these governments?
> Did you not debate Shaykh 'Abdul'Azīz bin Bāz ؒ over the kufr of these governments within audio tapes and in regards to the legality of these governments, including the Saudi government, and you made takfīr of it? Your books and tapes still testify to this against you (O Safar and Salmān)! Then today comes and you and the government are in the same ditch!
> Did you not say before that these governments, and in particular the Interior Ministry of Saudi Arabia, are not able to ever open the avenue for whoever wants good for the dīn, except for a small few of deceived elements from the Council of Senior Scholars?
> So do not reject and deny this, for we will bring forth your statements from your audios which you now reject today! 'Afwàn for this exposè but you were the ones who caused us to do this.[1]

So this man, Yūsuf al-'Ayrī, and Allāh knows best, was but a victim of the seeds which Safar and Salmān sowed, and he became disillusioned by the shifts of Safar and Salmān, as too did many of their former diehard followers in the UK who should have actually attached themselves to the credible and well-known scholars of Ahl us-Sunnah.

---

[1] Refer to the lecture of Shaykh 'Abdul'Azīz bin Rayyis ar-Rayyis, after 38 minutes and 48 seconds into the lecture *Inkashaf ul-Qinā': Haqīqat Du'āt us-Sahwa [Uncovering the Mask: The Reality of the Preachers of the 'Islamic Awakening]*: http://www.islamancient.com/lectures,item,71.html.

Chapter 2

In 'Awlakī's "explaination" of 'Ayrī's book entitled *'Thawābit 'ala Darb il-Jihād'* [Constants on the Path of Jihād] stated[1]:

> These people can come in the form of Shuyūkh and they will tell you that it is not the time for Jihād fī Sabīlillah, and because they are scholars you would listen to them. Allāh says, "And there would have been some among you who would have listened to them." Why would they listen to these people? Because of the status they have. They are leaders in their community, they're scholars, they're people who know how to speak. **They discourage a Muslim from doing Jihād fī Sabīlillah and they are Munāfiqūn; whoever discourages a Muslim from doing Jihād fī Sabīlillah is a Munafiq since this ayah is referring to the Munafiqoon.** A Muslim who has become a Mujahid since this ayah is these people; **he doesn't care about their status, "how good you are at speaking or how scholarly you claim to be. This is what Allāh wants from me and I'm gonna do it"**. And this is one of the most, I would say today, serious fitnas today that the young brothers face. That their scholars are not encouraging them instead they are discouraging them...

The ironic thing about this quote is that it aptly fits al-'Awlakī himself, since all one needs to do is to singularize the pronouns and re-direct the question: **"Why would they listen to 'Awlakī?" Answer: Because of the status he has.** However, the difference here is that the status of scholars is creditable due to their vast amounts of knowledge, but the status that is erroneously afforded to al-'Awlakī, then this is not the case. Al-'Awlakī then sets out on his vague campaign by claiming **"They discourage a Muslim from doing Jihād fī Sabīlillah; whoever discourages a Muslim from doing Jihād fī Sabīlillah is a Munafiq."** Al-'Awlakī here gives the impression that there are absolutely no occasions

---

[1] Transcribed and edited by "Mujadhid fi Sabīlillah" and is available online here: http://downloads.islambase.co.uk/booksEN/Constants.pdf on page 46 (after 40:12 of part 4 of the audio series).

wherein (armed) Jihād should be discouraged and that the one who discourages jihād (no matter the reason) should be labeled as a "Munāfiq". This blanket approach to understanding the dynamics of Jihād indicates clearly al-'Awlakī's obsession with all things "Jihād", and in particular the armed and martial aspect of it. It seems that al-'Awlakī, himself, is in need of a stiff reminder of the function of jihād, which serves as a means to the goal (i.e. Tawhīd) and it is not the goal itself.

So are there times in Islām when (armed) Jihād of an individual or jihād itself is discouraged? It is reported in *Kitāb ul-Jihād* of the Sahīh of Imām al-Bukhārī; *Kitāb ul-Birr wa's-Silah wa'l-Ādab* in the Sahīh of Imām Muslim; *Kitāb ul-Jihād* in the Sunan of Imām at-Tirmidhī; *Kitāb ul-Jihād* in the Sunan of Imām an-Nasā'ī; *Kitāb ul-Jihād* in the Sunan of Imām Abū Dāwud and in the Musnad of Imām Ahmad that:

'Abdullāh Ibn 'Amr said: "A man came to the Prophet and asked for his permission to go for jihād. He said,

((أَحَيٌّ والداك؟))

'Are your parents alive?'
The man replied, 'Yes.' The Prophet said:

((ففيهما فجاهد))

'then your jihād is with them.'"

Imāms Ahmad and Abū Dāwud include the additional narrations from the Prophet:

((ارجع فاستأذنهما فإن أذنا لك فجاهد وإلا فبرهما))

"Go back and seek their permission and if they grant you permission (then wage armed jihād) and if they do not (grant you permission) then be dutiful to them (and their wishes)."

Hence, Ibn Hajar al-'Asqalānī stated in *Fath ul-Bārī*:

Chapter 2

قال جمهور العلماء يحرم الجهاد إذا منع الأبوان أو أحدهما بشرط أن يكونا مسلمين لأن برهما فرض عين والجهاد فرض كفاية.. أهـ.

> **The majority of the scholars say that it is prohibited to wage (armed) jihād if the parents, or one of them, prevent it. With the condition that they are Muslims because being dutiful to them is an individual responsibility while (armed) jihād is a collective responsibility.**[1]

So did not Allāh's Messenger discourage the Sahābī from going to armed Jihād and does this hadīth not demand al-Awlakī to provide detail for his vague dismissive claim? The fact is that al-'Awlakī cannot provide specifics in his quest to undermine the 'Ulamā in the eyes of the masses, so he does what is so typical of these neo-takfiris and argues his case on the vaguest of premises; hoping to recruit the gullible on his crusade against the inheritors of the prophets by mere means of blanket accusations. Incidentally, it is an uncanny fact how the people of innovation always base their unsteady arguments on broad accusations. Shaykh ul-Islām Ibn Taymiyyah (661-728 AH/1263-1328 CE) said when explaining the status-quo of the Muslims during the Makkan peroid:

فكان النبي ﷺ في أول الأمر مأمورا أن يجاهد الكفار بلسانه لا بيده فيدعوهم ويعظهم ويجادلهم بالتي هي أحسن ويجاهدهم بالقرآن جهادا كبيرا قال تعالى في سورة الفرقان وهي مكية الآية 51 52 وكان مأمورا بالكف عن قتالهم لعجزه وعجز المسلمين عن ذلك ثم لما هاجر إلى المدينة وصار له بها أعوان أذن له في الجهاد ثم لما قووا كتب عليهم القتال ولم يكتب عليهم قتال من

---

[1] Al-Imām, al-Hāfidh Ahmad bin 'Ali bin Hajar al-'Asqalānī, *Fath ul-Bārī: Sharh Sahīh ul-Bukhārī* (Beirut: Dār ul-Kutub al-'Ilmiyyah, 1421 AH/2000 CE, 3rd Edn., ed. Muhammad Fu'ād 'AbdulBāqī), *Kitāb ul-Jihād wa's-Sīr* [The Book of Jihād and Prisoners of War], vol.7, p.173.

Chapter 2

سالمهم لأنهم لم يكونوا يطيقون قتال جميع الكفار فلما فتح الله مكة وانقطع قتال قريش ملوك العرب ووفدت إليه وفود العرب بالإسلام أمره الله تعالى بقتال الكفار كلهم إلا من كان له عهد مؤقت وأمره بنبذ العهود المطلقة فكان الذي رفعه ونسخه ترك القتال وأما مجاهدة الكفار باللسان فما زال مشروعا من أول الأمر إلى آخره فإنه إذا شرع جهادهم باليد فباللسان أولى

The Prophet ﷺ at the beginning was instructed (by Allāh) to strive against the kuffār not with his hand (i.e. physically and militarily) rather via preaching to them, admonishing them and arguing with them in a way which is better. He strove against them with the Qur'ān with an immense striving [Jihādan Kabeera] as Allāh states in Sūrat ul-Furqān, ayah 51-52 which is a Makkan verse:

> ["And if We had willed, We could have sent into every city a warner. So do not obey the disbelievers, and strive against them with the Qur'ān a great striving." *{Furqān (25) 51-52}*]

The Prophet ﷺ was instructed to withhold from fighting against them due to his inability, and the inability of the Muslims, to do that. Yet when he migrated to Madīnah, wherein he had helpers, it was permitted for him to make (military) jihād. Then when they grew in strength fighting was prescribed for them and it was not prescribed for them to fight for their own safety as they were unable to fight against all of the disbelievers. When Allāh opened up Makkah and the Arab delegations arrived there to embrace Islām, Allāh instructed that all the disbelievers be fought against except those who had a temporal covenant and Allāh instructed to annul absolute covenants and that which annulled them was abandoning fighting. As for striving against the kuffār by the tongue (i.e. preaching etc.) then this will not cease to be legislated from the beginning of the matter to the end of it, for if it is legislated to strive against them by the hand (i.e. physically) then by the tongue (i.e. verbally) takes precedence.[1]

He also said:

> The reason for that tax upon them is only when the dīn is manifest and raised such as jihād and their adherence to paying the jizya and subjugation. So when the Muslims were in a state of weakness in the beginning, the duty (which the non-Muslims pay to the Muslim state) was not Divinely Legislated, only after the deen had been completed and manifest was that Divinely Legislated.[2]

Then he said:

> This was the result of patience and consciousness of Allāh which Allāh instructed (the Muslims to have) at the very beginning of Islām and during that time the jizya was not taken from any of the Jewish community, or other non-Muslim communities, who were living in Madīnah. Those verses are applicable to every Muslim in a state of weakness who is unable to aid Allāh and His Messenger with his hand or via his tongue (i.e. by speaking), but could help by using what he was able to by his heart and the likes. The verses about subduing those non-Muslims who have contracts with Muslims are applicable to every strong believer who is able to help the dīn of Allāh and His Messenger with his hand and tongue (i.e. via speaking). It is with these verses that the Muslims were applying during the last epoch of the Messenger of Allāh ﷺ and during the epoch of his rightly guided caliphs. And thus it will be until the Day of Judgement as there will never cease to be a group from this ummah who are well

---

[1] Shaykh ul-Islām Ibn Taymiyyah, *al-Jawāb as-Sahīh liman Baddala Dīn al-Masīh* (Riyadh: Dār ul-'Āsimah, 1414 AH, eds. 'Ali Hasan Nāsir, 'Abdul'Azīz Ibrāhīm al-'Askar and Hamdān Muhammad), vol.1, p.227.

[2] *Iqtidā' as-Sirāt ul-Mustaqeem*, vol.1, p.420.

established on the truth who help Allāh and His Messenger with complete help. So whoever from the believers is weak in the earth or is weak in the time in which he is living in, must apply those verses of the Qur'ān which mention patience and forgiveness against those who are seeking to harm Allāh and His Messenger from those who were given the scriptures prior and also from the polytheists. As for those people who are in a state of strength then they are to apply the verses regarding fighting the leaders of kufr who slander the dīn. They are also to apply the Qur'anic verses regarding fighting those who were given the scriptures prior until they pay the jizya and are subjugated.[1]

Ibn ul-Qayyim said:
The first thing which his Lord revealed to him was to read in the name of his Lord who had created. That was the beginning of his Prophethood, where Allāh commanded him to recite to himself but He did not yet command him to convey that. Then He revealed the words:

﴿ يَـٰٓأَيُّهَا ٱلْمُدَّثِّرُ . قُمْ فَأَنذِرْ ﴾

"O you (Muhammad) enveloped in garments! Arise and warn!"
{al-Muddaththir 74:1-2}

So he became a Prophet with the word 'Iqra (Read!) and he became a Messenger with the words, 'O you (Muhammad) enveloped in garments...' Then Allāh commanded him to warn his closest kinsmen, then to warn his people, then to warn the Arabs around them, then to warn all the Arabs, then to warn all

---

[1] Shaykh ul-Islām Taqiuddīn Abu'l-'Abbās Ahmad bin 'AbdulHalīm bin 'AbdusSalām Ibn Taymiyyah (661-728 AH), *as-Sārim al-Maslūl 'ala Shātim ir-Rasūl* [The Unsheated Sword Upon the Defamer of Allāh's Messenger]. Dammām, KSA: Dār ul-Ma'ārif, 2nd Edn., 1428 AH/2007 CE, eds. Muhammad bin 'Abdullāh bin 'Umar al-Halwānī and Muhammad Kabīr Ahmad ash-Showdrī, vol.2, p.413.

of mankind. He continued to call them for over ten years from the beginning of his Prophethood, without fighting or imposing the jizyah; **he was commanded to refrain,** to be patient and to be forbearing. Then permission was given to him to migrate, and permission was given to him to fight.[1]

Imām 'AbdurRahmān as-Sa'dī ﷺ said:

These verses include the order to fight in the way of Allāh and this was after the hijra to Madīnah. So when the Muslims became strong, Allāh instructed them to fight after they were instructed to abstain from it.[2]

He then said:

And from it: is that if fighting was obligated upon them, with their small numbers and many enemies, that would have led to Islām disappearing. Some of the believers held that fighting during that condition was improper. What is actually suitable in such a period of weakness is to establish what Allāh has instructed from tawhīd, prayer, giving charity (zakah) etc. As Allāh said,

﴿ وَلَوْ أَنَّهُمْ فَعَلُواْ مَا يُوعَظُونَ بِهِۦ لَكَانَ خَيْرًا لَّهُمْ وَأَشَدَّ تَثْبِيتًا ﴾

"But if they done what they had been instructed to do it would have been better for them and would have strengthened (their faith)." {an-Nisā (4): 66}

So when they migrated to Madīnah and Islām became powerful, Allāh prescribed fighting for them at the suitable time.[3]

Imām Muhammad bin Sālih al-'Uthaymīn ﷺ said:

---

[1] Ibn ul-Qayyim, *Zād al-Ma'ād*, vol.3, p.159
[2] *Tafsīr*, p.89
[3] *Tafsīr*, p.188

There is a necessary condition within this which is that: the Muslims have ability and power that enables them to fight. If they do not possess the power yet put themselves forward to fight, they will be destroyed.[1] For this reason, Allāh did not obligate the Muslims to fight whilst they were in Makkah as they were unable due to their condition of weakness. But when they migrated to Madīnah and established the Islamic state they assumed power and were instructed to fight. Based upon this there is no escape from this condition and if not the remaining obligations would be redundant as all of the obligations have the condition of ability based on Allāh's saying,

﴿ فَٱتَّقُوا۟ ٱللَّهَ مَا ٱسْتَطَعْتُمْ ﴾

"Fear Allāh as much as you can…"
{Taghābun (64): 16}

And Allāh's saying,

﴿ لَا يُكَلِّفُ ٱللَّهُ نَفْسًا إِلَّا وُسْعَهَا ﴾

---

[1] [TN]: This is what has occurred with many of the so-called "leaders of jihād" that were based in London, which serves as an excellent example of where such misguided actions in the name of "jihād" materialised into nothing, largely due to not taking the advice of the scholars of Ahl us-Sunnah and *Salafiyyah*. They have either openly freed themselves from such desperate terrorist actions committed in the name of jihād or their hasty and naive plots have been completely destroyed leaving no positive benefits whatsoever from their actions and only bringing about harm to their own selves. Whether it be running websites from shed hide-outs to plotting to hijack trans-Atlantic airliners to planning to kill nightclub-goers to hatching plots to kill women and children – the end results have not reaped anything positive and have only brought about greater harms. Yet oddly enough despite all of these terrorist intrigues against those whom they claim to hate so much, when the going gets tough these terrorists begin to evoke how "British" they are and the rights that they should deserve as a result?! If this is not the case then such imprisoned individuals all of a sudden request "sympathy" from those Muslims who they showed no sympathy to whatsoever and in fact had described as being "spies", "Jews", "hypocrites" and "sell-outs".

Chapter 2

"Allāh does not burden a soul more than it can bear…"
{Baqarah (2): 286}.[1]

Then Imām 'Uthaymīn ؒ said in response to a question related to the Islamic society's need for jihād in the path of Allāh which asked:

The virtue of jihād and its lofty status in the Divine Legislation of Islām is in order for the dīn to be entirely for Allāh. In addition to this I ask: is fighting obligated or permissible without being prepared for it?

The answer from Imām 'Uthaymīn ؒ:

It is neither obligatory nor permissible without being prepared for it. Allāh did not obligate on His Prophet ﷺ whilst he was in Makkah to fight the Mushrikīn and permitted His Prophet in the Treaty of Hudaybiyah to make an agreement with the Mushrikīn.[2] This was an agreement which if a person read would

---

[1] *Sharh ul-Mumti'*, vol.8, p.9
[2] [TN]: The *Hudaybiyah Treaty* was made between the Muslims and the polytheists of Quraysh. When the *mushrikīn* of Quraysh witnessed the determination of the Muslims to risk their lives, properties, wealth and families for their faith in order to spread it peacefully, they realised that the Prophet Muhammad ﷺ and his followers ؓ could not be bullied or frightened by mere scare tactics. Therefore, a treaty of reconciliation and peace was made between the Quraysh and the Muslims. The clauses of the treaty were:
- The Muslims would return and come back in the following year (7 AH) but they would not stay in Makkah for more than three days and without arms except those concealed.
- War activities were to be suspended for ten years, during which both sides will live in security with neither side waging war against the other.
- Whoever wishes to join Muhammad ﷺ was free to do so and likewise whoever wished to join the *mushrikīn* of the Quraysh was also free to do so.
- If anyone from the Quraysh joins Muhammad ﷺ without his parent's or guardian's permission, he should be sent back to the Quraysh, but should any of Muhammad's followers return to the Quraysh, he was not to be sent back. (Safiur-Rahman al-Mubarakpuri, *The Sealed Nectar (ar-Raheequl-Makhtum)* Darusalam, 2002, p.403).

think that within it was a setback for the Muslims. Many of you know how the Treaty of Hudaybiyah was - to the extent that 'Umar ibn al-Khattāb ﷺ said "O Messenger of Allāh! Are we not upon the truth and our enemies upon bātil?" The Messenger of Allāh ﷺ said "Yes." 'Umar said "Then why should we accept such difficult terms in the affairs of our dīn?" 'Umar thought that there was a setback for the Muslims within the treaty. However, there is no doubt that the Messenger of Allāh ﷺ has more understanding than 'Umar and Allāh permitted the Messenger to do that. The Messenger of Allāh said "Indeed, I am the Messenger of Allāh and I would not disobey him and He will help me;" so if it was clear that the treaty was a setback for the Muslims then this indicates to us brothers an important issue which is the strength of a believer's trust in his Lord. So what is important is that it is obligatory upon Muslims to wage jihād in order to make the word of Allāh the most high and so that the dīn will be entirely for Allāh. However, currently we do not possess as Muslims that which can enable us to wage jihād against the kuffār, even if is defensive. As for offensive jihād then there is no doubt that this is not possible right now until Allāh brings consciousness to the ummah which prepare the ummah in

---

The treaty was significant in that the Quraysh began to recognise the Muslims legitimate existence and began to deal with them on equal terms. Safiur-Rahman al-Mubarakpuri notes in his biography of the Prophet Muhammad ﷺ, pp.407-408: "The Muslims did not have in mind to seize people's property or kill them through bloody wars, nor did they ever think of using any compulsive approaches in their efforts to propagate Islam, on the contrary their sole target was to provide an atmosphere of freedom in ideology or religion, **'Then whosoever wills, let him believe, and whosoever wills, let him disbelieve.'** *{al-Kahf (18): 29}*" The Muslims on the other hand had the opportunity to spread Islām over areas not then explored. When there was the peace agreement, war was abolished, and men met and consulted each other, none talked about Islām intelligently without entering it; within two years following the conclusion of the treaty, twice as many people entered Islām than ever before. This is supported by the fact that the Prophet ﷺ went out to al-Hudaybiyah with only 1400 men, but when he set out to liberate Makkah, two years later, he had 10,000 men with him.

Chapter 2

terms of īmān, personally and militarily. As for us today in this regard we are not able to wage jihād.[1]

What also proves that strength is a primary condition to establishing offensive jihād (to spread the borders of Islām) is that Allāh made it a condition in a number of obligations where one Muslim man would be opposed to two, as Allāh said,

﴿ ٱلْـَٰٔنَ خَفَّفَ ٱللَّهُ عَنكُمْ وَعَلِمَ أَنَّ فِيكُمْ ضَعْفًا ۚ فَإِن يَكُن مِّنكُم مِّا۟ئَةٌ صَابِرَةٌ يَغْلِبُوا۟ مِا۟ئَتَيْنِ ۚ وَإِن يَكُن مِّنكُمْ أَلْفٌ يَغْلِبُوٓا۟ أَلْفَيْنِ بِإِذْنِ ٱللَّهِ ۗ وَٱللَّهُ مَعَ ٱلصَّـٰبِرِينَ ﴾

"Now Allāh has lightened your (task), for he knows that there is weakness in you. So, if there are a hundred of you that are steadfast, they will overcome two hundred. And if there are a thousand of you, they will overcome two thousand, by the permission of Allāh. And Allāh is with those who are patient."
{al-Anfāl (8): 66}

So if the *kuffār* are three times the number of Muslims, fighting would not be obligated on the Muslims and it would be correct for them to runaway as the Sahābah did at Mu'tah. This makes it certain that strength is a condition and also from this is what has been reported by Muslim from an-Nawwās bin Sam'ān in the story of the 'Īsā's killing of the Dajjāl, he narrated: The Messenger of Allāh said

Allāh will reveal to 'Īsā "I have brought forth from my servants some people who no one will be able to fight against; take these people safely to Mount Tūr" and then Allāh will send Yajūj and Majūj...

Imām Nawawī said:

---

[1] Liqā' (open session) Thursday, 33 during the Month of Safar 1414 AH'1/1994 CE

> The scholars have said that the meaning of this *hadīth* is that when there is no power or ability due to his inability to defend himself and the meaning of their flight to Mount Tūr is: to gather the people all together and establish a fortified place for them.[1]

Within this *hadīth* it can be seen that when the strength of 'Īsā ﷺ will be weak in relation to the power of Yajūj and Majūj, Allāh will order 'Īsā not to fight or to wage *jihād* against them, this indicates that strength is a condition (for waging armed military *jihād*).[2]

So we have to assess al-'Awlaki's words in light of the words from the Prophetic Methodology, which was handed down by Allāh and commented on by the great Imām Ibn al-Qayyim, and this is enough to render al-'Awlaki's claims as futile. Al-'Awlakī claims that **"whoever discourages a Muslim from doing Jihād fi Sabīlillah is a Munafiq"**. However, this presents a problem because the Sunnah and Islamic history are replete with examples of jihād, or the jihād of a person, being discouraged for various reasons – thus how many of the Salaf has he smeared with his general indictment? How can a Muslim, who is familiar with the Book of Allāh and the Authentic Sunnah, not care about the status of the people of Knowledge?! There is no doubt that when al-'Awlaki encourages the Muslim youth not to care about the status of the scholars, he intends to drive a wedge between them and the inheritors of the Prophets. This is because, as long as the youth listen to their noble scholars, never will al-'Awlaki's obsession with everything (armed) "Jihād" be adopted and followed. To undermine the status of the scholars is to undermine the following verse of Allāh:

---

[1] *Sharhu Muslim*, vol18, p.68.
[2] More on this is discussed by our Shaykh 'Abdul'Azīz bin Rayyis ar-Rayyis (*hafidhahullāh*) in this ebook, pp.30-39, translated by 'AbdulHaq ibn Kofi ibn Kwesi al-Ashantī here:
http://www.salafimanhaj.com/pdf/SalafiManhaj_TakfeerAndBombing.pdf.

Chapter 2

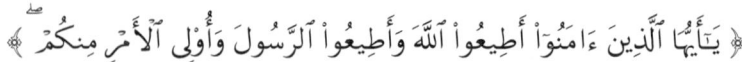

"O you who believe! Obey Allah and obey the Messenger, and those of you who are in authority." *{An-Nisā' (4):59}*

We should be aware that Ibn 'Abbās said that a *Ūli al-Amr* refers to the people of knowledge, therefore how are we to undermine the status of the scholars when Allāh has commanded us to obey them?! To undermine the status of scholars includes undermining the rights of the scholars. The Messenger of Allāh ﷺ said:

> *Not from us is the one who does not honour our elders, or the one who does not have mercy for our young or who does not recognize the right of our scholars.*[1]

'Awlakī continues (after 44:50 of part 4 of the audio series):

> A great majority of our youth want to please Allāh the proper way, but because of these Shuyūkh and Muslim celebrities, they are holding back these youth from doing Jihād fī Sabīlillah. Look at how much sin that these people are accumulating! **What they are doing falls under the service of the kuffār; their da'wah is in service of the kuffār.** Whether they are paid for it or not, whether they meet with Intelligence Agencies or not, it doesn't make a difference. **If what you are doing is serving the kuffār, then you have become one of them.** Whether you're doing for a pay, or for free, whether you are doing it in co-ordination with them or you're doing it on your own, it doesn't make a difference the end result is the same!

Here, once again, he argues on the fallacious premise of an *argumentum ad populum*, appealing to his audience through imaginary masses: "**A great majority of our youth want to please Allāh the proper way**". So by

---

[1] Sahīh al-Jāmi' No. 5443.

this is he claiming that the youth know how to please Allāh 'the proper way' but the inheritors of the Prophets, who have studied twice the life span of most of these youth, know not?! Al-'Awlakī here claims to be speaking on behalf of the masses, and even if this were true, he still would be a worthy candidate for a practical example of the hadith of Abū Hurayrah who said that the Messenger of Allāh ﷺ said:

> *"There shall come deceptive years. The truthful shall be deemed liars, while the liars shall be believed. The honest shall be deemed dishonest, while the dishonest shall be deemed honest; and the Ruwaybidah will begin to speak."* The companions asked: "What is Ruwaybidah O Messenger of Allāh?" He replied: *"An insignificant foolish man who speaks on general affairs."*

Another subtle approach of 'Awlakī is his uniform knack to place names to the scholars he wishes to wage war against without actually having to verbally mention a single name. He does this by silhouetting those who he wishes to attack through the use of pronouns and general terms like "Shuyūkh" or "scholars", just suggesting enough for his audience to know exactly who he is referring to. This underhanded method protects him from completely exposing himself but at the same time it permits him to speak out against the people of knowledge.

In relation to al-'Awlakī's translation the book of Yūsuf bin Sālih al-'Ayrī's (who was killed in a shoot-out with Saudi police), Shaykh Sālih al-Fawzān was asked:

> **A publication has been spread among the youth which permits killing the security forces and especially the inspectors and it is based on a fatwa from one of the students of knowledge, which rules these security forces to be apostates. We request from you respected Shaykh to explain the Shari' ruling with regards to this and the effects that will arise from this dangerous action.**

Answer from Shaykh Sālih al-Fawzān:

> This is the madhdhab of the Khawārij, for the Khawārij killed 'Ali bin Abī Tālib ؓ who was the best of the Sahābah after Abū Bakr, 'Umar and 'Uthmān. The one who killed 'Ali bin Abī Tālib ؓ did he not kill a man of security? **This is the madhdhab of the Khawārij and the one who gave them the fatwa allowing this is like them and one of them,** we ask Allāh for good health. Inspectors are from the armies of the Muslims and they work to safeguard security.[1]

When Imām Bin Bāz ؓ was asked: "**Is the work of the Mutawwa'īn along with the security forces considered to be from the actions of being posted at the frontline (ribāt) or not?**" He answered:

> The work of the Mutawwa'īn in every country along with the security forces against corruption and vice is considered to be jihād in the path of Allāh for whoever has rectified their intention.[2]

Also with regards to **"meeting with Intelligence Agencies"** then those who are guilty of this most are the likes of the takfīrīs and their minions! The likes of Omar Bakri, Abū Qatādah al-Filistīnī, Abū Hamza and a whole host of other *takfīrī-jihādīs* are well-known for their meetings with not even the police, but with Intelligence Services! Some of them have even been protected and sheltered by them! As in the case of Abū Qatādah al-Filistīnī after *9/11* which is perhaps the most well-known example in the UK of being sheltered by the Intelligence Services! What is all the more ironic is that 'Awlakī himself stated in a documentary on Ramadān in 2001/02:

---

[1] Shaykh, Dr Sālih bin Fawzān al-Fawzān, Muhammad bin Fahd al-Husayn (editor and compiler), *al-Ijabāt al-Muhimmah fi'l-Mashākil al-Mumilah* (Riyadh: Matābi' al-Humaydī, 1425 AH/2004 CE, Second Edition), pp.94-95.
[2] *Majmū' al-Fatāwā Shaykh Bin Bāz*, vol.6, p.123.

Chapter 2

"I think that in general Islām is presented in a negative way, I mean there's always this association between Islām and terrorism when that is not true at all, **I mean Islām is a religion of peace**"[1]!?

Only to then later translate and "explain" the work of one who was counted among the terrorists!

---

[1] See 2:45 here: http://www.youtube.com/watch?v=3BgG2ZLm2M8.

CHAPTER 3

'AWLAKI MOCKS THE DA'WAH OF TASFIYAH AND TARBIYAH, HEREBY MOCKING THE DA'WAH OF IMAM AL-ALBANI

'Awlaki also states in *'Thawābit 'ala Darb il-Jihād'* [Constants on the Path of Jihād], as per the transcript of the lecture (and in part 1 of the six-part audio series):

> Many say before Jihād, there must be tarbiyah; they say tarbiyah is a prerequisite of jihād, so without tarbiyah there is no jihād. Others say that we are at the Makkah stage, therefore there should not be any fighting, is this justified? If someone starts practising Islam, or someone reverts to Islam, would we tell them that they have to have tarbiyah before they start fasting? Or, that we are now in the Makkah period so there is no need to fast? There is no difference in this matter and Jihād fee Sabilillah. The instruction for Siyām and Jihād is no different, it came in the same form (surah baqarah). Fasting was prescribed after Jihād, it took longer. **Why must we require tarbiyah, when our rasool (saw) did not?**

Here 'Awlakī clearly attacks the people who claim Tarbiyyah is needed before Jihād. From these attacks is a subtle attack of the noble scholar of Hadīth, Imām Muhammad Nāsiruddeen al-Albānī , who popularised *Tasfiyyah wat-Tarbiyyah* in a famous lecture and in some of his books and was mentioned often by his well known students.[1] Imām al-Albānī stated:

> We have to begin with at-Tasfiyah and at-Tarbiyah; any movement which is not based on this foundation has no benefit whatsoever.[2]

Also, the analogy that 'Awlakī depends on when he argues his case for Jihād without tarbiyyah is a flawed analogy and, as a consequence, so is his conclusion, because fasting and Jihād *ad-Difā'* do not share the same rulings; fasting (Ramadhān) is *fard 'ayn* whereas jihād (in its *asl*) is *fard kifāyah*. Imām 'Abdul'Azīz ibn Bāz said:

> We have previously explained on more than one occasion that Jihād is a fard kifāyah, not a fard 'ayn. All Muslims must endeavour to support their brothers with their selves (i.e., physically, by joining them), or with money, weapons, da'wah and advice. If enough of them go out (to fight), the rest are free from sin, but if they abandon it (i.e. Jihād), then all of them are sinners.[3]

Therefore fasting (Ramadhān), due to its ruling, remains an individual obligation, but as for offensive Jihād, then obviously this is not the case. How can he even allow his lips to move and claim that our Messenger ﷺ never performed tarbiyyah?! So what was he doing with the Muslims for ten years <u>before</u> the verses for *qitāl* descended?! So when 'Awlakī asks

> "If someone starts practising Islam, or someone reverts to Islam, would we tell them that they have to have tarbiyyah before they start fasting?"

---

[1] For example, Shaykh 'Ali bin Hasan al-Halabī al-Atharī authored *at-Tasfiyah wa't-Tarbiyah*.
[2] Muhammad Ibrāhīm ash-Shaybānī, *Hayāt ul-Albānī*, (Kuwait: Markaz ul-Maktūtāt wa't-Turāth wa'l-Wathā'iq, 1425 AH/2004 CE, 2nd Edn.), vol.1, p.388.
[3] *Fatāwa Shaykh Ibn Bāz*, vol.7, p.335.

Then we reply: no, we would not tell them that they **"have to have tarbiyyah"**, but rather we would teach them the prophetic method of fasting, which in itself is tarbiyyah, because how else would he know how to fast correctly except through means of tarbiyyah?! All pillars in Islām have prerequisites; the Shahāda has prerequisites; the Salāh has prerequisites, so why would jihād or Siyām be exempt from having prerequisites?! Is it not a prerequisite for a Mujāhid to have correct *'aqīdah* and *ikhlās* in Allāh in order to make sure his *qitāl* is for Allāh, upon the *sabīl* of Allāh? But how can one have a correct *'aqīdah* in Allāh or fight jihād upon the *sabīl* of Allāh except through means of tarbiyyah? How can one separate true jihād waged for the sake of Allāh from jihād-nullifying acts like nationalism, patriotism or terrrorism except through tarbiyyah? Even one of the leaders of the Ikhwān ul-Muslimīn recognises the prerequisite for tasfiyyah and tarbiyyah upon the correct *'aqīdah* when he said:

> *'Establish the Islamic state in your hearts and it will be established for you on the earth.'*[1]

When the Mongols invaded Shām, the Muslims went out to confront them, yet they had some practices of *Shirk* amongst their ranks. Shaykh ul-Islām Ibn Taymiyyah ؒ emphasised correcting the *'aqīdah* of the Muslims and calling the Muslims to *tawhīd*, as is mentioned in his refutation of al-Bakrī which has been published as *Talkhīs Kitāb ul-Istighātha* (vol. 2, pp. 731-732):

> Some of the senior scholars from our companions were saying that tawhīd is the greatest thing, knowing that it is the basis of the dīn. Yet on the other hand, others were calling upon the dead and asking them for help, supplicating to them, humbling themselves to them and maybe even what they were doing with the dead was the worst thing, calling upon the dead in times of

---

[1] This famous statement was relayed often by Imām al-Albānī ؒ and was stated by the former Murshid of the Ikhwān, Hasan al-Hudaybī.

need. They were therefore calling upon the dead hoping for a response to their request or they make a supplication by the grave of the dead as opposed to worshipping Allāh and calling upon only Him. They call upon the dead most of the time to the extent that when the enemies, who were outside the Divine Legislation of Islām, entered Damascus, some of the people went out to seek help from the dead at the graves which people hoped could remove afflictions. Some of the poets said:

> *O those who are scared of the Mongols,*
> *go to the grave of Abū 'Umar*

and:

> *seek refuge in the grave of Abū 'Umar,*
> *it will save you from harms and afflictions"*

Then Ibn Taymiyyah said:

I said to them - those who were seeking help and assistance from the dead in the graves - that even if they were with you in the battle they would be defeated as the Muslims at Uhud were defeated.[1] As it was certain that the army was destroyed due to reasons that necessitated that, Allāh's wisdom is in that...

So therefore the people of knowledge of the dīn and those possessing insight did not fight on that occasion alongside the

---

[1] Shaykh 'AbdulMālik ar-Ramadānī al-Jazā'irī in his book *as-Sabīl ilā 'Izz wa't-Tamkīn* (Riyadh, KSA: Dār at-Tayyibah, 2000) commented on this from Ibn Taymiyyah saying: Contemplate on these two matters:
FIRST: The necessity of purifying the beliefs of those striving in the way of Allāh, even if there are righteous people amongst them this will not benefit them at all so long as innovations and idolatrous practices are rampant within the ranks of the Muslims. How can an army that seeks nearness to Allāh with *shirk* and is stubborn towards the *muwahhideen* be aided?!
SECOND: The sound deduction of Ibn Taymiyyah wherein he deducted the low with the lofty. The Muslims at Uhud did not fall into *shirk* yet they disobeyed the Messenger ﷺ and were thus defeated. So is it reasonable to think that Muslims will be aided by Allāh if they have innovations, idolatrous practices, *Sufism*, denial of Allāh's attributes (*tajahhum*), *rafd* (rejection of the rightly guided caliphs) and great tribulations?!

practices of innovations and shirk. This was due to the fact that the fight was not a Divinely Legislated fight that Allāh and His Messenger have commanded, as evil and corruption would have been achieved as opposed to the desired victory from the fight. **There would not have been any rewards in this life or in the next for whoever knows this.** As for many of those who believed that this was a Divinely Legislated fight then they will be rewarded for their intentions. After that we began to command the people to have sincerity to the dīn of Allāh and to seek help from Him and that they should not seek help from anyone other than Allāh, whether it be an angel or prophet, as Allāh said on the Day of Badr:

﴿ إِذْ تَسْتَغِيثُونَ رَبَّكُمْ فَٱسْتَجَابَ لَكُمْ ﴾

"(Remember) when you asked for help from your Lord, and He answered you..." {al-Anfāl (8): 9}

It is also narrated from the Messenger of Allāh ﷺ, who said on the day of Badr: *"O Ever-Living, O Self-Sufficient, there is no god worthy of worship except You, with Your Mercy I ask You for help."*[1] In another wording: *"Rectify all of my affairs and do not make me occupied with myself, or to anyone from Your creation."*[2] Ibn Battah narrated in his *al-Ibānah* (no. 1848) that 'Umar ibn Abdul'Azīz said: *"Do not do battle alongside the Qadariyyah, for they will not be helped."*

---

[1] The verifier mentioned seeking help in this *hadīth* which was reported by an-Nasā'ī (hadīth no. 611); al-Hākim (vol. 1, pp.222) and al-Bayhaqī in his *Dalā'il un-Nubuwwah* (vol. 3, p.49). It is authenticated in the narration of Tirmidhī (*hadīth* no. 3524) and others, and from Anas ؓ with the words: "The Prophet ﷺ whenever he was worried about a matter would say: *"O Ever-Living, O Self-Sufficient, with Your Mercy I ask You for help."*

[2] The verifier also mentioned that this is a narration from Ahmad (vol. 5, p. 42); Abū Dāwūd (hadīth no. 590) and al-Bukhārī in *al-Adab ul-Mufrad* (hadīth no. 701), and it is *sahīh*.

Chapter 3

Then Ibn Taymiyyah concludes with:

When the people rectified their affairs and were truthful in seeking help from only Allāh, Allāh gave them victory over their enemy with a mighty victory indeed. The Mongols had not suffered such a defeat as they did on that occasion.[1] **The realisation of the tawhīd of Allāh was corrected and obeying the Messenger from whence they did not beforehand. Allāh gave victory to His Messenger and those who believed with him in this life and in on the day when the witnesses will be established.**

Hence, the importance of Tarbiyah and Tasfiyah, despite 'Awlakī's aspersions to its importance, yet this is not surprising from one who has no experience in the practicalities of jihād!

---

[1] i.e. The decisive Battle of Shaqhab in Southern Damascus on 21 April 1303 CE wherein the Mongols were massively defeated and crushed and the invasion of Ghazan bin Arghun bin Abaqa bin Hulagu bin Tolui bin Chingiz [Genghis] Khan (1271-1304 CE) was put to an end.

CHAPTER 4

'AWLAKI CLAIMS JIHAD DOES NOT NEED THE PERMISSION OF A LEADER

'Awlaki also states in *'Thawābit 'ala Darb il-Jihād'* [Constants on the Path of Jihād], in part 1 of the six-part lecture series:
"This 'ibadah which the kuffār are trying to cover and are calling it 'terrorism' and criminal acts, and they are branding the followers of this path as terrorists, extremists and revolutionary, these names deceive us. Wherever you see the word 'terrorist' replace it with the word 'jihād', the reason they are not saying 'Jihād' is because these are words in the Qur'ān. **But in reality it's jihād.** And the hypocrites are helping them. They do this in the following ways:
- They say that Jihād is defensive and not offensive
- They say Jihād is only allowed to free Muslim lands
- **It must be performed by the permission and instruction of the imām**
- Jihād has ended at the time of prophet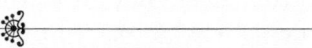
- Jihād is not applicable at this time of global peace."

Herein, as 'Awlaki is unable to present a detailed academic study of these matters in light of the *Usūl* and what has been outlined by Muslim scholars in history, he instead presents arguments which appeal to emotions. Yet in 'Awlakī's "explanation" of Ibn an-Nahhās' book *Mashāri' ul-Ashwāq ilā Masāri ul-'Ushshāq* which we will discuss in

Chapter 4

further detail later, Awlakī himself quotes (in CD 12, Track 9) Ibn an-Nahhās as saying

> The oppression of an Imām should not prevent from jihād with him. It is acceptable to fight with the Imām who drinks or commits major sins.

'Awlakī briefly comments on this by saying:

> "...so jihād is so important that it is even allowed to fight with a leader who drinks! So jihād should never stop."

Here however, 'Awlakī glosses over this issue and does not discuss it in depth due to it not only exposing his own stance on the rulers but also as it will expose that in fact 'Awlakī makes takfīr on all the Muslim leaders in the world today and views them as being "apostates" and not sinners. Jihād requires an Imām, or Muslim Leader, whom Muslims will fight under his leadership. This is an important condition for which the Sunnah has provided ample evidence. Also, the conduct of the *Salaf* shows that this indeed is a requirement. Al-Bukhārī, Muslim, Abū Dawūd and an-Nasā'ī reported that the Messenger of Allāh ﷺ said, what translated means,

> "The Imam is only Junnah (shield, barrier, refuge, etc.); fighting is raged by his authority and he serves as a shield. When he enjoins what involves the Taqwa (fear) of Allāh, and if he is just, he will gain a reward. If he enjoins otherwise, he will carry the burden of his actions."

Further, Imām Al-Bukhārī reported that Ibn 'Abbās narrated:

> "The Messenger of Allāh said, 'There is no Hijrah after al-Fat'h (meaning the capture of Makkah by the Prophet in 8 A.H.), but only Jihād and Niyyah (intention), and if you were called upon (by the Muslim Leader), then mobilize.'"

Chapter 4

These Texts are clear and direct in their meaning. As for the *Salaf*, they have similar statements concerning this subject. In his *I'tiqād Ahl us-Sunnah*, Imām Abū Bakr al-Ismā'īlī (d.371 AH) states in point no.43:

...ويرون الصلاة -الجمعة وغيرها- خلف كل إمام مسلم، براً كان أو فاجراً، فإن الله -عزّ وجلّ- فرض الجمعة وأمر بإتياها فرضاً مطلقاً مع علمه تعالى بأن القائمين يكون منهم الفاجر والفاسق، فلم يستثن وقتاً دون وقت، ولا أمراً بالنداء للجمعة دون أمر، ويرون جهاد الكفار معهم، وإن كانوا جورة، ويرون الدعاء لهم بالإصلاح والعطف إلى العدل، ولا يرون الخروج بالسيف عليهم، ولا القتال في الفتنة، ويرون الدار دار إسلام لا دار كفر -كما رأته المعتزلة- ما دام النداء بالصلاة والإقامة بها ظاهرين، وأهلها ممكنين منها آمنين.

They (Ahl us-Sunnah) view that the prayer, whether it is congregational or any other, should be made behind every Muslim Imām, good or sinful, because Allāh made the congregational prayer obligatory specifically and absolutely. This is even though Allāh knew that some of those who establish it will be immoral and sinful, and he did not exempt any time or instruct to make another congregation.

Then he states:

44 – They view jihād against the kuffār with the leaders even if the leaders are sinful and immoral.
45 – They view that du'ā should be made for the leaders so that they be righteous and just.
46 – They do not view that khurūj be made against the leaders with the sword (i.e. with weapons).
47 – Nor should there be any fighting during fitna (tribulations).
48 – They view that the transgressing group be fought against with the just Imām.

Chapter 4

49 – They view that the [Muslims] abodes are places of Islām (Dār ul-Islām) and not Dār ul-Kufr as the Mu'tazilah say. As long as the call to prayer is made and the prayer established apparently and the people are established (with their dīn) in it with safety.¹

Imām Abū Ja'far at-Tahāwī, author of *'Aqīdah Tahāwiyyah*, which was explained by Ibn Abi'l-'Izz al-Hanafī, states:

ولا نرى الخروج على أئمتنا وولاة أمورنا وإن جاروا ولا ندعوا عليهم، ولا ننزع يداً من طاعة، ونرى طاعتهم في طاعة الله عز وجل فريضة ما لم يأمروا بمعصية، وندعو لهم بالصلاح والمعافاة.

We do not view (that it is permissible to) revolt against our leaders or those who are responsible for our affairs and even if they transgress we do not make du'ā against them² and we do not take back the covenant of obedience from them³ and we view that obedience to them is from obedience to Allāh and obligatory⁴ as long as they do not command to disobedience and

---

¹ See al-Hāfidh Abī Bakr Ahmad bin Ibrāheem al-Ismā'īlī, intro. By Shaykh Hammād bin Muhammad al-Ansārī, *Kitāb I'tiqād Ahl is-Sunnah* (Riyadh, KSA: Dār Ibn Hazm, 1420 AH/1999 CE, ed. Jamāl 'Azūn), pp.55-56.
² Shaykh 'Ali bin Hasan al-Halabī al-Atharī stated regarding this, in a lesson with some brothers from London on Thursday 16th March 2006 at the *Imām al-Albānī Centre* in Ammān, Jordan: "Some people make du'ā against the Muslim leaders or curse and slander them and this is not from the characteristics of the people of truth."
³ Shaykh 'Ali bin Hasan al-Halabī al-Atharī further said: "This obviously means by extension removing themselves from the obedience of Allāh as the Prophet ﷺ said *'There is no obedience to the creation in disobedience to the Creator'* and he ﷺ also said *'Obedience is only in that which is good.'* If the issue is in regards to that which opposes the Divine Legislation and the affair of the Allāh and His Messenger, then obedience in this regard is not permissible."
⁴ Meaning: responding in obedience to the leader is as if you have responded in obedience to Allāh, it is obligatory.

we make du'ā to Allāh for them to have correctness and good health.[1]

As for the consensus which indicates this clearly is that which was stated by Imām an-Nawawī ﷺ in his explanation of *Sahīh Muslim* wherein he stated:

وأما الخروج عليهم وقتالهم فحرام بإجماع المسلمين وإن كانوا فسقة ظالمين

As for revolting against the rulers and leaders and fighting against them then it is **harām (impermissible) according to the consensus of the Muslims** even if they are sinful transgressors.[2]

Al-Hāfidh Ibn Hajar al-'Asqalānī transmitted this in his book *Fath al-Bārī* (vol.13, p.7) from Imām Ibn Battāl, who has an explanation of *Sahīh Bukhārī* which has been published:

وفى الحديث حجة على ترك الخروج على السلطان ولو جار، وقد أجمع الفقهاء على وجوب طاعة السلطان المتغلب والجهاد معه، وأن طاعته خير من الخروج عليه لما فى ذلك من حقن الدماء وتسكين الدهماء.

The fuquhā (Islamic jurists) have reached consensus that obedience must be made to the leader who becomes dominant (mutaghallib)[3] and making jihād with him and that obeying him

---

[1] Instead of making *du'ā* against them we make *du'ā* for them as Imām Ahmad ﷺ mentioned.
[2] Meaning: even if those Muslim rulers are sinners and transgressors.
[3] Shaykh 'Ali bin Hasan al-Halabī al-Atharī stated: "Here we must stop at this word **'mutaghallib (the one who overpowers and becomes dominant)'** for a while. In the next session it will be made apparent to us that the paths for a ruler acquiring power are numerous and from the paths are in the case of a ruler who becomes dominant and overpowers others *(al-Mutaghallib)*. It is when a person opposes the Divine Legislation and revolts against the Muslim leader and thus becomes dominant, and this has happened in Islamic history and the scholars noted that this opposes the Divine Legislation. However, the one who revolted against the Muslim ruler has established and settled security and command now and is able to control the Muslim lands as he obviously is a Muslim yet has opposed the consensus of the Muslims by revolting in the

is better than revolting against him due to the blood which would be spilt in that and this would not be permissible unless there was clear kufr from the leader.[1]

Imām Abū 'Uthmān as-Sābūnī (d.449 AH) stated in *'Aqīdat us-Salaf wa As-hāb ul-Hadīth*:

> The People of Hadīth view that the establishment of the Jumu'ah and the two 'Eids and other than that from all of the prayers that are made behind a Muslim Imām, **righteous or sinful, as long as he is not a disbeliever who is outside the fold of the religion.**[2] They (the People of Hadīth) make du'ā for the Muslim rulers for success and righteousness,[3] and they[4] do not view (that it is permissible to make) revolt against them (the

---

first place yet has seized the reins of power from the first bearers of it. The scholars have reached agreement that the leader who overpowers the reins of authority from another leader is to be obeyed and this is Divine Legislated. Why? Because it is feared that revolting against this one again will only cause a worse tribulation. For that reason, the greatest intents of the Divine Legislation is that preventing the harms takes precedence over enforcing the benefit."

[1] Shaykh 'Ali bin Hasan al-Halabī al-Atharī stated: "As now the leader would have been expelled from the condition of being a Muslim due to falling into clear *kufr*. For this reason, the Prophet ﷺ said: *'Until you see clear (buwāhan) kufr, for which you have with you evidence from Allāh.'* Pay attention here: *"you have with you ('indakum)"* meaning that this evidence is firmly settled in you hearts and is clear in front of your eyes, not any type of *kufr* rather it must be clear, explicit and apparent!"

[2] Shaykh 'Ali bin Hasan al-Halabī al-Atharī stated: "If such a person is a disbeliever who is outside the fold of the religion then the issue of revolting against him is not something that would need to be researched at all. The issue of revolting against a non-Muslim ruler has to be referred back to weighing up between the benefits and harms and it also has to be referred back to the *fatāwā* of the scholars." (*ibid.*)

[3] Shaykh 'Ali stated: "To the extent that Imām Ahmad ibn Hanbal ؓ would say **'If my du'ā would be accepted, I would make du'ā for the sultān (governer/ruler)'**, as if the ruler is rectified then so would the people under him and also the affairs of the society."

[4] i.e., the people of *hadīth* who are the saved sect and the aided group.

Muslim rulers) even if they see from the deviation from justice towards injustice, oppression, transgression and its likes.[1]

Imām Ahmad bin Hanbal (d. 241 AH) mentions in his *Usūl us-Sunnah* that revolt against a Muslim leader is not to be made. He states under point 53:

> And whoever revolts against a leader from among the leaders of the Muslims, after the people had agreed upon him and united themselves behind him, after they had affirmed the khilāfah for him, in whatever way this khilāfah may have been, by their pleasure and acceptance or by (his) force and domination (over them), **then this revolter has disobeyed the Muslims, and has contradicted the narrations of the Messenger of Allāh ﷺ. And if the one who revolted against the ruler died he would have died the death of ignorance.**

Then point 54:

> And the killing of the one in power is not lawful, and nor is it permissible for anyone amongst the people to revolt against him. **Whoever does that is an innovator,** (and is) upon other than the Sunnah and the (correct) path.[2]

Ibn Abī Hātim said:

> I asked my father and Abū Zur'ah (concerning various aspects of Islam, including Jihād, and they gave their answers), until they said, 'We have witnessed the scholars in all provinces, in 'Hijaz (Western Arabia), 'Irāq, ash-Shām (the Levant) and Yemen, and their Madhhab (way) was...' until they said, 'Jihād shall always

---

[1] See translaton: Abū 'Uthmān Ismā'eel ibn 'AbdurRahmān as-Sābūnī, *'Aqīdat us- Salaf wa As-hāb ul-Hadīth* [The Creed of the Pious Predecessors and the People of Hadīth], London: Brixton Mosque Islamic Centre, 1420 AH/1999 CE, pp.93-4.

[2] For both and Arabic and English texts see *Foundations of the Sunnah by Imām Ahmad ibn Hanbal* (Birmingham: Salafi Publications, 1417 AH/1997 CE), pp.37-38.

be performed, ever since Allāh has sent His Prophet until the commencement of the Hour, with the Muslim leaders from among the Muslim Imams, and nothing shall stop it (Allāh willing).'

Further, Imām Abū Ja'far at-Tahāwī had stated that:

والحج والجهاد ماضيان مع أولي الأمر من المسلمين برّهم وفاجرهم إلى قيام الساعة، لا يبطلهما شئ ولا ينقضهما.

Hajj and Jihād shall always be performed with Muslim Leaders, whether they were righteous or wicked, until the Hour commences, and nothing will invalidate or stop them (meaning Jihād and Hajj)." Refer to the explanation of the creed of Tahāwiyyah for further details.[1]

Also, Imām al-Barbahārī said:

و من قال: الصلاة خلف كل بر و فاجر و الجهاد مع كل خليفة و لم ير الخروج على السلطان بالسيف و دعها لهم بالصلاح فقد خرج من قول الخوارج أوله و آخره.

Whoever approves of praying behind every Barr (righteous) or Fājir (wicked, meaning from among Muslim leaders) and performs Jihād under every Khalīfah (Caliph), and does not deem it (correct) to rebel against the Muslim ruler with the sword, and who also ask Allāh to lead the Muslim leaders to righteousness, he will have discarded all of the ideology of Al-Khawarij (a misguided sect), from beginning to end.[2]

---

[1] *'Aqīdah Tahāwiyyah: Sharh Ibn Abi'l-'Izz* (Maktabah al-Islāmī), *tahqīq* Imām al-Albānī, p.437; also point no.77 of *'Aqeedah Tahāwiyyah*, *tahqīq* Shaykh 'Ali Hasan al-Halabī al-Atharī, p.143.

[2] *Sharh as-Sunnah* p. 123

He also states:

> واعلم أن جور السلطان لا يُنقص فريضة من فرائض الله عزّ و جلّ التي افترضها على لسان نبيه جوره على نفسه و تطوعك و برك معه تامّ لك — إن شاء الله تعالى و الجمعة معهم و الجهاد معهم و كل شيء من الطاعات فشاركه فيه فلك نيتك.

And know that a ruler's oppression does not reduce or lessen anything which Allāh has made obligatory upon the tongue of his Messenger ﷺ because his oppression is against himself. Your acts of obedience and good deeds along with good behaviour towards him will be complete, if Allāh wills. The congregational and Friday prayer is performed with them (i.e. Rulers) and so is Jihād, so accompany them in all acts of obedience for you have independent intention in that.[1]

In addition, Shaykhul-Islām Ibn Taymiyyah said:

> يَجِبُ أَنْ يُعْرَفَ أَنَّ وِلَايَةَ أَمْرِ النَّاسِ مِنْ أَعْظَمِ وَاجِبَاتِ الدِّينِ ؛ بَلْ لَا قِيَامَ لِلدِّينِ وَلَا لِلدُّنْيَا إِلَّا بِهَا . فَإِنَّ بَنِي آدَمَ لَا تَتِمُّ مَصْلَحَتُهُمْ إِلَّا بِالِاجْتِمَاعِ لِحَاجَةِ بَعْضِهِمْ إِلَى بَعْضٍ وَلَا بُدَّ لَهُمْ عِنْدَ الِاجْتِمَاعِ مِنْ رَأْسٍ حَتَّى قَالَ النَّبِيُّ ﷺ إِذَا خَرَجَ ثَلَاثَةٌ فِي سَفَرٍ فَلْيُؤَمِّرُوا أَحَدَهُمْ . رَوَاهُ أَبُو دَاوُدَ مِنْ حَدِيثِ أَبِي سَعِيدٍ وَأَبِي هُرَيْرَةَ . وَرَوَى الْإِمَامُ أَحْمَد فِي الْمُسْنَدِ عَنْ عَبْدِ اللَّهِ بْنِ عَمْرٍو أَنَّ النَّبِيَّ ﷺ قَالَ : ((لَا يَحِلُّ لِثَلَاثَةٍ يَكُونُونَ بِفَلَاةٍ مِنْ الْأَرْضِ إِلَّا أَمَّرُوا عَلَيْهِمْ أَحَدَهُمْ)) فَأَوْجَبَ ﷺ تَأْمِيرَ الْوَاحِدِ فِي الِاجْتِمَاعِ الْقَلِيلِ الْعَارِضِ فِي السَّفَرِ تَنْبِيهًا بِذَلِكَ عَلَى سَائِرِ أَنْوَاعِ الِاجْتِمَاعِ . وَلِأَنَّ اللَّهَ تَعَالَى أَوْجَبَ الْأَمْرَ بِالْمَعْرُوفِ وَالنَّهْيَ عَنْ الْمُنْكَرِ وَلَا يَتِمُّ ذَلِكَ إِلَّا بِقُوَّةٍ

---

[1] *Sharh as-Sunnah* p. 107.

Chapter 4

وَإِمَارَةٍ . وَكَذَلِكَ سَائِرُ مَا أَوْجَبَهُ مِنْ الْجِهَادِ وَالْعَدْلِ وَإِقَامَةِ الْحَجِّ وَالْجُمَعِ وَالْأَعْيَادِ وَنَصْرِ الْمَظْلُومِ . وَإِقَامَةِ الْحُدُودِ لَا تَتِمُّ إِلَّا بِالْقُوَّةِ وَالْإِمَارَةِ ؛ وَلِهَذَا رُوِيَ : ((أَنَّ السُّلْطَانَ ظِلُّ اللَّهِ فِي الْأَرْضِ)) وَيُقَالُ ((سِتُّونَ سَنَةً مِنْ إِمَامٍ جَائِرٍ أَصْلَحُ مِنْ لَيْلَةٍ وَاحِدَةٍ بِلَا سُلْطَانٍ)). وَالتَّجْرِبَةُ تُبَيِّنُ ذَلِكَ.

It should be known that appointing a leader for the affairs of the people is one the greatest religious duties without which religious or worldly matters can be established, since the best interests for mankind cannot be fulfilled except through coming together, owing to their need of one another. When they come together, it is essential to have a leader. The Prophet ﷺ said:

> "When three people set out on a journey, let them appoint one of them as a leader."

Imām Ahmed narrated in his Musnad from 'Abdullāh Ibn 'Amr that the Prophet ﷺ said:

> "It is not permissible for three people to be in some remote place unless that they appoint over themselves a leader."

The fact that it is necessary to appoint a leader over a small temporary group, whilst travelling, indicates that this is essential for all types of groups. Allāh has commanded enjoining good and forbidding evil and such cannot be achieved except through means of strength and authority. The same applies to the rest of the things that Allāh has enjoined, such as Jihād, justice, establishment of Hajj, Friday and Eid prayers, supporting those who have been wronged and enactment of al-Hudud (penal codes); all of which cannot be achieved except through means of power and authority. Hence it was narrated that "the ruler is the Shadow of Allāh on earth." And "sixty years under a tyrannical ruler are better than a single night without one." Experience proves this to be the case.[1]

Ibn Qudāmah in his *al-Mughnī* states:

وأمر الجهاد موكول إلى الإمام واجتهاده ، ويلزم الرعية طاعته فيما يراه من ذلك

The matter of Jihād is entrusted to the ruler and his ijtihād therefore his subjects must obey him in whatever he sees fit in regards to that.[2]

These Texts prove that having a leader or Imām is a condition for Jihād to commence, so that Muslims will fight under his banner and lead. This is a matter which has been explicitly stated within the books of *fiqh* of jihād yet 'Awlakī mocks it and deems it as akin to denying jihād in totality. As for 'Awlakī saying:

"Wherever you see the word 'terrorist' replace it with the word 'jihād', the reason they are not saying 'Jihād' is because these are words in the Qur'ān. **But in reality it's jihād."**

Then this is an aspect of al-'Awlakī's wilful intellectual denial. 'Awlakī's evidence, based upon bizarre emotional-contaminated rationale, is as follows: wherever the Kuffār use the term 'terrorism', this is a genuine case of Jihād, no matter how much it violates the prophetic methodology. For example, the following acts, according to 'Awlakī's thesis therefore, are noble acts of Jihād:

- Saudi Arabia - in 2003-2004 CE there were about five attacks upon civilian compounds and civilian places of residence;
- Jordan - the suicide bomb attack at the hotel in 'Ammān, killing a whole load of people that had nothing to do with any kind of war and were just at a *walīmah*;

---

[1] *Majmū' al-Fatāwā* (v.28 p. 390, 391).
[2] *Al-Mughnī*, vol.10, p.368

Chapter 4

- Morocco - like the bombings conducted by the Takfīrī-Jihādī youth of Sidi Momin in Dār ul-Baydā'/Casablanca in 2003 CE;
- Egypt - such as the Sharm e-Sheikh bombings in 2005 CE;
- 'Irāq - wherein it has been estimated that around a million or so Irāqīs have been killed largely by *Khawārij* and *Rawāfid* killing each other.
- Mumbai Bombings – where there were ten co-ordinated bombings and shootings that resulted in the death of 164 people and the wounding of 308 people.
- Pakistan and Afghanistan – wherein hundreds have been killed in such attacks.
- With regards to the effects of such operations upon Muslims who live in non-Muslim countries and how it has affected the image of Islām, then the treatment against Muslims after such 'operations' have become much more draconian. This increased after *7/7*, *9/11* and the Madrid bombings, and the attempted suicide bombing at Glasgow Airport on Saturday 30th June 2007.

Wars against Muslims have actually been justified via reference to such terrorist attacks, why is 'Awlakī therefore still in intellectual denial as to the nature of these atrocities being 'terrorist'?! Indeed, 'Awlakī himself stated (!!!) in a documentary on Ramadān in 2001/02:

I think that in general Islām is presented in a negative way, I mean there's always this association between Islām and terrorism when that is not true at all, **I mean Islām is a religion of peace**[1]!?

---

[1] See 2:45 here: http://www.youtube.com/watch?v=3BgG2ZLm2M8.

CHAPTER 5

'AWLAKI'S ERRORS IN THE FIQH OF JIHAD AND HIS OPPOSITION TO THE CLASSICAL AND CONTEMPORARY SCHOLARS OF AHL US-SUNNAH IN MANY ISSUES

Bukhārī reports in his Saḥīḥ on the authority of 'Abdullāh Ibn 'Amr Ibn al-'Āṣ ﷺ: I heard Allāh's Messenger ﷺ saying: *"Allāh does not take away the knowledge by taking it away from (the hearts of) the people, but He takes it away by the death of the scholars till when none of the (scholars) remains, people will take as their leaders ignorant people who when consulted will give their verdict without knowledge. So, they will go astray and will lead the people astray."*

There is no doubt that such serious matters in the religion such as jihād and the likes have to be referred back to credible scholars of the Sunnah. Yet what we find today unfortunately is that these issues, which involve life being taken, are referred to people who not only lack the requisite knowledge but also have their own agendas and axes to grind. There is also an issue with 'Awlakī, who is neither a scholar nor one who is known to have extracted knowledge from the well known scholars of Ahl us-Sunnah, presenting such major topics to the Muslim youth. Al-'Allāmah, Shaykh Dr. Sāliḥ al-Fawzān ibn 'Abdillāh al-Fawzān *(ḥafidhahullāh)* stated, with words which are especially relevant to al-'Awlakī:

> It is obligatory for the jāhil (ignoramus) to not speak, to keep quiet, fear Allāh, The Exalted and Majestic, and to not speak without knowledge. Allāh says,

Chapter 5

﴿ قُلْ إِنَّمَا حَرَّمَ رَبِّيَ ٱلْفَوَٰحِشَ مَا ظَهَرَ مِنْهَا وَمَا بَطَنَ وَٱلْإِثْمَ وَٱلْبَغْىَ بِغَيْرِ ٱلْحَقِّ وَأَن تُشْرِكُوا۟ بِٱللَّهِ مَا لَمْ يُنَزِّلْ بِهِۦ سُلْطَٰنًا وَأَن تَقُولُوا۟ عَلَى ٱللَّهِ مَا لَا تَعْلَمُونَ ﴾

"Say, My Lord has only forbidden immoralities - what is apparent of then and what is concealed - and sin,[1] and oppression without right, and that you associate with Allāh that for which He has not sent down authority, and that you say about Allāh that which you do not know." {al'A'rāf (7): 33}

So it is not permissible for the jāhil to speak in issues of knowledge especially in regards to major issues such as takfīr, jihād and al-walā wa'l-barā'. As for slander and backbiting in regards to the honour of the people in authority and the honour of the scholars, then this is the most severe type of backbiting and as a result is not permissible. As for current events which have passed or are taking place then these are affairs for the people in authority to research and seek counsel over and it is for the scholars to explain its Divinely Legislated ruling. As for the general and common people and beginning students it is not their issue. Allāh says,

﴿ وَإِذَا جَآءَهُمْ أَمْرٌ مِّنَ ٱلْأَمْنِ أَوِ ٱلْخَوْفِ أَذَاعُوا۟ بِهِۦ ۖ وَلَوْ رَدُّوهُ إِلَى ٱلرَّسُولِ وَإِلَىٰٓ أُو۟لِى ٱلْأَمْرِ مِنْهُمْ لَعَلِمَهُ ٱلَّذِينَ يَسْتَنۢبِطُونَهُۥ مِنْهُمْ ۗ وَلَوْلَا فَضْلُ ٱللَّهِ عَلَيْكُمْ وَرَحْمَتُهُۥ لَٱتَّبَعْتُمُ ٱلشَّيْطَٰنَ إِلَّا قَلِيلًا ﴾

"And when there comes to them something (I.e. information) about (public) security or fear, they spread it around. But if they

---

[1] Any unlawful action.

had only referred it back to the Messenger or to those in authority among them, then the ones who can draw correct conclusions from it would have known about it. And if not for the favour of Allāh upon you and His mercy, you would have followed Satan, except for a few." {an-Nisā (4): 83}

So it is incumbent to refrain the tongue in speaking about the likes of such issues, especially takfir, allegiance and disavowal. And humans are mostly ignorant of its application and can apply it incorrectly and thus judge a person with misguidance and kufr, and the ruling could thus return upon the claimant. So if a person says to his brother "O kāfir, O fāsiq" and the man is not like that (i.e. neither a kāfir nor a fāsiq) the ruling can return upon the one who said it, and Allāh's refuge is sought. This is a very dangerous issue, so it is upon the one who fears Allāh to refrain his tongue except if he is from those who are entrusted to deal with such issues, from the people in authority or the scholars. It is these who look into issues and find a solution to it, as for one who is from the common people or from the minor students (of Islamic knowledge) they do not have the right to issue rulings on people and slander the honour of people while he is an ignoramus (jāhil) who backbites and speaks about issues regarding takfir, tasfiq and other matters, this only harms the one who does this. So it is for the Muslim to withhold his tongue and not get involved in what does not concern him. Such a person should make dua' for the Muslims for them to be victorious and make dua against the kuffār for them to be punished, this is obligatory. As for discussing rulings of the Divine Legislation, falling into error and speaking about the honour of people in authority and the scholars and judging them with kufr or misguidance, this is very dangerous for you O speaker. Those you speak about will not be harmed by your speech, and Allāh knows best.[1]

Yet 'Awlakī has risen to the occasion to discuss such matters and is now taken as a "hero" by some of the Muslims even though his method is questionable as we shall see and his approach dubious. One such example of 'Awlakī taking it upon himself to discuss such delicate topics is in his series wherein he "explains" a classical book on jihād by one of the scholars of the past Abū Zakariyyā Ahmad bin Ibrāheem bin Muhammad ad-Dimishqī ad-Dumyātī (aka Ibn an-Nahhās), who died in 814 AH/1411 CE, entitled *Mashāri' ul-Ashwāq ilā Masāri ul-'Ushshāq (fi'l-Jihād wa Fadā'ilihi)*. Ibn an-Nahhās authored the book at a time when the Mediterranean shores of the Mamluk sultanate were the theatre of an ongoing fight between Christian naval forces and Muslims and also against the Mongols. Ibn an-Nahhās himself, along with many people from Shām had to flee Shām to Egypt due to the conquest of Damascus and sacking of Halab (Aleppo) at the hands of the dreaded and tyrannical Taymurlang bin Taraghāy bin Abghāy,[2] defeating the Mamluk armies. He first went to Manzalah (North-Eastern Egypt) in 804 AH (1401 CE) and then later resided in Dumyāt; such an environment was what motivated him to write *Mashāri' ul-Ashwāq* so as to exhort the Muslims to jihād in the Way of

---

[1] Shaykh, Dr Sālih bin Fawzān al-Fawzān, *op.cit.* pp.56-58.
[2] Tamerlane (circa 1370-1405 CE) was descended from the Mongols and conquered most of west and central Asia in the 14th Century CE. He is also the founder of the Mughal Empire and aspired to rebuild the Mongol Empire of his ancestors. His conquests were characterised by immense brutality and it is reported that he massacred 70,000 people of Isfahān after the people revolted against his taxes and killed his tax collectors. In 1395 CE at the Battle of the Terek River, his 100,000 strong force defeated the Mongol Golden Horde headed by Tokhtamysh. In 1398 CE he invaded Delhi and it is said that all Hindus were either killed or taken as captives while the Muslims were left. He invaded Baghdad in 1401 and massacred the people.

Allāh due to what was happening to the Muslims at the time.[1] There are a number of points about the work itself:
- The book was abridged by Ibn an-Nahhās himself and there is a Microfilm version of it at the *Markaz al-Bahth al-'Ilmī* [Centre for Academic Research] at *Umm ul-Qurā University*, Makkah.
- It was also abridged by Shaykh Mahmūd al-'Ālim al-Manzalī of Manzalah in Egypt, as *Fakahāt ul-Adwāq* (1873 CE).
- It was checked and revised by Salāh 'AbdulFattāh al-Khālidī as *Tahdhīb Mashāri' ul-Ashwāq ilā Masāri' il-'Ushshāq fī Fadā'il il-Jihād* (Ammān, Jordan: Dār un-Nafā'is, 1999), 407 pgs.
- The major edit of the work however is the most recent edit of *Mashāri' ul-Ashwāq ilā Masāri ul-'Ushshāq* by Idrīs Muhammad 'Ali and Muhammad Khālid Istanbūlī first published in 1410 AH/1989 CE with the Third Edition in Beirut in 1423 AH/2002 CE by Dār ul-Bashā'ir, 1228 pgs. The edit was originally a Masters Thesis submitted to the Sharī'ah College of Umm ul-Qurā University in 1405 and was published after. The edit also has an introduction, dated 1406 AH, by Dr 'Abdul'Azīz bin 'Abdullāh al-Humaydī the then head of College of Da'wah and Usūl ud-Dīn at Umm ul-Qurā University.
- As highlighted in the edit by the two editors above, Idrīs Muhammad 'Ali and Muhammad Khālid Istanbūlī, there are some stories, dreams and accounts in the book which exhort to the virtue of jihād but are unauthentic. There are also some ahādīth mentioned in it which are unauthentic.

---

[1] Abū Zakariyyā Ahmad bin Ibrāheem bin Muhammad ad-Dimishqī ad-Dumyātī (aka Ibn an-Nahhās), *Mashāri' ul-Ashwāq ilā Masāri' il-'Ushshāq fī'l-Jihād wa Fadā'ilihi* (Beirut: Dār ul-Bashā'ir in 1423 AH/2002 CE, Third Edition, eds. Idrīs Muhammad 'Ali and Muhammad Khālid Istanbūlī), pp. 11-12.

Chapter 5

'Awlakī however in his audio "explanation" is not using the edit by Idrees Muhammad 'Ali and Muhammad Khālid Istanbūlī and is possibly using the shorter abridged version or the *Tahdhīb*. In contrasting some of 'Awlakī's statements we however will be referring to the complete version, yet we will bring attention to this later in the study. In another lecture entitled *'Allāh is Preparing us for Victory'* which has been transcribed online by "Amatullah" and edited by "Mujahid fe Sabeelillah"[1], on page 18 we read:

> There will always be in this Ummah an at-Tā'ifah, but what is happening is that people will try to find a way out of responsibility and they will hang it on the 'Ulema saying, "This 'Alim did not give this fatwa", "This 'Alim did not tell us to fight Jihād fi Sabīlillah." So they would blame it on the 'Ulema when there are 'Ulema who are telling you otherwise; they are telling you to do the right thing and there are 'Ulema carrying the right Manhaj. **They might be in jail, they might be killed, they might be underground**[2] or they might not be famous because no television station will broadcast their Khutbah but they are 'Ulema. Another issue is that we are living in an interesting time were the 'Ilm of a person is in accordance to how famous he is and that is not a right standard for 'Ilm.

The above lecture can be found Online. Shaykh Sālih al-Fawzān ibn 'Abdullāh *(hafidhahullāh)* was asked:

> **There are those who see that the hadīth of the Prophet ﷺ: "Jihād is continuous until the Last Hour is established"[3] and then say**

---

[1] See http://www.salaattime.com/anwar.html.
[2] This in itself is the archetypal *ikhwānī modus operandi*, to only praise those who have been jailed, "underground" (meaning by this secretly hiding out in order to be elusive) or have been killed by Muslim security forces in Muslim countries.
[3] Shaykh Muhammad ibn Fahd al-Husayn says in his commentary and editing of Shaykh Sālih al-Fawzān's treatise on *jihād*, with regards to this *hadīth*: I did not find this *hadīth* with this wording and what Abū Dāwūd transmitted with the wording *"Jihād is continuous from the time Allāh sent me until the last part of this ummah fight the*

"why do the scholars say that the Ummah is not able to make offensive jihād during our present era and that this time resembles the first Makkan period? And the Prophet ﷺ said that "Jihād is continuous until the Last Hour is established"?

Answer from Shaykh Sālih al-Fawzān:
Yes, jihād is continuous if the conditions and basics have been fulfilled then it is continuous. As for when the conditions and basics have not been fulfilled then it is to be awaited for until power, capability and readiness returns to the Muslims, so then they can fight their enemies. So for example, if you have a sword or a gun, can you face airplanes, bombs and rockets?? No, because this face what they have prepared then will lead to severe harm; if you have that which is ready to face what they have prepared, or the likes of it, then face them. As for you not having anything to face them, then Allāh says,

﴿ وَلَا تُلْقُواْ بِأَيْدِيكُمْ إِلَى ٱلتَّهْلُكَةِ ﴾

"...and do not throw (yourselves) with your own hands into destruction." *{Baqarah (2): 195}*
And this will harm the Muslims more than benefiting them, if indeed there is any benefit in it at all.

Al-'Allāmah Sālih al-Fawzān *(wafaqahullāh)* also stated:
How many Muslims have been killed due to ignorant adventures which have angered the kuffār, who have been stronger than

---

Dajjāl" has within the chain of transmission Yazīd ibn Abī Tushbah about whom Ibn Hajar said in *at-Taqrīb "majhūl."* For this reason, he stated in *Fath al-Bārī* (vol.6, p.67) that in its chain of transmission is weakness. The wording that the scholars mention in the books of creed is as what at-Tahāwī ؒ said *"Hajj and jihād are both continuous with the leader of the Muslims, good or evil, until the Hour is established. They are not annulled at all or diminished."* Sharh 'Aqīdah Tahawiyyah, 387. See: Shaykh, Dr. Sālih bin Fawzān al-Fawzān, *al-Jihād wa Dawābithuhu ash-Shar'iyyah* (Riyadh: Maktabah ar-Rushd, 1424 AH/ 2003 CE, ed. Muhammad bin Fahd al-Husayn), p.48.

them in such instances, and have led to death, displacement and destruction, *la hawla wa la quwwata ilabillāh*! They also claim that such ventures are jihād when they are not jihād because the conditions of jihād have neither been met and nor have the pillars of jihād been achieved. Therefore, such ventures are not jihād rather they are transgressive actions which Allāh does not command to do.[1]

---

[1] *Al-Jihād: Anwā'uhu wa Ahkāmuhu*, p.92

CHAPTER 6

'AWLAKI CLAIMS CNN AND BBC HAVE SPREAD ISLAM ENOUGH TO HAVE ESTABLISHED THE HUJJAH ON HUMANITY TODAY!?

In the lecture *The Story of Ibn al-Akwa*, part 12 of the CD set,[1] 'Awlakī states after 38 minutes[2] into the lecture (as is also found in CD 12, Track 8 of the same series but entitled as the "explanation" of Ibn an-Nahhās' book *Mashāri' ul-Ashwāq ilā Masāri' il-'Ushshāq*):

> In the time of Rasoolullāh ﷺ the delivering of the da'wah wouldn't teach them everything about Islām and try to convince them with every single method, it would be a brief letter of two or three lines (saying) "become Muslim, if you do this is what will happen, if you don't this is what will happen." That was it, that was considered to be the da'wah that was delivered to the disbeliever and they hadn't heard anything about Islām because he didn't have mass media in those days to teach them anything about Islām people were only living in their own settlements in the desert separated and secluded...
> So to say now that the world has not heard of Islām is not true, they have heard a lot more than the reciepients of the letters of Rasoolullāh ﷺ, a lot more. **Overall, the entire population of earth**

---

[1] This edition was produced by Dar Ibn al-Mubarak (Beirut, August 2003) and distributed by al-Khandaq media.
[2] Track no.8 of this part. It can also be heard after 21 minutes here: http://www.muslimvideo.com/tv/watch/62db72d1fd2c007c5753/12.The-Book-of-Jihād-by-ibn-Nuhās---Commentary-by-Al-Awlaki.

today must have heard of Islam, they must have heard the name of Muhammad ﷺ and must know something about Islam, Salah, Hajj **and that is a sufficient form of da'wah.** The thing (that is said) is that "they have heard stereotypes about Islam", "they have heard the wrong message", "they have not been taught the truth about Islam", well that's what they used to say during the time of the Prophet ﷺ! All that they heard was that the Prophet ﷺ was "insane", "a magician", "a sorcerer", "a liar" that's what they heard about Muhammad ﷺ. **And the Sahābah did not argue with them, proving to them, they just told them "become Muslim!" So CNN has done the job, BBC has done the job in spreading the da'wah, they have all done it!** They've talked about Islam and they've raised the issue to the forefront so that's what people talk about today over their dinner table.

La hawla wa la quwwata ila billāh! So CNN and BBC have spread Islamic *da'wah*?!! First of all 'Awlakī himself in some of his other lectures has said the opposite to this and that the media have presented the wrong image of Islām!? Yet this was before his takfīrī-Khawārij phase, when the Khārijiyyah remained dorment in the ideological Qutbī-Ikhwānī paradigm only to be revived later! 'Awlakī stated after nine minutes into the lecture entitled *It's a War Against Islām*:

> ...**this will only send a ripple effect among the community around us and will add to the distorted image that already exists!**

Thanks Anwar! We couldn't have said it better ourselves! 'Awlakī's own words refute his own later words! Then 'Awlakī says in the same lecture:

> **This association is very dangerous, to associate between the mainstream Muslim community, Mosques, institutions and what is happening, is wrong and very dangerous.**

Secondly, this is a nonsensical assertion. As for saying that the Sahābah did not give *da'wah* to people first, then this is against the clear *hadīth* as the Prophet sent the Companions out with specific duties in regards to giving the *da'wah*. The Companions did not just say to people "become Muslim!", there is no evidence for such a method, rather we find it is reported on the authority of Ibn 'Abbās ؓ that Allāh's Messenger ﷺ said when he sent Mu'ādh ؓ to Yemen:

> *"You are going to a people who are from the People of the Book: So the first thing to which you call them should be the testimony that none has the right to be worshipped except Allāh."* - And in another narration: *"that they testify to the Oneness of Allāh."* – *"And if they obey you in that, then inform them that Allāh has made compulsory upon them five prayers every day and night. And if they obey you in that, then inform them that Allāh has made incumbent upon them a charity (Zakah) which is to be taken from the rich among them and given to their poor. And if they obey you in that then be careful not to take the best of their wealth (as Zakah), and be careful of the supplication of those who have suffered injustice, for there is no obstacle between it and Allāh."*[1]

Therefore, this hadīth indicates that it is not sufficient to merely "believe" without: knowledge, certainty, acceptance, compliance, sincerity, truthfulness and love.

Also the Prophet ﷺ had *jawāmi' al-kalim* (comprehensive speech of a few words that carried extensive meanings) which was from the *khasā'is* that Allāh had given him ﷺ and the Companions understood and if it was necessary they asked for further clarity. As for us, and the times we live in, we have to use technical arguments and vast words in order for people to understand and it is not sufficient for us to merely say "here's CNN, now believe in Islam!" We have to clarify further in fact. Furthermore, when the Prophet wrote letters to Mawqawqis, Kisrah, Qaysar and the likes there were details in these letters. When he

---

[1] Reported by Bukhārī (in *Kitāb uz-Zakat*) and Muslim (in *Kitāb ul-Īmān*); the *hadīth* is also reported by Imām Ahmad in his *Musnad*, and in the chapters of *Zakat* in an-Nasā'ī, ad-Dārimī and Ibn Mājah.

sent the Companions to different areas he sent specific people who understood as they had *fiqh* and a reciter of the Qur'ān, so it can be seen that the Prophet sent out people to give the *da'wah* who had good understanding, it was not a mere issue of: **"here's what the enemies say about us, now you know about Islam, so become Muslim or we kill you!"** Shaykh ul-Islām Ibn Taymiyyah ؒ said in *al-Jawāb us-Sahīh*:

> It is well known that Islām manifested with knowledge and exposition before its manifestation via the hand and the sword. For the Prophet ﷺ remained in Makkah for 13 years manifesting Islām with knowledge, exposition, verses and clear proofs and the Muhājireen and Ansār believed in it out of obedience and choice, without the use of the sword. When the verses, clear proofs and miracles were shown to them, then they manifested the sword. So if it is obligatory for us to primarily wage jihād against the kuffār with the sword (i.e. militarily) it is rather more worthy of us to firstly explain Islām and its signs to those who attack it.[1]

Imām Ibn ul-Qayyim ؒ said in explaining the *hadīth* of the Prophet's ﷺ leaning during the *Jumu'ah khutbah*:

> It is not preserved that he used to lean on a sword. Many ignoramuses think that the Prophet ﷺ used to hold his sword on the minbar as a sign that the deen is based on the use of the sword – this is disgraceful ignorance from two aspects: firstly: It is preserved that he ﷺ used to lean on a staff or on a bow. Secondly: The deen is based on revelation and as for the sword then it is established on the people of misguidance and shirk. The Madeenah of the Prophet ﷺ wherein he used to give khutab was conquered by the Qur'an and not by the sword.[2]

---

[1] Ahmad bin 'AbdulHaleem bin Taymiyyah, *al-Jawāb us-Sahīh liman Badal ad-Dīn al-Masīh* (Cairo: Matba' al-Madanī, n.d.), vol.1, p.75.
[2] Ibn ul-Qayyim, *Zād ul-Ma'ād* (Beirut: Mu'asash ar-Rosālah, 1405 AH, ed. Shu'ayb al-Arna'ūt, 7th Edn.), vol.1, p.190.

Ibn ul-Qayyim ﷺ said:

Conveying his Sunnah ﷺ to the Ummah is more virtuous than conveying arrows against the enemy, because many people do the latter while the former (conveying the Sunan) this is something which is only established by the inheritors of the Prophets and their successors within their nations – may Allāh make us from them with His Blessing and Virtue.[1]

He also said in *al-Qasīdah Nūniyyah*: "*Jihād* with the clear proofs and the tongue; Comes before *Jihād* with the sword and the spear." It is also well known that *da'wah* to the *kuffār* comes before fighting them.[2] When the Prophet ﷺ instructed the leader of an army, he would advise him and those Muslims with him to have *taqwā* of Allāh, he ﷺ would say to such a leader:

When you meet your enemies from the Mushrikeen call them to three virtues; mention Islām to them and if they do not accept it then the jizya (must be paid by them to the Muslims) and if they do not pay it, then fight.

Sahnūn said:

I asked 'AbdurRahmān bin al-Qāsim: "did Mālik instruct to give da'wah before fighting?" He said: "Yes, he (i.e. Imām Mālik) used to say: 'I do not view that the Mushrikeen be fought against until they are called to Islām.' I (Ibn ul-Qāsim) asked him (Mālik): 'so they (i.e. the Muslims) are not to plan against them and remain there until they are called to Islām?' He (Imām Mālik) said: 'Yes.'" I said: So whether we confront them or they

---

[1] Ibn ul-Qayyim, *Jalā' ul-Afhām fī Fadl as-Salah wa's-Salām 'alā Muhammad Khayr ul-Anām* (Dammām: Dār Ibn ul-Jawzī, 1420 AH/1999 CE, ed. Mashhūr Hasan), p.582.
[2] See Hamad bin Ibrāhīm al-'Uthmān, *Jihād: Anwā'ahu wa Ahkāmuhu, wa'l-Hadd al-Fāsil Baynahu wa Bayna'l-Fawda* ('Ammān: Dār ul-Athariyyah, 1428 AH/2007 CE), pp.260-62.

accept coming to us and have entered our lands, we do not fight them (firstly) until we have called them (to Islām), we are upon the saying of Mālik.[1]

Imām ash-Shāfi'ī ﷺ stated:

> Inviting the Mushrikīn to Islām or to the jizyah (primarily) is obligatory for whoever has not had the da'wah conveyed to him. As for the one who has the da'wah conveyed to him then the Muslims can fight them before giving da'wah to them… as for the one who has not had the da'wah of the Muslims conveyed to him then it is not permissible to fight them until they are called to īmān, if they are not from Ahl ul-Kitāb. Or they are called to īmān or to give the jizyah if they are from Ahl ul-Kitāb.[2]

Shaykh ul-Islām Ibn Taymiyyah ﷺ viewed that the command to convey the *da'wah* was obligatory and he also viewed the sanctity of the blood of the *kuffār* who had not had the *da'wah* conveyed to them, he said:

> The blood of the disbeliever during the early history of Islām was sanctified and inviolable just like the original sanctity of a person. Allāh prevented the Muslims from killing such a disbeliever. The blood of those is just like the blood of the Copt who Mūsā killed and like the blood of the disbeliever who has not had the message conveyed to him during our times.[3]

---

[1] *Al-Mudawannah al-Kubrā li-Imām Mālik Ibn Anas: the narration of 'AbdurRahmān bin Qāsim*, (Makkah al-Mukarramah: Dār ul-Bāz, 1415 AH/1994 CE, ed. Ahmad 'AbdusSalām, 1st Edn.), vol.1, p.496.
[2] Muhammad bin Idrīs ash-Shāfi'ī, *Al-Umm*, (Beirut: Dār ul-Ma'rifah, ed. Muhammad Zuhrī an-Najjār, n.d.), vol.4, p.239.
[3] Ahmad bin 'AbdulHalīm bin Taymiyyah al-Harrānī, *as-Sārim al-Maslūl 'alā Shātim ir-Rasūl* (Beirut: Dār ul-Kutub al-'Ilmiyyah, ed. Muhammad Muhiyydīn 'AbdulHamīd, n.d.), p.104.

Chapter 6

So the issue is: has the *da'wah* been conveyed adequately to the vast majority of non-Muslims? Let us see what one of the Imāms of the era, the Shaykh, al-'Allāmah, Muhammad bin Sālih al-'Uthaymīn ﷺ states about this important topic. Upon commenting on the saying of Allāh the Elevated:

﴿ وَأُوحِىَ إِلَىَّ هَٰذَا ٱلۡقُرۡءَانُ لِأُنذِرَكُم بِهِۦ وَمَنۢ بَلَغَۚ ﴾

"This Qurān has been revealed to me that I may therewith warn you and whomsoever it may reach." {al-An'ām (6): 19}

The Shaykh said:

"...that I may therewith warn you..." [Meaning] To warn you from defiance by it, His saying: "...and whomsoever it may reach." This indicates that the evidences are not established upon those whom the Qurān has not been conveyed to. Likewise are those whom the Qurān has been conveyed to in a distorted manner, the evidences are not established upon them either, but their excuse is not the same as the excuse of those whom the Qurān has not been conveyed to at all, because it is upon those whom the Qurān has reached in a distorted manner to further investigate. However they may trust the person who conveyed the Qurān to them to a point where they do not need to investigate [for themselves]. <u>The question is</u>: Has the Islāmic religion been conveyed to the masses of non-Muslims in a manner that is not distorted? <u>The Answer</u>: No! Never! And when the affair of those who act without wisdom emerged, it distorted the picture of Islām even further in the eyes of the westerners and other than them. Those who plant bombs in the midst of people claiming that this is Jihād. The truth is that they harm Islām and further turn people away from it.[1]

---

[1] *Fatāwā al-'A'immah*, p.55, originally translated by Abu 'AbdulWāhid Nadir Ahmed, see article *'Has Islam been properly conveyed to non-Muslims?'*: http://www.madeenah.com/article.cfm?id=1191.

CHAPTER 7

'AWLAKI'S VIEW ON LEAVING THE ARENA OF BATTLE IF THE MUSLIMS ARE OVERWHELMED

'Awlakī also states after 45 minutes into the lecture[1] of *The Story of Ibn al-Akwa* (as is also found in CD 12, Track 9 of the series when it is entitled as the "explanation" of Ibn an-Nahhās' book *Mashāri' ul-Ashwāq ilā Masāri' il-'Ushshāq*) that if there are too few Muslims fighting on the battlefield then they can barricade themselves into a fortified building and wait for reinforcements!!? This is incorrect as rather the Muslims are allowed to flee! If at that point there are too few Muslim soldiers then this is an instance wherein it is allowed for the Muslims to leave the arena of the Battlefield and regain reinforcements, however 'Awlakī is trying to assert that the Muslims must persist on fighting and barricade themselves into a building and carry on fighting even though they will be overwhelmed. Shaykh, Dr 'AbdusSalām as-Sihaymī stated in his lessons explaining his book on jihād:[2]

---

[1] After 2 and half minutes on track 9 of the Dar Ibn al-Mubarak (Beirut, August 2003) CD, part 12.
[2] From the Shaykh's explanation of his book *al-Jihād fi'l-Islām: Mafhūmuhu, Dawābituhu wa Anwāuhu wa Ahdāfuhu*. The lesson was held in Jeddah, 5/6/ 1427 AH and was translated from the recording that was available online. For the book reference see 'AbdusSalām bin Sālim bin Rajā' as-Sihaymī (Associate Professor, Fiqh Department, Sharī'ah College, Islamic University of Madīnah), *al-Jihād fi'l-Islām: Mafhūmahu wa Dawābitahu wa Anwā'ahu wa Ahdāfahu* [Jihād in Islām: Its Understanding, Rules, Types and Aims]. Madīnah an-Nabawiyyah, KSA: Maktabah Dār un-Nasīhah, 1430 AH/2009 CE, 2nd Edn., pp.76-77. The book has introductions by al-'Allāmah Sālih bin Fawzān al-Fawzān and Shaykh 'AbdulMuhsin bin Nāsir Āl 'Ubaykān.

The second principle has preceded which mentioned the Divinely Legislated evidences which made the conditions of having strength and ability (to make jihād) but this is not sufficient itself as there also has to be added to this the issue of not bringing about a greater harm than leaving jihād. The Fuqahā have also mentioned this wherein they say "if the kuffār increase their numbers (on the battlefield) and it is most likely that we will be destroyed then we have to flee (al-Firār) based on the saying of Allāh,

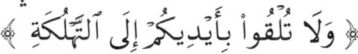

'…and do not throw (yourselves) with your own hands into destruction.' *{Baqarah (2): 195}*

Or if we are not able to harm them, then it is recommended to flee (al-Firār)."

"Recommended to flee (the battle)", pay attention to this principle of the Fuqahā that if the kuffār increase in number in the battle and their numbers are more than that of the Muslims, if the Muslims are sure that they will be triumphant they continue but if they are sure that they will be defeated and not able to harm the enemy then it is obligatory for them to flee the battle. If they cannot harm the enemy and all what will happen is Muslims getting killed then they have to flee the battle based on the saying of Allāh,

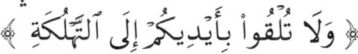

"…and do not throw (yourselves) with your own hands into destruction." *{Baqarah (2): 195}*

Or if the Muslims are not able to harm them then it is recommended to flee, because the intended aim is not merely killing people or (sacrificing) the souls of the Muslims or aiming to be martyred, rather the intended aim (of jihād) is to achieve benefits for Islām and avert harms which may affect the Muslims.

Ibn Juzayy al-Mālikī stated that when the Muslims are being killed on the battlefield, then for them to flee is primary, Abū Ma'ālī stated "there is no difference of opinion in this."[1]

There is no difference of opinion in this with the *Fuqahā* ؓ that if the Muslims are being killed, to withdraw takes precedence than standing to face the enemy because standing to face them will result in a greater harm and the harms of participating in jihād here will be worse than the harm of leaving off fighting.

Ash-Shawkānī said "If it is known for sure that the kuffār are overpowering and getting the better of the Muslims, then the Muslims have to avoid fighting them and get more fighters and gain the help of the people of Islām", he based this on the saying of Allāh,

$$ \text{﴿ وَلَا تُلْقُوا بِأَيْدِيكُمْ إِلَى ٱلتَّهْلُكَةِ ﴾} $$

"...and do not throw (yourselves) with your own hands into destruction." *{Baqarah (2): 195}*

And this is taken generally even within a specific reason, and it is oft-repeated in Usūl that the general expression takes precedence and not a specific reason. It is well-known that whoever goes forth while seeing that he is

---

[1] Muhammad bin Ahmad bin Juzayy al-Kalbī (d. 741 AH/CE), *Qawānīn ul-Ahkām ash-Shar'iyyah wa Masā'il ul-Furū' al-Fiqhiyyah* (Beirut: Dār ul-'Ilm, 1979 CE), p.165.

going to be killed, defeated or overpowered has thrown himself into destruction.[1]

Shawkānī deduces from the *ayah*:

﴿ وَلَا تُلْقُوا بِأَيْدِيكُمْ إِلَى ٱلتَّهْلُكَةِ ﴾

"...and do not throw (yourselves) with your own hands into destruction." *{Baqarah (2): 195}*

...that in regards to "throwing oneself into destruction" then when one knows for sure that the kuffār are overpowering the Muslims, the Muslims should leave off fighting in this instance, until they get stronger power and stronger force so that the challenge will be stronger. However, when the Muslims are weakened and still fight, it will not be known when the reinforcements will come, so it is not a matter of merely trying to gain victory and martyrdom, rather it depends on the benefits that will be gained by the Muslims. Preventing the harms takes precedence over achieving the benefits and Shawkānī used as a proof for this the well-known principle of the general meaning taking precedence over the specific reason, so even though this ayah was about a specific reason the general meaning of it is looked at and not the specific reason. So the ayah in its general words indicates that when Muslims will be destroyed (in any scenario) then they should stay away from what will cause destruction.

However, 'Awlakī does later say in the series, quoting Ibn an-Nahhās ؒ, that it is allowed to flee if the enemy are more than double the Muslim forces. Ibn an-Nahhās states in *Mashāri' ul-Ashwāq ilā Masāri'*

---

[1] Muhammad bin 'Ali ash-Shawkānī (1250 AH/CE), *as-Sayl al-Jarār Mutadaffiq 'ala Hadā'iq il-Azhār* [The Torrential Profuse Flood of the Blooming Gardens]. Beirut: Dār ul-Kutub al-'Ilmiyyah, 1405 AH, first edn., ed. Muhammad Zāyid, vol.4, p.529.

Chapter 7

il-'Ushshāq in the edit of Idrees Muhammad 'Ali and Muhammad Khālid Istanbūlī (first published in 1410 AH/1989 CE with the Third Edition in Beirut in 1423 AH/2002 CE by Dār ul-Bashā'ir), p.570 that:

> The madhhab of Ahmad is that if the enemy is more than double (the Muslim forces) and the Muslims think that it is probable that they will be destroyed by remaining and that there is salvation for them if they flee, then it takes precedence for them to flee, but if they remain it is allowed for them to do that so as to achieve martyrdom. This is what was mentioned by the author of al-Mughnī[1] and he did not relay any difference of opinion over this, and he did not make a condition of harming the enemy by remaining. Upon my life, the one who stays in his place yet does not effect the enemy at all, and there is no other outcome except for total destruction (Mahdh ul-Halāk) - such as for the one who is blind and faces the enemy with no weapons, or one or two stationed on the coastline without anything to deflect the (enemy) weapons while the enemies are many in their approaching ships and their arrows reach the coastline (where the two are stationed) - **then their remaining there will not achieve anything and the one who remains until he is killed (by the enemy) has sinned and this falls under the general ayah of throwing oneself into destruction (Tahlukah).** The words of al-Ghazālī have preceded in a previous chapter and is clear on this. I do not think that anyone differs on this side of it, as for one who is brave and has a sincere intention for martyrdom and is able to attack them with arrows, fire, stones or the likes and effect the enemy and is killed in this process then this is what has to be looked into: is it better in regards to him to remain stationed or flee? The previous evidences in the chapter are clear in that in

---

[1] Ibn Qudāmah al-Maqdisī, *al-Mughnī* (Beirut: Dār ul-Kitāb al-'Arabī, 1392 AH/1972 CE), vol.8, pp.485-486.

this case it is recommended to remain stationed and Allāh knows best.

These words from Abū Hāmid al-Ghazālī ؒ will be mentioned later on. Then Ibn an-Nahhās ؒ relays straight after this (p.571):
Shaykh ul-Islām Abū Hafs al-Bulqīnī ash-Shāfi'ī ؒ was asked about two men who go out with the intention of being stationed in Ribāt on some coasts. Then (while they are stationed in Ribāt) the enemy kuffār forces attack them and they are more in number than the two of them. One of the two suggests to the other that they should flee saying "there is nothing in us remaining stationed except total destruction without us affecting any harm on the enemy!" While the other one says "we will rather fight on even if it is most likely that we will be destroyed!" Which one is correct and free from sin? Answer: **"The one who is correct is the one who indicates to flee and there is no sin on either of them and Allāh knows best."** Ar-Rāfi'ī said: "if a Muslim comes across two Mushriks and they seek him out, he can flee, yet to remain and face them is better." If he goes after the two of them can he flee after that? This has two sides and the most accurate view of the two is that: yes he can flee, **because the obligation of jihād and remaining stationed is for a Jama'ah.**

So here we find a number of benefits such as:
- The emphasis on there being a benefit in a Muslim remaining stationed to challenge the enemy, and remember it is talking about those fighting against the Muslims in a war which the 'Ulamā are behind and support.
- That one can flee if there is no benefit in remaining.
- That Jihād is to be waged as a collective action not merely on what an individual wants to do to the detriment of the whole.
- All of the above is in regards to enemy troops and not civilians!

CHAPTER 8

'AWLAKI SAYS 'IRAQ IS "NEW JIHAD FRONT FOR THE MUSLIMS"!?

'Awlakī says in the lecture *Allāh is Preparing us for Victory* (as documented in the Online transcription of the lecture which is abridged from the actual lecture):

> "Look at al-Irāq – who would imagine that Irāq would be a land of jihād? Who would have even imagined that a few years ago?! Who would have thought that the land of Saddam turn in to a land of jihād?...**it turns out to be the new jihād front for the Muslim Ummah today and the most important one. The land of Iraq is being prepared by Allāh,** Azza wa Jall. **The Iraqi people - without that twelve year sanctions and without the First Gulf War- would not have become the new Mujahideen front today**...They took away Saddam and Abu Mus'ab az-Zarqawi (rahimahullah)[1] replaced him."[2]

La hawla wa la quwwata ila billāh! So 'Irāq has become "the new and most important jihād front for the Muslim Ummah"!? So over a million souls have been lost and this is supposed to be **"the new jihād front for the Muslim Ummah and the most important one"**? There are bombings everyday in which hundreds of people are murdered and this

---

[1] This *tarāhum* (having mercy on him) is mentioned in the transcript of the lecture but not in the actual lecture by 'Awlakī himself.
[2] See page 24-5 of the transcription of the lecture here:
http://downloads.islambase.co.uk/books/AllāhPreparingVictory.pdf.

is the **"the new jihād front for the Muslim Ummah and the most important one"**? The enemies of Islām have encroached further into the land and this is supposed to be **"the new jihād front for the Muslim Ummah and the most important one"**? Women and children are killed nearly every day and this is supposed to be **"the new jihād front for the Muslim Ummah and the most important one"**? There is absolutely no safety to even go to the local market place and this is supposed to be **"the new jihād front for the Muslim Ummah and the most important one"**? By what stretch of the imagination did al-'Awlakī manage to deduce that 'Irāq is **"the new jihād front for the Muslim Ummah and the most important one"**?

As for 'Awlakī's saying that **"'Irāq is being prepared by Allāh"** then indeed it is being prepared for kindling *fitna*! In his *al-Kabīr* (vol.12, p.384, no.13422), at-Tabarānī narrated via a good chain of narrators traced back to Nāfi' ؓ who said:

The Prophet ﷺ said: *"O Allāh! Bless our Shām for us, O Allāh bless our Yemen for us"* many times. On the third or fourth time, the Sahābah said: "O Allāh's Messenger! And our 'Irāq?!" He ﷺ said: *"From there will appear earthquakes and fitan (tribulations, afflictions etc). From there the horn of Shaytān (satan) will appear."*[1]

---

[1] This narration is mursal, which is the strongest type of da'īf hadīth. Shaykh Mashhūr Hasan Āl Salmān stated in *'Irāq fī Ahādīth wa'l-Athār il-Fitan* (Dubai: Maktabat ul-Furqān, 1425 AH/2004 CE): "The isnād [Ismā'īl bin Mas'ūd narrated from 'Ubaydullāh bin 'Abdullāh bin 'Awn from his father from Nāfi'] is good and 'Ubaydullāh is well known in hadīth. Al-Bukhārī stated in *at-Tārīkh al-Kabīr*, vol.5, p.388, no.1247, as did Ibn Abī Hātim in *al-Jarh wa't-Ta'dīl*, vol.5, p.322, that 'Ubaydullāh from his father is 'sālih ul-hadīth.'" Adh-Dhahabī said about the hadīth in *as-Siyar*, vol.15, p.356: "This hadīth is Sahīh ul-Isnād Gharīb." It was authenticated by Abu'l-Ma'ālī al-Maqdisī in *Fadā'il Bayt ul-Maqdis*, p.430; Jamāluddīn al-Marrākushī in his Takhrīj to *Mashaykhat ul-Imām al-Marāghī*, p.414; at-Tirmidhī, Ahmad, Ibn Hibbān; al-Baghawī in *Sharh us-Sunnah*, vol.14, p.206, no.4006; and Ibn Jamī' in the Mu'jam of his Shaykhs, pp.324-325.

Chapter 8

Other hadīth scholars such as: al-Fasawī, al-Jurjāni, Abū Nuʿaym and Ibn ʿAsākir narrated via a sahīh (*authentic*) chain of narrators traced back to Sālim ؇ who said:

> Allāh's Messenger said: *"O Allāh! Bless our Makkah for us, bless our Madīnah for us, bless our Shām for us, bless our Sāʿ for us and bless our Mudd for us."* One of the Sahābah said: "O Allāh's Messenger! And our 'Irāq?!" The Prophet ؇ did not answer him. The man repeated his statement three times but the Prophet did not answer him and finally he ؇ said: *"From there will appear the earthquakes and fitan (tribulations) and from there will appear the horn of Shaytān."*[1]

Imām Ahmad narrated in his *Musnad* (vol.5, p.33) and his *Fadāʾil us-Sahābah* (p.719)[2] via a sahīh chain of narrators from Ibn Huwālah that the Prophet ؇ said:

> *"O Ibn Huwālah! What would you do when fitan spreads throughout the land like the horns of bulls?"* Ibn Huwālah answered: *"What should I do, O Allāh's Messenger?"* He ؇ said: *"Go to Shām!"*

Ibn ʿAsākir (vol.1, p.159) narrated a long conversation that took place between 'Umar ؇ and Kaʿb al-'Ahbār tracing it back to Abū Idrīs who said:

> Once 'Umar ؇ came to Shām and said: *"I intend to go to 'Irāq."* Kaʿb al-'Ahbār then said: *"I seek Allāh's refuge for you from such a thing, O Ameerul Mu'minīn."* 'Umar then exclaimed: *"Why do you hate my going there?"* Kaʿb answered: *"In it ('Irāq) there are nine tenths of evil, the incurable ailment, the deviants amongst the*

---

[1] The hadīth is narrated through many authentic ways of narration mentioned in Mashhūr Hasan Āl Salmān, *Irāq fi Ahādīth wa'l-Athār il-Fitan* (Dubai: Maktabat ul-Furqān, 1425 AH/2004 CE).

[2] And many others; all mentioned in Mashhūr Hasan Āl Salmān, *Irāq fi Ahādīth wa'l-Athār il-Fitan* (Dubai: Maktabat ul-Furqān, 1425 AH/2004 CE).

Jinn and Hārūt and Mārūt and in there Iblīs has laid his eggs and had his chicks."[1,2]

Shaykh Mashhūr Hasan Āl Salmān stated in his book of *'Irāq fī Ahādīth wa'l-Athār il-Fitan* (Dubai: Maktabat ul-Furqān, 1425 AH/2004 CE):

In his *Sahīh* (vol.7, p.77), Imām al-Bukhārī narrated and so did Ahmad (vol.2, pp.85, 153) from Ibn Abī Nu'aim to have said: "I was in the presence of Ibn 'Umar ؓ when a man from 'Irāq came and asked him regarding a *Muhrim* who kills a fly. Ibn 'Umar said: "O people of 'Irāq! You ask me about the *Muhrim* who kills a fly and you killed the son of the daughter of Allāh's Messenger ﷺ about whom he ﷺ said: *"They (i.e. al-Hasan and al-Husain) are my two sweet basils in this world."* And his book *Mukhtasar Sahīh al-Bukhārī* (vol.1, pp.130-311) Shaykh al-Albānī ؓ commented on Ibn 'Umar's *hadīth* which includes "and our *Najd*" saying:

> "I say that the words "and our Najd" refer to 'Irāq as some authentic narrations state. This was interpreted as such by al-Khattābī and al-'Asqalānī, as I clarified in my *Takrīj Fadā'ilush-Shām* (pp.9-10, hadīth no.8).

So the word 'Najd' mentioned in al-Bukhārī's narration refers plainly to 'Irāq as stated in the other narrations.

---

[1] Narrated by: Ibn 'Asākir via many ways of narrations (vol.1, pp.120-121, 121, 121-122, 159). All these narrations include praise of Shām. For more clarification on this, kindly refer *to al-Hinnā'iyyāt*. Some of the narrations mention 'Irāq such as the one (vol.1, p.121) that states: *"I seek refuge with Allāh for you from 'Irāq, O Amīrul Mu'minīn; it is the land of deceit and witchcraft, it includes nine tenths of evil, the ailment and every disobedient devil."* This narration was also narrated by Ibn al-Murji in *Fadā'il-Baitil-Maqdis*, pp. 64-65, 442-443.

[2] This narration was also narrated by Imām Mālik in his *al-Muwatta'* via an authentic chain of narration. Another narration was narrated by al-Balāthurī in his *Ansābul-Ashrāf* (vol.10, p.387) via a weak chain of narrators. For more details, refer to the original Arabic text.

Chapter 8

Having stated the same thing regarding Najd being 'Irāq and the surrounding area, al-Kirmānī said in his interpretation of *Saḥīḥ al-Bukhārī* (vol.24, p.168):

> The word '*Fitnah*' may encompass earthquakes, turmoil and afflictions that take place amongst people; this interpretation would be more comprehensive. The word was also interpreted to mean that people of the east were disbelievers at that time hence it is they who would excite enmity amongst Muslims. **Besides, it was the people of 'Irāq and the people of the eastern surrounding terrain who excited the Jamal and Siffin crises and from amongst them the Khawārij emerged and from amongst them the Dajjāl (Pseudo Messaiah) and Ya'jūj and Ma'jūj (Gog and Magog) will come out. As for the word "horn", it was interpreted to refer to that which is evil.**

Ibn Battal stated the same in his interpretation of *Saḥīḥ al-Bukhārī* (vol.10, p.44).[1] Interestingly, al-'Awlakī appears to promote jihād yet these *khawārij* of 'Irāq are in fact just the type of Khawārij against whom jihād should be also waged, for Shaykh ul-Islām Ibn Taymiyyah noted;

> Ahl us-Sunnah, and all praise is due to Allāh, are agreed on the fact that they (the Khawārij) are misguided innovators and that it is obligatory to fight them according to the authentic texts. The best of actions of leader of the believers 'Ali ﷺ was his fight against the Khawārij.[2]

---

[1] Most of the translations here regarding the scholars explanations of the hadīth are from the forthcoming translation by Iman bint Zakaria Abu Ghazie of Shaykh Mashhūr's book on 'Irāq.

[2] Ibn Taymiyyah, *Minhāj us-Sunnah*, vol.6, p.116

As for the 'Irāq being "the new Mujahideen front" then the majority of the country is controlled by extremist *Rawāfid!* Is it among these whom the Muslim Ummah should take the lead from?[1]

---

[1] For more on the correct Islamic stance regarding the situation in Irāq refer to the book *Who's in for Irāq?* by Shaykh 'Abdul'Azīz bin Rayyis ar-Rayyis available from salafimanhaj.com.

CHAPTER 9

'AWLAKI TRIES TO MAKE AN ANALOGY BETWEEN THE MARTYRDOM AND BRAVERY OF THE SAHABAH AND THE CONTEMPORARY MANIFESTATION OF SUICIDE BOMBING: AN ANALYSIS[1]

Mudrak bin 'Awf ﷺ reported:

I was with 'Umar when he received a Messenger (from a battle). 'Umar asked him about the condition of the soldiers. The Messenger kept on mentioning to 'Umar some of the well-known people who died and then he said: *"And others died whom I don't know."* 'Umar said: *"But Allāh knows them!"* The Messenger said: *"And men who sold themselves to Allāh."* Mudrak said: *"Among those is my uncle. People claim he killed himself by throwing himself into the enemy's army."* 'Umar said: *"Whoever claims that is a liar! He (your uncle O Mudrak) is one of those who sold this world for the next."*[2]

'Awlakī in his "explanation" of Ibn an-Nahhās' book *Mashāri' ul-Ashwāq ilā Masāri' il-'Ushshāq*, CD 6, Track 15 states after relaying the above story:

So here you have a man who jumps into the army, seeking martyrdom. Might as well just put on an explosive belt, what's

---

[1] Some aspects of this section are from 'AbdurRahmān Mahdī, *Martyrdom in Jihād Versus Suicide Bombing* (London: Islamic Knowledge and Jamiah Media, 2011), pp.62-73.

[2] Recorded by Ibn Jarīr and Ibn ul-Mundhir.

the difference!? Jump in with an army of thousands?! So... (either way) it's definite death."

'Awlakī also says in his "explanation" of Ibn an-Nahhās' book *Mashāri' ul-Ashwāq ilā Masāri' il-'Ushshāq*, CD 2, Track 15:
> ...otherwise the suicide bomber would be committing suicide – but what makes it jihād is because the intention is done for the sake of Allāh.

In the lecture series *Stories from Hadīth*, part 4, after 21 minutes here; http://www.halaltube.com/stories-from-hadith, Awlakī is asked about the permissibility of suicide bombings and also makes reference to the story of al-Barā' ibn Mālik al-Ansārī ؓ at the Battle of Yamāma as proof of suicide bombings, or what has been called "martyrdom operations".

The Martyrdom and Bravery of the Companions

From the many historical narrations and ahādeeth extolling the battlefield jihād of the Companions of Allāh's Messenger ﷺ are:

- **Al-Barā' ibn Mālik al-Ansārī** ؓ **at the Battle of Yamāma** (which was arguably the most fierce battle that the Muslims had fought up until that point). The army of the true Prophet, Muhammad ﷺ, who had recently left this world, met the army of the false prophet Musaylama al-Kadhdhāb, on the territory of Banū Hanīfah at Yamāma in Najd, Central Arabia. In what was becoming an all-or-nothing battle for the survival of Islām itself, Musaylama and his men were devastating the Muslim forces, forcing the latter's retreat from their positions and even storming the tent of their commander, the brilliant Khālid ibn al-Walīd ؓ. As the battle raged with ever greater intensity, Khālid ordered al-Barā': *"Charge, O young man of the Ansār!"* Al-Barā' ؓ turned to his men saying: *"O Ansār, let not anyone of you think of returning to Madīnah! There is no Madīnah for*

Chapter 9

you after this day. There is only Allāh, then Paradise!" He and the Ansār ؐ then rushed the lines of the disbelievers, breaking both their ranks and their spirits, and forcing them to withdraw. Musaylama and his still thousands-strong forces barricaded themselves behind a high-walled fruit garden, which later became known as The Garden of Death. From this fortified position, the army of the false prophet began raining down arrows on the Muslims, ripping apart their flesh with iron barbs on chains and burning their skins with boiling oil. Al-Barā' ؐ said to his fellow soldiers: **"I shall sit upon a shield and you shall raise the shield with the help of your spears to the height of the outer wall of the garden. Then you shall propel me inside. Either I will die as a martyr or I will open the gate for you."** Thus, al-Barā' ؐ descended upon the enemy hoards and slew many of their number sustaining blows and injuries before eventually managing to open the gate. The Muslims charged through the open gate, flooding through the garden with some soldiers opening other gates and fought bitterly in close combat until Musaylama was finally killed and victory was attained.[1] Al-Barā' ؐ was carried to Madīnah where he spent a month in the care of Khālid ibn al-Walīd ؐ who tended to his eighty or so wounds.[2]

- 'Abbād ibn Bishr ؐ was one of the eminent Companions and he was martyred on the Day of Yamāmah at the age of forty-five. As a member of the Ansār he embraced Islām at the hands of Mus'ab ibn 'Umayr ؐ. One of the miracles which happened to him was when he was in the company of the Prophet ؐ on a very dark night making it difficult to know the route back and the direction. By Allāh's Permission 'Abbād's stick lit up for

---

[1] Reported by Ibn Ishāq and in Ibn Hajar's *al-Isābah*. Also refer to Shawqī Abū Khalīl, *Hurūb ur-Riddah* (Damascus: Dār ul-Fikr), p.92.
[2] Bayhaqī.

him making it easy for him to find his route back home.[1] Due to 'Abbād's integrity the Prophet ﷺ trusted him a great deal and thus put him in charge of collecting Zakāt from the Muzaynah and Banū Salīm tribes. During the Tabūk expedition the Prophet made him his personal guard and 'Abbād also participated in the execution of Ka'b ibn Ashraf.[2] 'Ā'ishah ؓ said: "One night as the Prophet ﷺ was performing Tahajjud at my house, he heard the voice of 'Abbād ibn Bishr. He ﷺ then said to me: 'O 'Ā'ishah, is that the voice of 'Abbād?' I replied: 'Yes.' He ﷺ said 'O Allāh forgive him'."[3] At the Battle of Yamāmah, 'Abbād showed his exquisite and formidable skill on the battlefield leaving certain marks on the Banū Hanīfah. To the extent that if any of their number were injured they would say "It looks as if he has been hit by 'Abbād ibn Bishr."[4] Their reason for this expression was due to the losses 'Abbād personally had inflicted on them. At the start of the battle 'Abbād ؓ stood on a small mound and said: *"I am 'Abbād ibn Bishr! Come O people of the Ansār! Come O people of the Ansār! Rally around me!"* Responding with the words *"We are here answering your call!"* the Ansār gathered around him and 'Abbād broke the sheath of his sword to indicate that his sword will remain unsheathed until he achieved victory or martyrdom and the Ansār followed suit and did the same. Then 'Abbād bin Bishr said to them: *"Let us attack with sincerity and determination, follow me!"* He led his brothers from the Ansār straight towards the heart of the opposing army changing the whole momentum of the battle and forcing Banū Hanīfah to

---

[1] Bukhārī.
[2] Bukhārī.
[3] Bukhārī.
[4] Abu'r-Rabī Sulaymān al-Khilā'ī al-Andalūsī, *al-Iktifā' bimā Tadammanahu min Maghāzī Rasūlullāh Wa Thalātha al-Khulafā* (Beirut: Ālam ul-Kutub, 1417 AH/1997 CE), vol.3, p.53.

retreat until they went back to the large enclosed garden. When the gates were opened, thanks to the earlier courage and bravery of al-Barā' ibn Mālik al-Ansārī ﷺ, 'Abbād raced inside and continued to engage enemy fighters until he could no longer fight. He was inflicted with so many wounds that his body was unrecognisable and only due to a distinguishing mark on his body he was able to be identified.[1]

- Mu'ādh ibn 'Afrah asked Allāh's Messenger: *"What makes Allāh laugh (with approval) at His slave?"* He ﷺ replied: *"His (the slave's) immersing himself into the enemy without armour."* Mu'ādh ﷺ then took off his armour and fought until he was killed.[2]

- Thābit bin Qays al-Ansārī, the standard bearer of the Ansār during the Battle of Yamāma, dug himself into a pit and planted himself in it. He fought until he was killed and the pit became his own grave.

- Sālim ﷺ, the freed slave of Abū Hudhayfah ﷺ, was the standard bearer of the Muhājirūn during the Battle of Yamāmah. Demonstrating valour for his people, Sālim proclaimed: *"If you manage to overtake me, what a miserable bearer of the Qur'ān I shall be."* He then plunged into the enemy ranks and fought until he too attained martyrdom.

- In the Battle of Yamāmah, Zayd ibn al-Khattāb ﷺ, brother of 'Umar ibn al-Khattāb ﷺ, called out to the Muslims: *"Men, bite with your teeth, strike the enemy, and press on. By Allāh, I shall not speak to you after this until either Musaylama is defeated or I meet Allāh."* Zayd then charged the enemy and continued fighting until he was killed. Before being killed, Zayd killed Musaylamah's number one commander ar-Rajjāl ibn 'Unfuwah who was described as being more evil than Musaylamah. The one who killed Zayd was Abū Maryam al-Hanafī who later

---

[1] Ibid.
[2] Ibn Abī Shaybah, *al-Musannaf*, vol.5, p.338.

embraced Islām and when he encountered 'Umar ibn al-Khattāb after his Islām he said: *"O leader of the believers, Allāh has indeed honoured Zayd by my hand and Allāh has not humiliated me at the hands of Zayd."* Meaning Zayd achieved martyrdom when I killed him and if Zayd had killed me I would have died as a disbeliever and suffered eternal humiliation. Upon learning of Zayd's death 'Umar said: *"He beat me to goodness twice! He embraced Islām before I did and he was the first of us to be martyred."*[1] The appointed brother to Zayd from the Ansār was Ma'an ibn 'Adī al-Balwī ﷺ who had participated in the battles of Badr, Uhud, Khandaq and all of the battles which the Prophet ﷺ took part in.

- At-Tufayl ibn 'Amr ad-Dawsī al-Azdī ﷺ was wise poet of noble lineage and upright character. Before the Battle of Yamāmah Tufayl had a vision and said about it: *"I saw that it was as if my head was being shaved, and that a bird came out of my mouth, and that it was as if a woman inserted me into her private part. I interpreted the dream as follows: the shaving of my head signified it being chopped off; the bird represented my soul (coming out of my body) and the woman represented the earth in which I would soon return to be buried."* Tufayl was then martyred on the Day of Yamāmah.[2]

- On the third day of the Battle of al-Qādisiyyah, known as the Day of 'Imas, 'Amr ibn Ma'dikarib as-Sulamī (d.21 AH/642 CE) said: *"I am going to attack the elephant (of a group of the Persian forces) and the people around it. Do not leave me for longer than the time it takes to slaughter a camel. If you come late, you will lose Abū Thawr (meaning himself), and how could you find another man like Abū Thawr? If you come on time you will*

---

[1] Ibn Kathīr, *al-Bidāyah wa'n-Nihāyah*, vol.6, p.240; also see Dr 'Ali Muhammad Muhammad As-Sallābī, *The Biography of Abu Bakr as-Siddīq* (Riyadh, KSA: Darusalam, 2007) p.502.

[2] Sallābī, *op.cit.*, p.p.507-508.

117

find me with my sword still in my hand." So he charged and did not look back until he started striking them and disappeared into a cloud of dust.[1]

- During the Conquest of Damascus, Wāthilah ibn al-Asqa' ﷺ said: *"I heard the squeaking of the gate of al-Jābiyah, which was one of the gates of Damascus, so I waited and then I saw a huge (Byzantine) cavalry. I waited for a while, then I rushed at them, saying takbīr and they thought they were surrounded and thus they fled back to the city abandoning their leader. I grabbed their leader and threw him off his steed and then I grabbed the reins of the steed. The rest of his cavalry turned around and saw that I was alone so they came after me. I killed one horseman with my spear and then another came close to me and I killed him too. I then later got away and went to Khālid ibn al-Walīd telling him there is now a Byzantine leader with him seeking safety for the people of Damascus."*[2]

- During the Conquest of Caesarea, 'Ubādah ibn as-Sāmit ﷺ was on the right flank of the Muslim army during the siege of Caesarea. He exhorted his troops and called on them to check on themselves and beware of sin. Then he led an attack in which many of the Byzantines were killed, but he did not manage to achieve his goal. He went back to the place from which he had set out and urged his companions to fight,

---

[1] *Tārīkh ut-Tabarī* (Beirut: Dār ul-Fikr, 1407 AH/1987 CE), vol.4, p.378; also see Dr 'Ali Muhammad as-Sallābi, *'Umar ibn al-Khattāb: His Life and Times* (Riyadh, KSA: International Islamic Publishing House, 2007), vol.2, pp.192-193.

[2] *Tārīkh al-Islāmī* (Dār ul-Kitāb al-'Arabī, 1407 AH/1987 CE), vol.10, p.319; *Siyar A'lām un-Nubalā'* (Mu'assasat ar-Risālah, 1410 AH/1990 CE, 7th Edn.), vol.3, pp.386-387; Ibn 'Asākir reports it with his chain of transmission from al-Hasan bin Yahyā al-Khushanī ad-Dimishqī from Zabd bin Wāqid from Busr bin 'Ubaydillāh. Al-Hasan bin Yahyā al-Khushanī ad-Dimashqī is "Sudūq (a truthful narrator), but makes many errors." see *Taqrīb ut-Tahdhīb*, p.72; Zabd bin Wāqid al-Qurashī ad-Dimishqī is Thiqah, see *Taqrīb ut-Tahdhīb*, p.114; Busr bin 'Ubaydillāh al-Hadramī ash-Shāmī is Thiqah and a Hāfidh, see *Taqrīb ut-Tahdhīb*, p.43. See Ibn an-Nahhās, *op.cit.*, p.534.

expressing his astonishment that he had not managed to achieve the aims of this attack. He said: *"O people of Islām! I was one of the youngest of those who came to give the oath of allegiance, and I have been one of the longest-lived. Allāh has dreceed that I should remain alive until I fight this enemy with you. By the One in Whose Hand is my soul, I have never launched an attack with a group of believers against a group of Mushrikīn but they fled from us and Allāh caused us to prevail. What is wrong with you that you attacked these people but did not cause them to flee?"*[1]

- In the Battle of Mu'ta, Ja'far ibn Abī Tālib ☙ took the standard and fought until he became immersed in the fighting, whereupon he turned to his light-coloured horse and wounded it (so he could not escape), then he fought until he was killed.[2]

Analysis

As bomb-making materials, devices and explosives were not known during the early centuries of Islām, all the arguments advanced to justify suicide bombings through reference to the Sunnah of Allāh's Messenger ﷺ and the practice of his Companions ☙ are by way of tremendously fragile analogy. What should be immediately apparent from the above ahādeeth of the Prophet ﷺ and *athār* of his Companions ☙ is that they all clearly extol the virtue of the Mujāhid fighting the enemy until he is killed by them. Pay attention here: the narrations are praising the one who fights until he is killed by his enemy – not the one who kills himself in order to fight the enemy. Hence, Allāh says:

$$\text{﴿ يُقَٰتِلُونَ فِى سَبِيلِ ٱللَّهِ فَيَقْتُلُونَ وَيُقْتَلُونَ ﴾}$$

---

[1] Dr Hāmid Muhammad al-Khalīfah, *al-Ansār fi'l-'Asr ir-Rāshidī*, p.209.
[2] Narrated by Ibn Jarīr at-Tabarī in his *Tārīkh*, vol.2, p.151.

Chapter 9

"They fight in the path of Allāh, they kill and are killed."
{at-Tawbah (9): 111}

Thus, the battlefield martyr, according to the divinely-revealed texts and consensus of jurists, is the one who fights and then dies by other than his own hand; the exception to this being the one who kills himself accidently. As for the lone warrior charging the enemy ranks during Jihād, he never sets out to kill himself – unlike the suicide bomber.

'Awlakī in his "explanation" of Ibn an-Nahhās' book *Mashāri' ul-Ashwāq ilā Masāri' il-'Ushshāq*, CD 12, Track 1 refers to the story of al-Barā' ibn Mālik al-Ansārī ؓ at the Battle of Yamāma. The bravery and valour of al-Barā' ibn Mālik al-Ansārī ؓ at the Battle of Yamāma is a favourite of the Takfīrī-Jihādī suicide bombing apologists; al-Qā'ida in Irāq even have squads entitled the *'al-Barā' bin Mālik Battalion'* and the *'al-Barā' ibn Mālik Martyrdom Brigade'*. Perhaps another reason why the story of al-Barā' at Yamāma is so celebrated by Takfīrī-Jihādīs is because the battle was fought against tribes who had apostated from Islām and Takfīrīs console themselves with their murderous antics, from Casablanca to Kabul, and from Riyadh to Rawalpindi, by declaring their victims to be apostates – either because they do not implement the Sharī'ah (according to their own particular interpretation) or because they refuse to support their own Jihādī ranks. Yet there are a number of issues related to attempting to use the story of the heroism of Al-Barā' ibn Mālik ؓ as a proof for actions such as suicide bombings or "martyrdom operations".

Firstly, any narrations from the Companions that are used as proofs have to be authentic as is well-known, Imām al-Albānī stated in *Silsilat Hudā wa'n-Nūr* (no. 350):

> We have to deal with the narrations of the Companions as we deal with the Prophetic hadīth by researching their authenticity.

Chapter 9

Within the historical writings and *Maghāzī* literature (related to the military expeditions and campaigns) however is material which is unauthentic.[1] For example, al-Wāqidī, is praised by some scholars for his *Maghāzī* and yet some scholars say that **"his works on Maghāzī should be regarded as his affair in hadīth, his hadīth are not accepted."**[2]

This is the same for *Sīrah*, as al-Hāfidh Zaynuddīn al-'Irāqī noted: **"the student should know that the Sīrah combines that which is authentic and that which is not recognised."** In *Tārīkh* of Tabarī for example there are accounts mentioned with their chains of transmission, yet we will find that the chain of transmission of a story that has been mentioned in it has been reported by one who is either a liar *(kadhāb)*, unknown *(majhūl)* or weak *(da'eef)*, this is sufficient in rendering such a story or report as being invalid. This error of taking stories and reports found in the Sīrah and historical works to be correct has been brought to attention by the people of knowledge such as Imām al-Albānī in his book *ad-Difa' 'an al-Hadīth in-Nabawī wa's-Sīrah* which is a good book that mentions many of the things unauthentic things related in the Sīrah.

Shaykh Akram bin Muhammad Ziyādah al-Fālūjī al-Atharī from the *Markaz Imām al-Albānī li'l-Buhūth il-'Ilmiyyah wa'd-Dirāsāt il-Manhajiyyah* [Imām al-Albānī Centre for Academic Research and Methodological Studies] in Jordan, has also discussed the importance of

---

[1] Al-'Awlakī himself, after 14 minutes into the lecture *Studying Sīrah is 'Ibādah* appears to recognise this. However, after 20 minutes into the lecture he recommends certain books on Sīrah and cites:
- Al-Būtī (!!!?)
- Salmān al-'Awda (!!!?)
- Muhammad al-Ghazālī (!!!?)
- Muhammad al-'Abda
- Sa'īd Hawwa (!!!?)

A clear Ikhwānī-Qutbī reading list! Topped off with al-Būtī!!!?

[2] Al-Wāqidī died in 207 AH/823 CE. T. Khalidi mentioned in his book *Arabic Historical Thought in the Classical Period* (Cambridge: Cambridge University Press, 1994), p.48 that: **"Waqidi was attacked for loose isnad usage by strict practitioners of Hadith…"**

Chapter 9

historical verification. Shaykh Akram noted in his book *Tarīkh ul-Madkhal ilā 'Ilm it-Tārīkh: Buḥūth Tārīkhiyyah* [Establishing the Entry to the Knowledge of History: Historiographical Research] when discussing the isnād:

> The writing and transmission of history in the way of the Muhaddithīn, which is the isnād, is firstly of the hallmarks of this Ummah and secondly of the hallmarks of Islamic history, rather it is of the most important features of Islamic history.[1]

Then Shaykh Akram highlights:

> What has been transmitted from Imām Ahmad ؓ is the famous quote wherein he said: "There are three matters which do not have (much authentic reliance on) isnād: tafsīr, al-Malāhim (the battles) and the Maghāzī, and they are (often) reported without any basis." Meaning: the isnād because they are mostly reported in the form of the Marāsīl.[2] Meaning therefore: their chains of transmission do not reach back to the Prophet ﷺ and they are most often traceable up to someone else lesser than him from the Sahābah and are thus Mawqūf; or they are traceable up to the Tābi'īn and are thus Maqtū'ah (broken). If the narrations are attributed to the Prophet ﷺ without mention made of the Companion between the two of them, then the chain is Munqati' (disconnected), Mursal (hurried) and Mu'dal (where two or more consecutive narrators are omitted from chain by a

---

[1] Akram bin Muhammad Ziyādah al-Fālūjī al-Atharī, *Tarīkh ul-Madkhal ilā 'Ilm it-Tārīkh: Buḥūth Tārīkhiyyah* [Establishing the Entry to the Knowledge of History: Historiographical Research] ('Ammān, Jordan: Dār ul-Athariyyah, 1427 AH/2006 CE), p.32. The book itself is based on one of the lectures given by Shaykh Akram during the Seventh Conference held at the *Markaz Imām al-Albānī li'l-Buḥūth il-'Ilmiyyah wa'd-Dirāsāt il-Manhajiyyah* [Imām al-Albānī Centre for Academic Research and Methodological Studies] in 'Ammān dated 10 Jumādā al-Ākhir 1426 AH/Sunday 17 July 2005 CE.

[2] As stated in *Majmū' al-Fatāwā Shaykh ul-Islām Ibn Taymiyyah*, vol.13, p.346.

Chapter 9

reporter) - depending on the number of narrators that have been omitted.[1]

'Awlakī therefore is of those speakers who mainly rely upon historical stories neglecting the fact that such stories and narrations have to be reliable and in accordance with the correct understanding of the dīn. Shaykh Sālih Āli Shaykh stated about this procedure in a lecture entitled *Dawābit fī Ma'rifat is-Sīrah* [Principles for Understanding the Sīrah]:

> Also from the errors in studying the Sīrah, which the callers to innovation and those who give no concern to knowledge yet attach themselves to da'wah err in, is that they base issues of da'wah on the Sīrah. As a result, they do not look at what is present in the texts or what the people of knowledge have stated in regards to such issues. For example, some of them deduce from the incident of Sa'd ibn Abī Waqqās ؓ[2] when he threw a stone which hit a mushrik in the face in Makkah, that this is an evidence for assassination operations and take this as an proof in their research on the permissibility of assassination plots. There is no doubt that this is not the correct and authentic methodology of knowledge wherein incidents of the Sīrah are taken for the basis of knowledge, as it needs to be taken from that which is authentic from the Prophet ﷺ or authentically

---

[1] Akram bin Muhammad Ziyādah al-Fālūjī al-Atharī, *op.cit.*, p.33.
[2] He is Sa'd ibn Mālik az-Zuhahyrī, better known as Sa'd ibn Abī Waqqās ؓ was one of the first people to accept Islām, accepting Islām when he was 17 years old and he was one of the ten whom the Prophet ﷺ promised Paradise. His grandfather was Uhayb ibn Manāf, the paternal uncle of Amīnah, the mother of the Prophet ﷺ. He was a skilled horseman and archer, participating in many of the battles and military expeditions and is noted for his contribution during the battles of Badr and Uhud. He was one of the six members of the *Shūra* counsel which 'Umar ibn al-Khattīb ؓ chose to appoint the *Khalīfah* after 'Umar was stabbed. Sa'd ibn Abā Waqqās ؓ was the first to shoot an arrow at the *mushrikīn* in *jihād* and he led the Muslims in taking over 'Irāq from the Persians after defeating them in the battle of *al-Qādisiyyah* in the 15th year after the *Hijrah* (corresponding to 634 CE). He died in 55 AH (circa 675 CE). See ath-Thahabī, *Tahthīb Siyār 'A'lam an-Nubala*, vol.1, no.5.

reported from his companions ﷺ and determined by the Prophet ﷺ during his lifetime. Another example what some of them mention is that the youth who gathered in the Masjid of the Prophet ﷺ in order to hear his opinion about the Battle of Badr is an evidence for the permissibility of staging sit-ins within Masājid and demonstrations. There is no doubt that this is against the correct and precise Islamic methodology and is mere searching for a way out to establish evidence between a worshipper and his Lord. A further example of this is what is found in some of the books of Sīrah regarding the secrecy between the Companions which some use to prove secrecy in giving da'wah and that such secrecy is the foundation of da'wah and organising da'wah. If this is assessed with correct knowledge, the speech of the people of knowledge and the scholars who can verify, it will emerge that this (such secrecy amongst the companions) is not a proof for such a method of da'wah, as secrecy in a (particular) issue does not indicate secrecy in everything.[1]

Secondly, the story [about al-Barā' ibn Mālik being catapulted over enemy lines] has been relayed by at-Tabarī, Ibn ul-Athīr, al-Bayhaqī in his *Sunan* and others. Yet there is an issue with the source of the story as the chain of transmission which is provided by Ibn 'AbdulBarr ﷺ in *al-Istī'āb fī Ma'rifat il-Ashāb* (Beirut: Dār ul-Jeel Print, 1412 AH/1992 CE), vol.1, p.154. The chain is as follows:

Aḥmad bin Muḥammad bin 'Abdillāh bin Muḥammad bin 'Ali narrated to us saying: my father narrated to us saying: 'Abdullāh bin Yūnus narrated to us saying: Baqī' bin Makhlid narrated to us saying: Khalīfah bin Khayyāt narrated to us saying: Bakr bin Sulaymān narrated to us from Abū Isḥāq who said: the Muslims

---

[1] Shaykh Sāliḥ Āli Shaykh, *Dawābit fī Ma'rifat is-Sīrah* (lecture given in 2002 at the Maktabat Da'wah wa'l-Irshad in al-Kharj), translated here by 'AbdulHaq al-Ashantī: http://salafimanhaj.com/pdf/SalafiManhaj_UnderstandingSeerah.pdf.

went to war against the Mushrikīn on the Day of Yamāmah until they game to the garden where the enemy of Allāh Musaylamah was and al-Barā' said: *"O gathering of Muslims! Throw me over..."* to the end of the narration.

The chain of transmission mentioned by both Ibn 'AbdulBarr and at-Tabarī is weak and contains a number of defects. Bakr bin Sulaymān, who is Abū Yahyā al-Basrī al-Aswārī is *majhūl* (unknown) and Abū Hātim said about him: **"majhūl"**. There is also *inqitā'* (discontinuity) in the transmission as Abū Ishāq did not meet al-Barā'. Also there is a *Mu'allaq* form of this narration, and this is a type of weak hadīth, wherein Khalīfah did not mention the narrators before him and sufficed with saying: "An Ansārī narrated to us from his father Thumāmah from Anas..." and then the narration mentions when al-Barā' is thrown over the garden wall and fights to open the gate for the Muslim soliders. In the *Musannaf* of Khalīfah, the chain of transmission contains 'Abdullāh bin Muthanna bin 'Abdullāh bin Anas who narrated from his uncle Thumāmah bin 'Abdullāh bin Anas. An-Nasā'ī said about 'Abdullāh bin Muthanna bin 'Abdullāh bin Anas: **"he is not strong"**, Yahyā bin Ma'een said: **"he is nothing"**, al-'Uqaylī said: **"many of his hadīth are not to be followed"**, ad-Dāraqutnī said: **"weak"** yet deemed him trustworthy in another instance and Abū Hātim said: **"Sālih (acceptable)"**. Such a narrator's reports by itself are not to be accepted, hence Ibn Hajar stated about him in *at-Taqrīb*: **"Sudūq, yet makes many errors"** and this is an indication of weakness, thus the chain of transmission is weak.[1]

Thirdly, even if the narration is authentic, and as we have seen there is some discussion about its authenticity, al-Barā' ibn Mālik ﷺ took a calculated risk when he plunged perilously behind enemy lines. His explicitly stated aim was to breach the enemy defences in what was a clear act of *iqtihām* and *inghimās*, and the risk paid off. Al-Barā' neither

---

[1] Refer to Shaykh Māhir bin Thāfir al-Qahtānī, *an-Nadhārah li Muntaharī Filistīn wa Atfāl il-Hijārah* (Cairo: Dār Kitāb wa Sunnah, 2007 CE), pp.16-17.

intended his own death nor did his actions necessitate it – unlike the case of a suicide bomber. Hence, Shaykh Dr Muhammad Bāzmūl stated in his book *al-Muhkam wa'l-Mutashābih fi't-Takfīr wa'l-Jihād*:

> As for the issue of there being some from the Salaf us-Sālih who were catapulted into enemy fortresses and then opened the fortress gates for the Muslims – then this istidlāl is incorrect as there is a difference between the state of a battlefield and the state of one who performs a suicide bombing![1]

Moreover, al-Barā' ibn Mālik ؓ actually survived the Battle of Yamāma and die a martyr's death years later in Tastar, Persia. In the same way, Wāthilah ibn al-Asqa ؓ also survived when he rushed the Byzantine cavalry and did not die and in fact the cavalry fled from him alone! This is further evidenced by what was stated by 'Ubādah ibn as-Sāmit ؓ during the Battle of Caesarea that in his experience of fighting, no group of believers charged into the enemy except that the enemy fled from him and those with him. The act of 'Abbād ibn Bishr ؓ was another clear example of *iqtihām* and *inghimās*. We return to 'Awlakī's statement in his "explanation" of Ibn an-Nahhās' book *Mashāri' ul-Ashwāq ilā Masāri' il-'Ushshāq*, CD 6, Track 15:

> "So here you have a man who jumps into the army, seeking martyrdom. Might as well just put on an explosive belt, what's the difference!? Jump in with an army of thousands?! So...(either way) it's definite death."

Well, the differences are many O 'Awlakī! The differences are that:
- Jumping into an army in an act of *iqtihām* and *inghimās* is Divinely Legislated, while putting on and detonating an

---

[1] Shaykh Muhammad bin 'Umar bin Sālim Bāzmūl (Professor at College of Da'wah and Usūluddīn, Book and Sunnah Department, Umm ul-Qurā' University, Makkah), *al-Muhkam wa'l-Mutashābih fi't-Takfeer wa'l-Jihād* (Cairo: Dār ul-Istiqāmah, 1429 AH/2008 CE). pp.401-411.

explosive belt wherein the user intends to end their lives with no possibility of survival, is not.
- Jumping into an army or enemy ranks is not definite death as we have seen with the examples of al-Barā' ibn Mālik, Wāthilah ibn al-Asqa *and* 'Ubādah ibn as-Sāmit ﷺ. Putting on an explosive belt however definitely is!
- 'Umar ﷺ considered whosoever accused the one who jumped into the enemy of having killed himself to be liars. While the one claiming martyrdom for whosoever detonates his explosive belt is the liar!
- The difference is that the one who jumped into the army of thousands, like Mudrak's uncle and those who were martyred alongside him, aided Islām against their enemies. While the suicide bomber ultimately aids the enemies of Islām, examples of which have been mentioned previously.

Furthermore, the Companions ﷺ launched themselves against dense groupings of the enemy in blatant and overt acts of jihād. They did not covertly mingle amongst a crowd of non-Muslims, as if part of them, in order to attack them treacherously. They did not, as many suicide bombers do, wear a woman's Jilbāb and Niqāb, or wear the clothing of a Jewish Rabbi, and nor did they trade their beard and armour for clean-shaven faces and pair of tight-fitting and non-Islamic attire of the disbelievers; the Companions did not pretend to be irreligious and un-Islamic, impious Muslims or indifferent non-Muslims. They wore their Islām on their sleeves, so-to-speak, in a manifest act of jihād, open war and declared open hostility between the followers of Islām and the followers of disbelief. However, the overwhelming majority of suicide attacks are carried out against soft targets: women shopping in market place bazārs, commuters waiting at bus cues, employees in their offices, and so on. This is certainly the case in Irāq (and to a lesser extent, Afghanistan) where the heretical Takfīrī ideology of the bomber makes the blood of innocent Muslim men, women and children worthy of spilling. Thus, the honoured, noble and illustrious al-Barā' ibn Mālik al-Ansārī, 'Abbād ibn Bishr, Thābit bin Qays al-Ansārī, Mu'ādh ibn 'Afrah, Abū 'Aqīl al-Balwī al-Ansārī al-'Awsī, Ma'an ibn 'Adī al-Balwī, Ja'far ibn Abī Tālib, Talhah ibn 'Ubaydullāh, Sa'd ibn Abī Waqqās or any other Companion ﷺ who fought in any of the battles of our beloved Prophet ﷺ are in no way the blueprint of a suicide bomber.

﴿ وَقَٰتِلُوا۟ فِى سَبِيلِ ٱللَّهِ ٱلَّذِينَ يُقَٰتِلُونَكُمْ وَلَا تَعْتَدُوٓا۟ إِنَّ ٱللَّهَ لَا يُحِبُّ ٱلْمُعْتَدِينَ ﴾

"Fight in the way of Allāh against those who fight you and do not transgress the limits (set by Allāh). Indeed, Allāh does not love those who transgress." *{Baqarah (2): 190}*

Also from the Battle of Uhud, with the brave and heroic actions of Talha ibn 'Ubaydullāh, Sa'd ibn Abī Waqqās, Abū 'Ubaydah ibn al-Jarrāh and Abū Dujāna we learn of brave warriors who put themselves into harms way as if they were human shields,[1] risking their lives in order to *save* the lives of others. The suicide bomber on the other hand puts himself into harms way in order to *take* the lives of others. There is no comparison to be drawn between saving lives and taking lives. As for trying to make a Qiyās from the issue of *Inghimās fi'l-'Adū* [Immersing Oneself Among the Enemy] and suicide bombing then there is a big difference as Shaykh 'Abdullāh al-Jarbū' mentioned in his book *al-'Amaliyāt al-Intihāriyyah at-Tafjīriyyah: A Jihād Hiya Am Fasād? Dirāsah Turakkiz 'ala'n-Nadhr fi'l-Istidlāl* [Suicide Bombing Operations, Are They Jihād or Corruption? A Study Focusing on Deductions and Inferences]:

1. The Munghamis if he is killed, then he is killed by the enemy.

---

[1] Saheeh ul-Bukhārī.

2. The 'Ulamā make the condition that it is only permitted to perform inghimās by charging into the enemy ranks and line of fire, with the permission of the commander or the leader.
3. This all differs from the one who blows himself up who directly sets out to kill himself neither going into enemy ranks for the line of fire.[1]

In relation to the verse where Allāh says:

﴿ وَمِنَ ٱلنَّاسِ مَن يَشۡرِي نَفۡسَهُ ٱبۡتِغَآءَ مَرۡضَاتِ ٱللَّهِ ۗ وَٱللَّهُ رَءُوفٌۢ بِٱلۡعِبَادِ ﴾

"And of the people is he who sells himself, seeking means to the approval of Allāh. And Allāh is kind to [His] servants." {Baqarah (2): 207}

Hence, Imām al-Albānī ﷺ ruled that a Muslim commander, only within an Islamic State, if he views it as appropriate can send troops to perform such operations. Yet this is only where there is an Islamic State and rulership implemented and not what how they are performed today by Takfīrī mavericks and Khawārij bandits. Imām al-Albānī was asked, as documented and transmitted by his prolific student Shaykh 'Ali Hasan al-Halabī al-Atharī *(hafidhahullāh)*:

Is it allowed to drive a booby-trapped car packed with explosives and drive it into the enemies? What is currently called 'suicide bombings', with evidence.

---

[1] Shaykh 'Abdullāh bin 'AbdurRahmān al-Mansūr al-Jarbū' in his book *al-'Amaliyāt al-Intihāriyyah at-Tafjīriyyah: A Jihād Hiya Am Fasād? Dirāsah Turakkiz 'ala'n-Nadhr fi'l-Istidlāl* [Suicide Bombing Operations, Are They Jihād or Corruption? A Study Focusing on Deductions and Inferences], introduction by Shaykh Sālih al-Fawzān, p.96. The book can be downloaded here at the website of our Shaykh, 'Abdul'Azeez bin Rayyis ar-Rayyis: http://islamancient.com/books,item,286.html.

Chapter 9

Answer from Imām al-Albānī ﷺ:
> We have said regularly and frequently about these questions that: during these times they are not allowed[1] because they are either individual and personal actions wherein the individual is unable to be outweigh the benefits over the harms, or the harms over the benefits; or, if it is not an individual action it is from an organisation, Jamā'ah or (group) leader – and this leader is not Divinely Legislated (Sharī'), and at this point such an action is considered suicide! As for the evidence: then this is well-known from the ahādīth in the Two Sahīhs,[2] that whoever commits suicide with any instrument will be punished with it (in the Hereafter). The likes of these suicide operations, as they say today, are only when there is Islamic rule headed by a Muslim ruler who rules by what Allāh has revealed and applies Allāh's Sharī'ah in all aspects of life, such as the military and soldiers which are also to be in line with the restrictions of the Shar' (Divine Legislation). The higher leader, and then those who represent him such as the Army General – if they view that there is a Maslahah for the Muslims by performing these suicide operations in order to achieve a Divinely Legislated benefit, then they are permitted. The Muslim ruler is the one who estimates this via seeking advice from those whom he seeks counsel in his

---

[1] Shaykh 'Ali Hasan al-Halabī al-Atharī *(hafidhahullāh)* says about this:
This is a clear and frank text on this issue which shows the error of some of our noble brothers who understand from some words of our Shaykh that such actions are allowed with "a number of restricted and detailed conditions!"

[2] In Bukhārī (hadīth no.5442) and Muslim (hadīth no.109) from Abū Hurayrah ﷺ from the Prophet ﷺ who said: *"Whoever throws himself off a mountain killing himself, will be in Hellfire throwing themselves off for ever and eternity. Whoever drinks poison to kill himself will drink poison in his hand eternally in the Hellfire for ever. Whoever kills himself with iron (a weapon) then this iron will be in his hand and he will be killing himself with it in Hellfire for ever and eternity."*

gatherings with them, only in these instances are they allowed and anything other than this is not allowed.¹

Furthermore, Ibn an-Nahhās himself has a chapter on the issue in *Mashāri' ul-Ashwāq ilā Masāri' il-'Ushshāq*, p.522-560 of the edit by Idrīs Muhammad 'Ali and Muhammad Khālid Istanbūli! Ibn an-Nahhās states:

> You should know that the 'Ulamā ﷺ have differed over the issue of a man making iqtihām during warfare and he alone going against a large enemy grouping and immersing himself among them. Statements and actions have been relayed prior regarding the recommendation and virtue of that, and that is sufficient. Imām Abū Hāmid al-Ghazāli ﷺ stated in *al-Ihyā'* in the 'Chapter of Commanding the Good and Forbidding the Evil':
>> There is no difference of opinion over a lone Muslim charging to attack the ranks of the kuffār and fighting, even if he knows that he will be killed. Just as it is allowed for him to fight the kuffār (enemy troops) until he is killed (by them) – this is also allowed in commanding the good and forbidding the evil. **However, if he knows that there will be no effect in harming the enemy in his attack against the kuffār, such as a blind or disabled person charging against the ranks, then that is harām and is included in the general meaning of the ayah of throwing oneself into destruction.** It is only allowed for him if he knows that he will not be killed until he is killed (by the enemy); or he knows that he will be able to crack the hearts of the kuffār by them witnessing his nerve and them believing that the Muslims do not care (to die in battle)

---

¹ From Shaykh 'Ali Hasan al-Halabī al-Atharī, *Su'alāt 'Ali bin Hasan bin 'AbdulHamīd al-Halabī al-Atharī li'sh-Shaykhihi Imām al-'Allāmah al-Muhaddith al-Faqīh Shaykh Muhammad Nāsiruddīn al-Albānī* ﷺ. Makkah al-Mukarramah, KSA: Dār 'Abdullāh Bū Bakr Barakāt, 1430 AH/2009 CE, First Edn. Vol.1, pp.389-390.

and have a love for martyrdom in the path of Allāh which breaks their will.[1]

Yet 'Awlakī did not mention this basis at all: if destruction is brought upon ones own self then such actions are not to be done. Indeed, and in the modern manifestation of suicide bomb attacks, harm is not only on the individual who does the attack but also on the whole of the Muslims as a result of the action! Ibn an-Nahhās also mentions in *Mashāri' ul-Ashwāq ilā Masāri' il-'Ushshāq*, p.558 (Idrīs and Istanbūlī edit) that Abū 'Abdullāh al-Qurtubī said in his Tafsīr:

> The 'Ulamā have differed over a man making iqtihām during warfare against the enemy ranks by himself. Al-Qāsim bin Mukhaymarah, al-Qāsim bin Muhammad and 'AbdulMalik from our 'Ulamā say: "there is no problem in a man by himself going against a large army if he has strength and a pure intention for Allāh. **If he does not have strength then that is from throwing oneself into destruction.**"

Then Ibn an-Nahhās relays (p.559) that Ibn Khuwayzmindād ﷺ[2] said:
> As for a man going against a hundred or against a grouping of soldiers or a group of thieves, bandits (Muhāribīn) **or Khawārij** then that is in two cases: if he knows and thinks that it is likely that he will kill those he is facing and will be saved (from death) then that is good; likewise if he knows and thinks that it is likely he will be killed yet be able to harm or affect them so as to benefit the Muslims – then that is allowed also.[3]

Another scholarly and academic case scenario mentioned by Ibn an-Nahhās which seems to have slipped 'Awlakī's "explanation" of his

---

[1] *Ithāf us-Sādat il-Muttaqīn fī Sharh Asrār Ihyā' 'Ulūm id-Dīn*, vol.7, p.26
[2] Abū 'Abdullāh Muhammad bin Ahmad bin 'Abdullāh bin Khuwayzmindād, the Imām and scholar, his Shaykh was al-Abharī who died in 395 AH.
[3] Tafsīr Qurtubī, vol.2, p.363-364.

Chapter 9

book!? Herein Ibn Khuwayzmindād ﷺ also notes that this *iqtihām* and *inghimās* can even be against bandits, highway robbers and, wait for it, Khawārij! Then Ibn an-Nahhās relays (p.560) that Muhammad bin al-Hasan said:

> If a lone man goes against a thousand men from the Mushrikīn and he is by himself there is no problem in that if he is assured of escape or harming the enemy. **If this is not the case then that is disliked (Makrūh) because he has placed himself into destruction without any benefit for the Muslims.**[1]

Finally, 'Awlakī always drones on about **"it's the intention"** and that **"the difference is the intention"** however we see here again Awlakī's lack of fiqh and Usūl, as

النية الصالحة لا تصلح العمل الفاسد.

"The good intention does not rectify the corrupt action."

Thus, a good intention does not change the sinful act into a virtuous action! Evidence for this is in the story found in the Musnad of ad-Dārimī, vol.1, pp.68-69, no.204:

> (Imām ad-Dārimī reported that:) Hakam bin al-Mubārak informed us: 'Amru bin Yahyā informed us saying: I heard my father talking about his father 'Amr bin Salamah who said: "We used to sit in front of 'Abdullāh Ibn Mas'ūd's house before Fajr prayer so that when he'd come out we'd go to the Masjid with him. One day, Abū Mūsā al-'Ash'arī came and asked us: 'Has Abū 'AbdurRahmān (Ibn Mas'ūd) left yet?' We replied: 'no.' So Abū Mūsā al-'Ash'arī stayed with us until Ibn Mas'ūd came out and then we all stood up. Abū Mūsā al-'Ash'arī said: 'O Abū 'AbdurRahmān I saw something in the Masjid which I thought was evil, but I did not see anything except good.' Ibn Mas'ūd asked: 'What was it?' Abū Mūsā al-'Ash'arī said: 'You will see it

---

[1] *Al-Jāmi' li-Ahkām wa'l-Hikam*, vol.2, p.364.

if you live. In the Masjid I saw a group of people sitting in circles waiting for the prayer, each circle is led by a person and everyone in the circle has small pebbles. The leader of the circle would say *"Allāhu Akbar"* a hundred times and the people would repeat this after him a hundred times. Then he'd say *"La ilaha il Allāh"* a hundred times and the people would repeat it hundred times after him. Then he'd say *"SubhānAllāh"* a hundred times and the people would repeat it hundred times after him.' Ibn Mas'ūd said to Abū Mūsā: 'What did you say to them?' Abū Mūsā al-'Ash'arī said: 'I didn't say anything to them I wanted to wait for your view and instruction.' Ibn Mas'ūd said: 'Could you not have told them to count their evil actions and assured them of getting their reward?' Then Ibn Mas'ūd went ahead and we accompanied him as he approached one of these circles saying: 'What is this I see you doing?' They replied; 'O Abū 'AbdurRahmān, these are pebbles that we use to count when we say *"Allāhu Akbar," "La ilaha il Allāh"* and *"SubhānAllāh."'* Ibn Mas'ūd said: 'Count your evil actions and I assure you that you will not lose any of your reward. Woe to you O Ummah of Muhammad, how quickly you go to destruction! These are the companions of the Messenger ﷺ who are present, these are his clothes not worn out yet and his pots that have not broken yet. I swear by Him in Whose hand is my soul, that you are either following a religion which is better than the Prophet's religion or you are opening a door to misguidance.' They said: 'O Abū 'AbdurRahmān, we only intended to do good.' Ibn Mas'ūd replied: 'How many people intend good but never do it, the Messenger of Allāh ﷺ told us: "There will come a people who recite the Qur'ān yet it will not affect them other than passing through their throats." By Allāh I do not know but I fear that you may be from them.' Then Ibn Mas'ūd left them." 'Amr bin Salamah (the narrator) then said: "We saw most of those people from those circles fighting against us in the Battle of an-Nahrawān."[1]

So a good intention, let's say to gain martyrdom, cannot justify the corrupt actions of bida', lying, cheating, criminality, purposefully targeting those far from any warfare and a whole host of other aspects which are involved in these so-called "martyrdom operations", which

---

[1] Al-Haythamī authenticated two other routes of the hadīth (one from Sufyān ibn 'Uyaynah and the other from Sufyān bin Salamah bin Kahīl) in *Majma' az-Zawā'id*, vol.1, p.181, no.855; Imām adh-Dhahabī said in *Mīzān ul-I'tidāl*, vol.2, p.345 that Imām Ahmad, Ibn Hibbān (in *ath-Thiqāt*, vol.8, p.480) and Ibn Mandah held al-Hakam bin al-Mubārak al-Khāshī al-Balkhī to be trustworthy; also by Imām al-Albānī in *Silsilah as-Sahīhah*, vol.11, p.5, no.2005 and in *ar-Rad 'ala'l-Habashī*, pp.45-47; Husayn Asad in his edit of *Musnad ud-Dārimī*, vol.1, p.287, no.210. As for 'Amr bin Yahyā then Yahyā ibn Ma'īn stated about 'Amru bin Yahyā that "he is nothing" and Ibn 'Adiyy also accused al-Hakam of fabricating hadīth and *asānīd*. Refer to *al-Kāmil fī Du'afā' ir-Rijāl*, vol.5, p.122 and *Lisān ul-Mīzān*, vol.4, p.378. Ibn 'Adiyy also brings two separate transmissions of Ibn Hibbān deeming 'Amru bin Yahyā to be weak and Ibn Hajar al-'Asqalānī also brings a transmission from Ibn Khurāsh deeming 'Amru bin Yahyā to be a weak narrator. See: Ibn ul-Jawzī, *ad-Du'afā' wa'l-Matrūkīn*, vol.2, p.233. However, there is another transmission of the hadīth in *Tārīkh Baghdād* from: Muhammad bin Ibrāhīm bin Salamah al-Kahīlī (about whom Ibn ul-Jawzī said had authentic reports) from: Muhammad bin 'Abdullāh bin Sulaymān al-Hadramī (who ad-Dāraqutnī said was trustworthy to the utmost) from 'Abdullāh bin 'Umar bin Abān (who is also *thiqah*) from 'Amru bin Yahyā bin 'Amr bin Salamah al-Hamdānī who said: "I heard my father narrated from his father 'Amr bin Salamah..." and then he relayed the hadīth. It is also relayed by Bahshal in *Tārīkh Wāsit* (ed. Bashhār 'Awād), p.198. Ibn Abī Hātim in *Jarh wa't-Ta'dīl*, vol.3, p.1, no.269 and vol. 9, p.176 and mentions a group of scholars who deemed 'Amru bin Yahyā to be *thiqah* including Sufyān ibn 'Uyaynah and an authentic transmission from Yahyā bin Ma'īn wherein he said he is "Sālih" and "thiqah" in other manuscript copies, hence Imām al-Albānī's authentication of the report. Imām al-Bukhārī in *Tārīkh ul-Kabīr*, vol.6, p.382 also mentions 'Amru bin Yahyā. The *jarh* herein therefore is not *mufassir* and thus the attestation of the narrator is to be given precedence. When Yahyā bin Ma'īn says "he is nothing" this is not necessarily an indication of a severe disparagement as has been highlighted by Imām al-Albānī and Shaykh Salīm al-Hilālī.

Chapter 9

'Awlakī denies! Thus, our beloved Prophet ﷺ said, as narrated from Abū Mūsā al-'Ash'arī ؓ in a hadīth which is agreed upon:

((من قاتل لتكون كلمة الله هي العليا فهو في سبيل الله))

"Whoever fights so that the Word of Allāh will be Highest, he is the one in the Path of Allāh"

Not the one who fights to be seen, to show off or so that it is said "so and so is a Mujāhid". Or the one who fights for the sake of just fighting or merely because he wants to show that he is a rebel and hero, or the one who fights over party-spirit and politics.

CHAPTER 10

'AWLAKI EXHORTS OTHERS TO ARMED JIHAD YET DOES NOT DO IT HIMSELF!?

Allāh says about a particular blameworthy trait found in some:

﴿ وَلَوْ كَانُوا فِيكُم مَّا قَتَلُوٓاْ إِلَّا قَلِيلًا ﴾

"**And if they should be among you, they would not fight except for a little.**" *{al-Ahzāb (33): 20}*

Ibn Katheer ؒ said about this noble *ayah*:
Meaning: if they are among you, they will not fight alongside you very much, because they are so cowardly and weak, and have so little faith, but Allāh knows best about them.

'Awlakī states in his "explanation" of Ibn an-Nahhās' book *Mashāri' ul-Ashwāq ilā Masāri' il-'Ushshāq*, CD 5, Track 3:
The Muslim accepts the path of struggle as their path, intellectually they agree with it, they agree with the idea of it, but because they are far away from the events **it remains an intellectual activity to them. What happens is the brothers stay just talking about the issue of jihād for too long, they end up talking about it *only* for too long.** It carries on and on and on and what happens is a person accepts that state as being appropriate and he just carries on. So the whole issue becomes an intellectual discourse and doesn't go beyond that."

Chapter 10

Indeed O Anwar! Then he states:
> Brothers have been talking about the issue of hijra **and the issue of going to fight for years and years and nothing is changing, it's just intentions and talk.**

Al-'Awlakī also states in part 3 of his explanation of *Thawābit 'ala'd-Darb il-Jihād* [Constants on the Path of Jihād], after 43 minutes:
> **We don't want brothers just talking about jihād fī sabeelillāh because jihād fī sabeelillāh is not talk!**

Al-'Awlakī also states in part 4 of his explanation of *Thawābit 'ala'd-Darb il-Jihād* [Constants on the Path of Jihād], after 33 minutes:
> **...they need to prove that, and the way to prove that is through action and not through words, and the action is: you become a Mujāhid!**

Then 'Awlakī says:
> **If you want to show that you love Allāh and love Rasoolullāh then go out and become a Mujāhid and you don't have to talk about it any more! You have proved it though your action! See this is not a religion of talk it's a religion of action.**

La ilaha il Allāh! 'Awlakī says all this from the comfort of university lecture theatres, or while he himself sits in Yemen! We ask again: upon which battlefield has 'Awlakī fought and where has he fought?! Where was he ever been stationed in Ribāt? What lands has he himself defended or protected and what Muslims has he gone to aid with his life? This is the clearest proofs of his Qa'diyyah. There is also an element of *isti'jāl* in his speech here which is not a hallmark of the believers who are praised by Allāh,

﴿ ثُمَّ إِنَّ رَبَّكَ لِلَّذِينَ هَاجَرُواْ مِنْ بَعْدِ مَا فُتِنُواْ ثُمَّ جَٰهَدُواْ وَصَبَرُوٓاْ إِنَّ رَبَّكَ مِنۢ بَعْدِهَا لَغَفُورٌ رَّحِيمٌ ﴾

"Then, indeed your Lord, to those who emigrated after they had been compelled [to renounce their religion] and thereafter fought [for the cause of Allāh] and were patient – indeed, your Lord, after that, is Forgiving and Merciful" {an-Nahl (16): 110}

Indeed, 'Awlakī himself, during his US Ikhwānī phase, stated in the lecture *Revivers of the Message*:

> ...dont be in a hurry, don't try to react before its time. You have to follow the plan, even if its gonna take a long time. You know sometimes we think that we can have the Islamic Khilāfah by Eight O' Clock tomorrow morning. It doesn't happen that easy. There is a lot of sacrifice that is involved.

So 'Awlakī's own words have refuted himself again! Also, Ibn an-Nahhās ؒ has excellent advice for those cowards who do not fight themselves. Ibn an-Nahhās in *Mashāri' ul-Ashwāq ilā Masāri' il-'Ushshāq* (!!) in the edit of Idrīs Muhammad 'Ali and Muhammad Khālid Istanbūlī, pp.953-960 has a good section on the cowardice of those who do not fight, yet 'Awlakī did not discuss the section in his own "explanation" of the book!!? And we also have to add here that: being thrown into prison over one's own irresponsible and Khawārij statements, or one's links to the Khawārij of the era, or being imprisoned for plotting to intentionally kill or blow up innocent women and children in stores, planes or other civilian quarters, does not qualify as **"armed jihād in the Path of Allāh"**.

CHAPTER 11

'AWLAKI INSINUATES THAT CIVILIANS CAN BE PURPOSEFULLY TARGETTED IN ARMED COMBAT

'Awlakī states in his "explanation" of Ibn an-Nahhās' book *Mashāri' ul-Ashwāq ilā Masāri' il-'Ushshāq*, CD 7, Track 8:

> So with these rules of civilians, trees, all of these issues, they're applied as long as they're not gonna end up harming the Muslims – as soon as they start harming the Muslims all of these rules are abrogated or overruled. (Someone in the audience interjects)…Yeah, ya'nī, the Hisār at Tā'if, Rasulullāh *(salasalam) {sic}* used Manjanīq, catapults. You can't control where the catapult will land! (Someone in the audience interjects) **This is a strong argument, it is a strong argument, that they are actually complacent in the crime.**

He means "complicit in the crime". However, Ibn an-Nahhās mentions in *Mashāri' ul-Ashwāq ilā Masāri' il-'Ushshāq* (!!) on page 1023 of the Idrīs and Istanbūlī edit that:

> **It is prohibited to kill women and children if they do not fight according to ash-Shāfi'ī, Mālik, Ahmad and Abū Hanīfah. If they fight (against the Muslim armies however) then they are to be killed (as they are combatants).**

Then 'Awlakī states:

> "When Rasoolullāh would give da'wah to a people he would not submit a brochure to every single member of the community.

He'd send a letter to the head of state and based on the response of the head of state Rasoolu (salasalam) {sic} **would react to the entire nation - based on what the head of state does...** Rasoolu (salasalam) {sic} would fight everyone in that nation based on the response of that leader.

'Awlakī also states in his "explanation" of Ibn an-Nahhās' book *Mashāri' ul-Ashwāq ilā Masāri' il-'Ushshāq*, CD 12, Track 9, when discussing the opinion on the permissibility (according to Imām ash-Shāfi'ī's view) of executing elderly war strategists and also those who give **"intellectual support"** to those fighting against the Muslims:
...so one might argue here for attacking the ones who pay taxes to the government that fights against Muslims.

Firstly, 'Awlakī equates a mere tax-payer (who is obliged to pay taxes) to one who has given **"intellectual support"** to kuffār during jihād, despite millions of them demonstrating against unjust wars like Irāq!? Not just that, but secondly 'Awlakī then says that on the basis of the view of the permissibility (according to Imām ash-Shāfi'ī's view) of executing the elderly who provide **"intellectual support"** this extends to a mere-tax payer who may in fact intellectually be against any wars against the Muslims!? So based on Awlakī's understanding, this elderly individual should be executed on the mere basis of paying taxes, which by the way he is obliged to pay, regardless if he is an anti-war campaigner or not!? Thirdly, this *shādh* view which is attributed to Imām ash-Shāfi'ī was opposed by many of the Shāfi'ī scholars which we will come across soon. Fourthly, why stop at the tax-payer? Why not extend this to all who contribute to the disbelieving state in terms of buying, selling and other forms of indirect contribution to government coffers? No matter how hard the one who resides in Dār ul-Kufr tries s/he will still be contributing to the treasury whether they like it or not. Not to mention VAT added on a variety of items purchased, alongside fuel duty, Vehicle Excise Duty and other motoring taxes, council tax, business rates etc! Fifthly, taxation, in the UK at least, does not account for mainly financing military expenditure, as taxation largely goes to: social protection, health and education (three services which many Takfīrī-Jihādīs have shown no aspersions towards utilizing whatsoever!?), with defence coming in after these in terms of the government's expenditure. Hence, a small fraction of a person's tax may go towards military expenditure, in the US the tax-payer however has about a third of his/her tax which goes towards the military. Sixthly, those who pay taxes do not exactly have a choice as they are compelled and forced to pay them otherwise they will be putting themselves into further harm and danger.

Finally, Shaykh 'Abdul'Azīz bin Rayyis ar-Rayyis was asked about al-'Awlakī's inclusion of a tax-payer to a Western government as one who has sided with the disbelievers against Muslims and said:

> **This is jahl (ignorance) and ghulū (extremism)!** A disbeliever who obligates that money be paid to him is one thing, yet supporting a disbeliever (for the sake of the deen) against a Muslim is another thing. Allāh knows best but it seems that the man (i.e. Anwar al-'Awlakī) is extreme and ignorant, and if he had intelligence and knowledge he would not say the likes of these things.[1]

Lastly, upon referral back to the actual text of the complete work Ibn an-Nahhās' book *Mashāri' ul-Ashwāq ilā Masāri' il-'Ushshāq* by Idrīs Muhammad 'Ali and Muhammad Khālid Istanbūlī, there is absolutely nothing about **"intellectual support"** mentioned by Ibn an-Nahhās (see p.1023 of the 1423 AH/2002 CE Dār ul-Bashā'ir print). Ibn an-Nahhās does not even mention the issue of them being war strategists who could possibly provide info to the enemy, he just mentions that Imām ash-Shāfi'ī allows it. The issue about them being war strategists who could provide possible info to the enemies is discussed in other

---

[1] Dated Monday 7 December 2009 CE.

Chapter 11

works which will be mentioned shortly and not in *Mashāri' ul-Ashwāq ilā Masāri' il-'Ushshāq*. So why then did al-'Awlakī add the issue of **"intellectual support"** when it was not mentioned at all by Ibn an-Nahhās ؟? Awlakī says in *Thawābit 'ala'd-Darb il-Jihād* [Constants on the Path of Jihād], part 3, after 15:58:

> Who said that if a particular people are in a state of war with you that this war needs to be limited to the piece of land that they occupy? If a particular nation or people are classified as "Ahl ul-Harb" (people of war) in the Sharī'ah then that applies to them on the whole earth. It is not restricted to a particular area.

First of all, 'Awlakī himself said that the war is limited to a particular people! You said it Anwar! 'Awlakī stated after 52 minutes into the lecture *Lessons Learned from the Sahābah Living as a Minority* (conducted at a JIMAS [!!!] conference in a Bank Holiday weekend during August 2002 in Leicester):

> ...the regular people, the laymen, are not the ones who make the decisions, just like we heard yesterday by our brother Abū Muntasir: 70% of the British population don't vote. **These are your nice neighbours, the decent people you meet on the street!** So Allāh is teaching us something about human nature that on the top the people who are making the planning and leading the people they might not necessarily be like the people you meet on the street. Not everybody in Makkah was evil, but the leadership was evil, not everyone among the people of Thamūd was evil, but the leadership was...

'Awlakī also stated after 10 minutes and 50 seconds into *The Life of Muhammad (The Medinan Period)*, track 23:

> **Akhlāq are important even with your enemy, even with your enemy the Muslim should deal with him in a good way with dignity. A Muslim is not cruel, a Muslim is not wicked, a Muslim is not deceptive, a Muslim is not a liar. A Muslim deals**

with everyone with honesty, dignity, straight-forwardness and kindness towards all of the creation of Allāh ﷻ except those who deserve to be dealt with cruelly...

'Awlakī also stated in a *khutbah* aired on PBS (USA) in October 2001 CE:

> Our position needs to be re-iterated and needs to be very clear: the fact that the US has administered the death and homicide of over one million civilians in Iraq, the fact that the US is supporting the deaths and killing of thousands of Palestinians does not justify the killing of one US civilian in New York City or Washington D.C. and the deaths of six thousand civilians in Washington D.C. does not justify the death of one civilian in Afghanistan![1]

What is all the more ironic is that 'Awlakī himself stated in a documentary on Ramadān in 2001/02:

> I think that in general Islām is presented in a negative way, I mean there's always this association between Islām and terrorism when that is not true at all, **I mean Islām is a religion of peace**[2]!?

Only to then later translate the work of one who was with the terrorists! *La ilaha il Allāh!* What confusion. 'Awlakī doesn't know whether he's coming or going, how yesterday was different from today! More ups and downs than a yo-yo! It's almost as if 'Awlakī became Jihādī for opportunist and populist reasons as he saw a tide of youth inclining towards that way after 9/11, so he also then jumped on the bandwagon of the Takfīrī mavericks and Khawārij bandits and ditched the wishy-washy Ikhwānī methodology. As for 'Awlakī's justification of attacking Ahl ul-Harb wherever they may be, then this clearly goes against what

---

[1] The video of this khutbah can be seen here: http://www.pbs.org/newshour/updates/religion/july-dec09/alawlaki_11-11.html.
[2] See 2:45 here: http://www.youtube.com/watch?v=3BgG2ZLm2M8.

the classical and contemporary 'Ulamā have stated in their works on Jihād, which we will mention later *inshā'Allāh*. This all indicates that 'Awlakī has no solid academic Islamic basis and knowledge hence such contradictions and major shifts. As for his referral to the hadīth of the attack of Tā'if with Manjanīq, it is a common *shubhah* used by the Takfīrī-Jihādīs to justify killing civilians; more on that hadīth will be mentioned later.[1] Yet Allāh says:

﴿ وَقَٰتِلُوا۟ فِى سَبِيلِ ٱللَّهِ ٱلَّذِينَ يُقَٰتِلُونَكُمْ وَلَا تَعْتَدُوٓا۟ إِنَّ ٱللَّهَ لَا يُحِبُّ ٱلْمُعْتَدِينَ ﴾

"Fight in the way of Allāh against those who fight you and do not transgress the limits (set by Allāh). Indeed, Allāh does not love those who transgress." *{Baqarah (2): 190}*

In Sahīh Muslim from Buraydah ؓ who narrated that whenever the Prophet Muhammad ﷺ commanded an army general, he ﷺ would exhort the army general to have fear and consciousness of Allāh. This is because an army leader is in need of having *taqwā* of Allāh and being reminded of it. In the same way the leader orders goodness for those under him and does not transgress against them. Therefore, the leader of an army has to be one of pious worship, correct dīn and good manners with his followers. The Prophet ﷺ said to an army:

"Do battle and do not steal from the spoils of war, do not betray, do not depart (from the battle), do not mutilate and do not kill young children."

In the Two Sahīhs it is mentioned that the Prophet ﷺ found a dead woman of the polytheists that had been killed during the battle. The hadīth mentions that he saw the companions surrounding something and then he found out that it was a woman who had been killed during

---

[1] We have dealt with this before in a separate paper here: http://www.salafimanhaj.com/pdf/SalafiManhaj_Fighting.

the battle. The Prophet was angered by this and said *"This is not one against who war is to be fought against"* clearly showing that this woman did not come to fight against you, so why did you kill her? He then instructed the other Companion: "Tell Khālid to not kill children, women or the elderly and frail." In the Two Saḥīḥs[1] Ibn 'Umar narrated:

> A woman was found killed in one of the battles so Allāh's Messenger prohibited the killing of women and children.

Shaykh 'Abdullāh al-Bassām stated in *Tawḍīḥ ul-Aḥkām*:

1. It has preceded that the Prophet prohibited the killing of women, old men, children, people in places of worship and the likes who have no concern with fighting.
2. These two ḥadīths affirm this meaning in regards to the prohibition of killing women and old people who do not aid in war via action or opinion (i.e. strategies).
3. The wars of Islām are neither about oppression nor corruption rather they are wars of mercy and to call to goodness. Al-Māwardī said in *al-Aḥkām us-Sulṭāniyyah*: "It is not permitted to kill women and children whether during warfare or outside of it, because the Prophet forbade killing them just as he prohibited killing the weak. The commander must order his troops with what Allāh has obligated in terms of adhering to His rulings."[2]

Therefore, the Prophet prohibited the killing of women and children and it is known that a clear forbiddance of something *(nahy)* indicates *taḥrīm* (prohibition). Imām ash-Shāfi'ī stated, as relayed in *al-Faqīh wa'l-Mutafaqih*, vol.1, p.69:

---

[1] Also in Abū Dāwūd, at-Tirmidhī and Ibn Mājah.
[2] 'Abdullāh bin 'AbdurRahmān al-Bassām, *Tawḍīḥ ul-Aḥkām min Bulūgh il-Marām* (Makkah al-Mukarramah: Maktabah al-Asadī, 1423 AH/2003 CE, 5th Edn.), vol.6, pp.371.

The basis of nahy from Allāh's Messenger ﷺ is that all which he forbids is prohibited until a proof comes which indicates that the meaning is not a prohibition.

Also, the argument which claims that the forbiddance of things which are related to acts of worship and dealings indicate *tahrīm* yet when related to manners (Ādāb) does not indicate *tahrīm* is a view which does not have any evidence. Rather the general evidences demonstrate the obligation of staying away from all that has been forbidden without making any distinctions.

Shaykh Abū Anas Hamād bin Ibrāhīm Āl 'Uthmān on the Prohibition of Transgression when Fighting[1]

From Buraydah ؓ that the Messenger of Allāh ﷺ used to say[2]:
Fight in the way of Allāh and fight those who disbelieve Allāh. Do battle and do not exceed the limits, do not depart (from the battle), do not mutilate and do not kill children or those in monasteries (i.e. places of worship).[3]

The reason due to which the killing of monks (i.e. those secluded in places of worship) and those who are within places of worship is prohibited has to be understood. The reason is due to them abandoning fighting not due to them being preoccupied with their worship for indeed they are leaders of *kufr*. Ibn ul-Habeeb ؓ said:

---

[1] From Hamd bin Ibrāhīm al-'Uthmān, *Jihād: Anwā'ahu wa Ahkāmuhu, wa'l-Hadd al-Fāsil Baynahu wa Bayna'l-Fawda* [Jihād: Its Types and Regulations and the Decisive Difference Between it and Chaos], ('Ammān: Dār ul-Athariyyah, 1428 AH/2007 CE), pp.220-28.
[2] Reported by Muslim in *Kitāb ul-Jihād* and within other chapters, vol.3, p.1356, *hadīth* no.1731.
[3] The addition of **"...and those in monasteries (or other places of worship)"** is from the *Musnad* of Imām Ahmad, vol.5, p.352.

Chapter 11

It was not prohibited to kill religious people due to their preoccupation with their worship, as they are the most distant from Allāh than others from the people of their dīn due to their intense insight into kufr. Rather, it was on account of their non-involvement with the people of their dīn in waging war against the believers whether that be via hand, thought or wealth. But as for when it is known that one of them guides the enemy against us secretly or the likes, then at such a point it would be lawful to execute such a person (during jihād).[1]

Ibn ul-Qayyim said:

Killing is only obligatory when facing warfare and armed combat not when facing kufr. For this reason, neither women are to be killed nor children, nor the elderly, nor the blind nor those worshippers who do not fight, rather we fight against those who fight us. This was the way of the Messenger of Allāh in dealing with the people of the earth, he used to fight those who fought against him until they either entered into the dīn, make an agreement or treaty with him or came under his authority via paying the jizya. This is what he used to instruct his armies if

---

[1] Abū Muhammad 'Abdullāh bin 'AbdurRahmān bin Abī Zayd al-Qayrawānī, *an-Nawādir wa'z-Ziyādāt'alā mā fī'l-Mudawanna min Ghayrihā min al-Ammahāt* (Beirut: Dār ul-Maghrib al-Islami, 1999 CE, ed. Muhammad Hijji) vol.3, p.60.

Translator's Note: Ibn ul-Habīb also stated that if women or children are fighting with swords, arrows and the likes against the Muslims then they can be killed out of self-defence, but if they are merely throwing stones and the likes at the Muslims from the turrets of fortified buildings then they should not be killed. See *adh-Dhakhīrah*, vol.3, p.399. Other companions of Imām Mālik said the same as this. See Imām al-Mujtahid Abū 'Abdullāh Muhammad bin 'Īsā bin Muhammad bin Asbagh al-Azdī al-Qurtubī (aka Ibn ul-Munāsif), *Kitāb ul-Injād fī Abwāb il-Jihād* (Beirut: Mu'assasah ar-Rayān, 1425 AH/2005 CE, eds. Shaykh Muhammad bin Zakariyyā Abū Ghāzī and Shaykh Mashhūr Hasan Āl Salmān), vol.1, p.235.

they fought against their enemies, as has preceded from the hadīth of Buraydah.¹

Rather, from the justice and fairness of the Muslims is that a boy was only to fight when he reached puberty and maturity. They used to distinguish between those who fought against them out of opposing and wanting to counter Islām and the one who fought against them out of play and jest, it is mentioned in Sahnūn's book:

> **If the child does not endure the fighting due to his young age then his fight is not (really) a (proper) fight, rather it is out of play and jest so he is not to be killed.²**

Abū Bakr as-Siddīq ﷺ said to Yazīd bin Abī Sufyān ﷺ when he sent him to Shām,

> *You will surely find a people who claim to have secluded themselves for Allāh, so leave them to what they claim they have secluded themselves for and I advise you with ten matters: do not kill women or children or the elderly and infirm. Do not chop down the fruit-*

---

[1] Muhammad bin Abī Bakr Ibn Qayyim al-Jawziyyah, *Ahkām Ahl udh-Dhimmah* (Beirut: Dār al-'Ilm Li'l-Malayyīn, 3rd Edn., 1983 CE, ed. Sahbī as-Sālih), vol.1, p.17.

Translator's Note: Imām Ibn ul-Munāsif states:

> As for the insane person then there should be no difference of opinion whatsoever over the issue of not killing them, even if the person has reached maturity, this is because the person is not responsible by agreement. The evidence that these types of people (are not to be fought against) is the saying of Allāh, "**Fight in the way of Allāh against those who fight you and do not transgress the limits (set by Allāh). Indeed, Allāh does not love those who transgress.**" *{al-Baqarah (2): 190}*
>
> From these types of people are those who are generally unable to fight such as the elderly, the decrepit, those who are secluded in worship, hired workers, mothers and the likes who are not to be transgressed against during fighting and Allāh gave them a special position in that it is prohibited to kill them due to His saying, "**...and do not transgress the limits (set by Allāh).**" *{al-Baqarah (2): 190}* Meaning: do not kill non-combatants such as women due to their inability to fight.

From Ibn ul-Munāsif, *op.cit.*, vol.1, p.228.

[2] *An-Nawādir wa'z-Ziyādāt*, vol.3, p.58

bearing trees. Do not destroy inhabited places. Do not slaughter sheep or camels except for food. Do not burn bees and do not scatter them. Do not steal from the booty and do not be cowardly.[1]

Killing women, children and the elderly who have no opinion in fighting (by recommending strategies and the like) is included as being transgression which is prohibited,

$$\text{﴿ وَقَاتِلُوا۟ فِى سَبِيلِ ٱللَّهِ ٱلَّذِينَ يُقَاتِلُونَكُمْ وَلَا تَعْتَدُوٓا۟ إِنَّ ٱللَّهَ لَا يُحِبُّ ٱلْمُعْتَدِينَ ﴾}$$

"Fight in the way of Allāh against those who fight you and do not transgress the limits (set by Allāh). Indeed, Allāh does not love those who transgress." *{Baqarah (2): 190}*

Al-Ḥāfidh Ibn Kathīr said:

Allāh's saying,

$$\text{﴿ وَلَا تَعْتَدُوٓا۟ إِنَّ ٱللَّهَ لَا يُحِبُّ ٱلْمُعْتَدِينَ ﴾}$$

---

[1] Reported by Mālik in the *Muwaṭṭa'*, *Kitāb ul-Jihād* in the chapter of the prohibition of killing women and children during warfare, vol.2, p.447, the *hadīth* is on the authority of Yaḥyā bin Sa'īd from Abū Bakr as-Siddīq that he said the *hadīth*. 'AbdurRazzāq also reported the *hadīth* in *Kitāb ul-Jihād* in the chapter of '*destroying the trees within the land of the enemy*', vol.5, p.199, *hadīth* no.9375 on the authority of Ibn Jurayj who said: Yaḥyā bin Sa'īd said that Abū Bakr said, then he mentioned the *hadīth*. The *isnad* is *munqati'* (disconnected) but the *'Ulama* have utilised it and referred to it as the meaning is correct and in agreement with other authentic *marfū'* narrations.

Translator's Note: Shaykh Mashhūr mentions that Yaḥyā bin Sa'īd did not hear directly from Abū Bakr as-Siddīq. The hadīth was also reported by Sa'eed bin Manṣūr, *Sunan*, (no. 2284); al-Bayhaqī, *Sunan*, vol.9, p.86; al-Balādhuri, *Ansāb ul-Ashrāf*, pp.108-09 via another route of transmission from Abū Bakr, see *al-Majālisah*, p.1535 and *Jāmi' il-Uṣūl*, vol.2, p.599. In the *Sunan* of Abū Dāwūd, *Kitāb ul-Jihād* is the following *hadīth* on the authority of Anas bin Mālik:

> The Prophet said: "*Go in Allāh's name, trusting in Allāh, and adhering to the religion of Allāh's Messenger. Do not kill a decrepit old man, or a young infant, or a child, or a woman; do not be dishonest about booty, but collect your spoils, do right and act well, for Allāh loves those who do well.*"

> "...and do not transgress the limits (set by Allāh). Indeed, Allāh does not love those who transgress." *{Baqarah (2): 190}*

Means: Fight for the sake of Allāh and do not be transgressors, such as, by committing prohibitions, as al-Hasan al-Basri stated that transgression (indicated by the ayah), "includes mutilating the dead, theft (from the captured goods), killing women, children and old people who do not participate in warfare, killing priests and residents of houses of worship, burning down trees and killing animals without real benefit." This is also the opinion of Ibn 'Abbās, 'Umar bin 'Abdul'Azīz, Muqātil bin Hayyān and others.[1]

Just like al-Hasan al-Basrī ؓ is utilised as a proof for the prohibition of transgression in fighting involving killing women, children and old people, likewise 'Umar bin 'Abdul'Azīz ؓ is used as proof wherein he said about the saying of Allāh,

﴿ وَقَٰتِلُوا۟ فِى سَبِيلِ ٱللَّهِ ٱلَّذِينَ يُقَٰتِلُونَكُمْ وَلَا تَعْتَدُوٓا۟ۚ إِنَّ ٱللَّهَ لَا يُحِبُّ ٱلْمُعْتَدِينَ ﴾

> "Fight in the way of Allāh against those who fight you and do not transgress the limits (set by Allāh). Indeed, Allāh does not love those who transgress." *{Baqarah (2): 190}*

> ...the killing of women and children is included within this, and so are those who are not involved in warfare.[2]

Ash-Shāfi'ī ؓ opposed this and viewed that it was permissible to kill a disbeliever who was not fighting and he did not exempt the monk (or person of religion) from this, he said:

---

[1] *Tafsīr al-Qur'ān al-'Adhīm*, vol.1, p.528.
[2] *An-Nawādir wa'z-Ziyādāt*, vol.3, p.57

If one was to say "what is the evidence that the mushrik who does not participate in fighting is to be killed?"[1] Then it can be said: the companions of the Messenger of Allāh ﷺ on the Day of Hunayn killed Durayd bin as-Samah who was thrown into a tree and was not able to sit, he was about 150 years old and the Messenger of Allāh ﷺ did not find this offensive.[2]

The *'Ulamā* of the Shāfi'ī madhhab opposed this view of ash-Shāfi'ī for the view of the majority and they neither found his view pleasing nor did they refer to it as a proof. Ibn Battāl ؒ stated:

> Ash-Shāfi'ī viewed it permissible to kill them as is found within one of his sayings on the issue and he used as a proof the fact that the Messenger of Allāh ﷺ ordered the killing of Durayd bin as-Samah on the Day of Hunayn.[3]

What is useful to us is Ibn Battāl's mention of **"…within one of his sayings…"** which indicates that Imām ash-Shāfi'ī had another view which concurred with the view of the majority which takes precedence due to it agreeing with the generality of *'Ulamā* and due to its strong

---

[1] **Translator's Note:** in any case this is in referral to a Mushrik so it could be deduced from Imām ash-Shāfi'ī's *shādh* view here that it is in referral to the Mushrikīn in any case and not Ahl ul-Kitāb, and Allāh knows best.

[2] Muhammad bin Idrīs ash-Shāfi'ī, *al-Umm* (Beirut: Dār ul-Ma'rifah, ed. Muhammad Zuhrī an-Najjār), vol.4, p.240.

Translator's Note: this opinion of Imām ash-Shāfi'ī ؒ is also reported in *Mukhtasar al-Muzanī*, p.272; *al-Wajīz*, vol.2, p.189; *al-Iqnā'*, p.176; *Mukhtasar ul-Khilāfāt*, vol.5, p.47, no.314; *Mugni ul-Muhtāj*, vol.4, pp.222-23; *Nihāyat ul-Muhtāj*, vol.8, p.64; *Rawdat ut-Tālibīn*, vol.10, p.243; *al-Muhdhab*, vol.2, p.299; *al-Majmū'*, vol.21, pp.154-55; *Hilyat ul-'Ulama*, vol.7, p.650 and al-Māwardī, *al-Ahkām us-Sultāniyyah*, p.41. See Ibn ul-Munāsif, *op.cit.*, vol.1, p.225. It is also found in Ibn an-Nahhās, *op.cit.*, p.1023.

[3] 'Ali bin Khalf bin 'AbdulMālik ibn Battāl, *Sharh Sahīh al-Bukhārī* (Riyadh: Maktabah Rushd, 1320 AH/2000 CE, ed. Yāsir bin Ibrāhīm, 1st Edn.), vol.5, p.171.

evidence.¹ As for using the killing of Ibn as-Samah as a proof then it is weak as Durayd was one of the military strategists and for that reason Ibn Battāl himself said:

> **Whoever compares the hadīth about the prohibition of killing shuyūkh from the Messenger of Allāh ﷺ will see that they refer to those who do no assist at all in warfare via participating in combat or strategies. The hadīth of Durayd relates to an old person who assisted in combat as indeed Durayd did, in such an instance there is no problem in killing such a person even if they do not participate in armed combat.² This is because such assistance is more severe than most fighting, this is the view of Muhammad bin al-Hasan and is the analogy of the saying of Abū Hanīfah and Abū Yūsuf.³**

Some scholars claim that there is a lack of evidence preventing the killing of worshippers and the elderly,⁴ Imām Abū Bakr Muhammad bin Ibrāhīm Ibn ul-Mundhir an-Naysābūrī ؒ – died 318 AH:

---

¹ **Translator's note:** Ibn Munāsif ؒ however asserts that this opinion was the most authentic of his sayings on the matter, see Ibn Munāsif, *op.cit.*, vol.1, p.225. Ibn Munāsif also says that this was the view of the Dhāhirī scholars such as Abū Muhammad Ibn Hazm in *al-Muhallā*, vol.7, p.296, issue no.928.

² **Translator's Note:** this is also the view of Shaykh 'Abdullāh bin 'AbdurRahmān al-Bassām in is explanation of the *hadīth* in Abū Dawūd regarding the use of catapults against the people of Tā'if, see *Tawdīh ul-Ahkām min Bulūgh il-Marām* (Makkah al-Mukarramah, KSA: Maktabah al-Asadī, 1424 AH/2003 CE, 5ᵗʰ Edn.), vol.6, p.385. Shaykh 'Abdullāh al-Bassām states:

> As for intending to attack those who are not fighting such as women, children, the elderly, those in monasteries, churches and the likes – then this is not permissible, as long as they neither provide a benefit (to the enemy troops) via their views or strategies nor have committed murder. For example, the Prophet ﷺ acknowledged the execution of Durayd bin as-Samah on the Day of Hunayn because he was a strategist, and just as the Qaradhiyyah woman was executed because she had murdered one of the Companions.

³ Ibid.

⁴ **Translator's note:** Ibn ul-Munāsif stated that the evidence that is used by Ibn Hazm and those of the view that it is permissible is the verse,

Chapter 11

> I do not know of decisive evidence which obligates withholding from killing worshippers, the elderly and the sick from the apparentness of the Book. Mālik, Layth bin Sa'd and a group of scholars viewed that killing them should be withheld due to the narration of Abū Bakr as-Ṣiddīq and his prohibition of that.[1]

However, the evidence from the Book is clear in refuting this as Allāh says,

﴿ وَقَٰتِلُوا۟ فِى سَبِيلِ ٱللَّهِ ٱلَّذِينَ يُقَٰتِلُونَكُمْ وَلَا تَعْتَدُوٓا۟ إِنَّ ٱللَّهَ لَا يُحِبُّ ٱلْمُعْتَدِينَ ﴾

"Fight in the way of Allāh against those who fight you and do not transgress the limits (set by Allāh). Indeed, Allāh does not love those who transgress." *{Baqarah (2): 190}*

Along with the understanding of al-Hasan al-Basrī and 'Umar bin 'Abdul'Azīz ؓ as has preceded. Shaykh ul-Islām Ibn Taymiyyah ؒ stated:

"Fight the Mushrikīn wherever you find them..."
{at-Tawbah (9): 5}

And they also use as a proof the saying of the Messenger of Allāh ﷺ: *"I was instructed to fight the people until they say "La ilaha il-Allāh"."* The *hadīth* is reported by Muslim and others. They also use the *hadīth*: *"Wage war in the names of Allāh, on the way of Allāh and fight those who disbelieve in Allāh..."*

[1] Abū Bakr Muhammad bin Ibrāhīm bin al-Mundhir an-Naysabūrī, *Al-Iqnā'* (n.p., 1408 AH, ed. 'Abdullāh al-Jibreen, 1st Edn.) vol.2, p.464.

Translator's Note: The view of Imām Mālik ؒ was documented in: *al-Mudawwana*, vol.1, p.370; *ar-Risālah*, p.189; *al-Ma'ūnah*, vol.1, p.624; *Ashal ul-Madārik*, vol.2, p.16; *al-Kāfī*, p.208; *Qawānīn ul-Ahkām*, p.164; *Bidāyat ul-Mujtahid*, vol.1, p.384; *Fath ul-Jalīl*, vol.3, p.144-46; *Hāshiyat ud-Dusuqī*, vol.2, p.177; *Sharh uz-Zurqānī*, vol.3, pp.111-12; *'Iqd ul-Jawāhir ath-Thamīnah*, vol.1, p.468; *adh-Dhakīrah*, vol.3, p.397; *Jāmi' ul-Amāhāt*, p.246; *an-Nawādir wa'z-Ziyādāt*, vol.3, pp.57-8; *al-Istidhkār*, vol.14, p.72, hadīth no.19435; *al-Ishrāf*, vol.4, p.419, issue no.1739; Ibn ul-Jawzī, *at-Tahqīq*, vol.10, p.149, *hadīth* no.728.

As for those who are not from the people who help and fight, such as women, children, the worshipper, the elderly, the blind, the disabled and the likes then they are not to be killed according to the majority of the 'Ulamā unless the person participates in fighting (against the Muslims) with speech or action. Even though some 'Ulamā permitted the killing of all merely on account of kufr, except for women and children which become for the Muslims. The first opinion (that non-combatants are not to be killed or fought against at all) is the most correct opinion, because fighting is only against whoever fights us when we want to manifest the deen of Allāh, just as Allāh says,

﴿ وَقَٰتِلُوا۟ فِى سَبِيلِ ٱللَّهِ ٱلَّذِينَ يُقَٰتِلُونَكُمْ وَلَا تَعْتَدُوٓا۟ إِنَّ ٱللَّهَ لَا يُحِبُّ ٱلْمُعْتَدِينَ ﴾

"Fight in the way of Allāh against those who fight you and do not transgress the limits (set by Allāh). Indeed, Allāh does not love those who transgress." *{Baqarah (2): 190}*

In the Sunan is a hadīth from the Prophet ﷺ that he passed by a woman who had been killed within a battle and the people had gathered around the body. The Prophet ﷺ said: "This is not one who should be fought against" and sent the men away saying to one of them: "Tell Khālid not to kill children or workers." Also reported from him ﷺ is that he said: "Do not kill a frail elderly man or a young child or a woman;"[1]

---

[1] *As-Siyāsah ash-Shar'iyyah*, pp.177.
Translator's Note: Shaykh Mashhūr *(hafidhahullāh)* highlights that the *hadīth* is reported by Abū Dāwūd from Rabāh bin Rabī' in *Kitāb ul-Jihād*, chapter *'qatl un-Nisā'*, hadīth no.2669; an-Nisā'ī, *al-Kabīr*, hadīth nos. 8625, 8628; Ibn Mājah, hadīth no.2842; at-Tahāwī, *Sharh ul-Ma'ānī*, vol.3, pp.221-22 and in *al-Mushkil*, 6138; Ahmad, vol.3, p.488 and vol.4, p.178; Ibn Hibbān, no.4789; al-Hākim, vol.2, p.122; at-Tabarānī, *al-Kabīr*, hadīth nos. 4617, 4618, 4619, 4620, 4621, 4622; al-Bukhārī, *Tārīkh ul-Kabīr*, vol.3, p.314; al-Bayhaqī, *al-Kubrā*, vol.9, p.82, 91; Ibn 'AbdulBarr, *at-*

Chapter 11

Ibn Taymiyyah also stated,

> Whoever neither prevents the Muslims from establishing the *dīn* of Allāh nor harmful with his *kufr* except to his own self.[1]

As for the underlying reason for the prohibition of killing women and children being due to them being under the ownership of the Muslims only then this is incorrect. This is because when the Prophet ﷺ saw a murdered woman during a battle he said, *"This is not one who should be fought against."*[2] This is a clear text indicating that a woman is not to be killed because she neither fights nor is the property of the Muslims. The disbeliever is only killed for helping and participating in fighting, not on account of their *kufr* only.

The conclusion of the matter is that the prohibition of killing women and children is clear as there is no evidence that opposes this.[3]

Tamhīd, vol.16, p.140; Ibn Abī 'Āsim, *al-Āhād wa'l-Ma'ānī*, *hadīth* no.2751; Abū Ya'lā, *hadīth* no.1546 – from the *hadīth* of Rabāh bin ar-Rabī'.
The *hadīth* with all its transmissions is *sahīh*, see Shaykh al-Albānī, *Sahīh Abū Dāwūd*. The narration from Ibn 'Umar with the wording *'the prohibition of killing women and children'* has been verified by al-Bukhārī, no.3015; Muslim, nos. 1744, 25; and from Ibn 'Abbās; al-Aswad bin Surī'ah; Hadhalah al-Kuttāb; Buraydah bin al-Hasīb; an-Nu'mān bin Muqrin and Anas bin Mālik. There are also other *hadīth* on this issue; refer to *Majma' az-Zawā'id*, vol.5, pp.315-18. Ibn ul-Munāsif stated that the *hadīth* "for those who authenticate it is a proof that the *'asīf* (hired workers or servants) and those like them are exempted from fighting and this is what the qiyās is extrapolated from." See Ibn ul-Munāsif, *op.cit.*, vol.1, pp.228029.

[1] *As-Siyāsah ash-Shar'iyyah*, pp.177-78
[2] Reported by Abū Dāwūd in his *Sunan, Kitāb ul-Jihād* in the chapter entitled *'Qatl un-Nisā'*, vol.3, p.121, *hadīth* no.2669.
[3] **Translator's Note:** It is amazing therefore to find the Khawārij of the current era feebly try to piece together all manner of *'dalīl'* to justify the killing of non-combatants. Then to make matters worse some of the *Qutbīs*, *ikhwānīs* and *hizbīs* then have the audacity to deny that any Muslims can even be involved in such actions and defer blame to conspiracy theories!? However, one does not need to be a conspiracy theorist to realise that the likes of Abū Qatādah al-Filistīnī gave *'fatāwā'* encouraging and inciting the murder and killing of women and children during the civil war in Algeria.

Chapter 11

As for old people, then there is another issue which is that Samurah bin Jundub ❧ reported that the Prophet ﷺ said: *"Kill the Shuyūkh of the Mushrikīn and keep their sharkh alive."*[1] Al-Baghawī stated: he intended

---

Furthermore, the *'al-Ansār'* magazine that Abū Qatādah used to write articles and *'fatāwā'* for used to feature stories which they considered praiseworthy of so-called 'Mujāhiddīn' "reviving the way of the Salaf" by killing their own parents who they had made takfīr of!!? Refer to *al-Ansār* magazine, issue no.147, p.4 dated: al-Khamīs (Thursday) 14th Dhu'l-Hijjah 1416 AH corresponding to 2 May 1996 CE, transmitting the story from an article from *al-Qitāl* (issue no.32), the mouthpiece of the *GIA* [the 'Armed Islamic Group'].

Therefore, even if we are arguing within the rubric of the Qutbī neo-conspiracy theorists (such as some of the *majāhīl* from the *'Islamic Awakening'* forum), Abū Qatādah is an "agent for the security services".

[1] Reported by Ahmad, vol.5, p.12, 20; Abū Dāwūd, *Kitāb ul-Jihād*, chapter *'Qatl un-Nisā"*, vol.3, p.122, *hadīth* no.2670; at-Tirmidhī, *Kitāb us-Seer*, vol.4, p.145, *hadīth* no. 1583 and at-Tirmidhī said: **the hadīth is hasan sahīh gharīb.**

Translator's Note: Shaykh Mashhūr also highlights that the *hadīth* is also reported by Ibn Abī Shaybah, vol.12, p.388, hadīth no.33138; at-Tabarānī, *al-Kabīr*, hadīth no.6900; Sa'īd bin Mansūr, *as-Sunan*, hadīth no.2624; al-Bayhaqī, *al-Kubrā*, vol.9, p.92 and *Ma'rifat us-Sunan wa'l-Āthār*, hadīth no.18099; Abū 'Ubayd, *Gharīb ul-Hadīth*, vol.3, p.16; ar-Ruwayānī, *Musnad*, hadīth no.802 – via Hajjāj bin Artā; at-Tabarānī, *al-Kabīr*, hadīth no.6902 and *Musnad ush-Shāmiyyīn*, hadīth no.2641 – via Sa'īd bin Bashīr via Qatādah from al-Hasan al-Basrī from Samurah in a *marfū'* form; al-Bazzār, *Musnad* (al-Kattāniyyah), hadīth no.253 and Abū Tāhir al-Mukhallas, *Fawā'id*, p.175, via Qatādah.

Hajjāj bin Artā is *sudūq* yet has many mistakes and *tadlīs* as al-Hāfidh stated in *at-Taqrīb*, he narrates much from Sa'īd bin Mansūr and Sa'īd bin Bashīr (who is al-Azdī), their freed slave and he is weak. See *Da'īf Abī Dāwud* and *Da'īf at-Tirmidhī* by Shaykh al-Albānī ❧. The scholars differed as to whether al-Hasan heard from Samurah and the more correct opinion is that he did, see Sharīf Hāim al-'Awnī, *al-Mursal al-Khafi' wa 'Alāqatuhu bi't-Tadlīs*, p.1301. Both transmissions (via Hajjāj bin Artā' and Sa'īd bin Bashīr) are weak but they strengthen each other and inshā'Allāh the hadīth is *hasan*. For this reason at-Tirmidhī said that the *hadīth* is: "hasan sahīh gharīb" and he reported it via al-Hajjāj bin Artā from Qatādah. It is probably due to this reason that at-Tirmidhī made the hadīth *hasan*. At-Tabarānī reported the hadīth (no. 7037) via Ja'far bin Sa'd bin Samurah from Khubayb bin Sulaymān ibn Samurah from his father from his father (Samurah). This *isnad* is weak because it contains more than one narrator who is either *da'īf* or *majhūl*. Ibn Munāsif, *op.cit.*, pp.226-27, ftn.4.

by *'sharkh'* – children and by *'Shuyūkh'* – the youth."[1] Upon referral to dictionaries[2] we do not find that the entry 'Shaykh' refers to youth except that al-Baghawī ؓ intends by *'Shuyūkh'* those of them who have youthful vigour as there is no doubt that these, if they are fought against, are to be killed. The same is for the weak Shaykh who has a strategy or is consulted with for fighting against the Muslims, then such an individual is to be killed (during warfare). Shaykh ul-Islām Ibn Taymiyyah ؓ said:

> The foundation is that the blood of Banī Ādam is sanctified and inviolable and no one is killed except with right. Killing due to kufr is not something which the legislations have agreed upon at any one time of the Sharī'ah, such as killing the one who sits out of combat, for this is something that the legislations and intellect do not differ over. The blood of the disbeliever during the early history of Islām was sanctified and inviolable just like the original sanctity of a person. Allāh prevented the Muslims from killing such a disbeliever.[3]

The prohibition of killing women and children is muhkam and the Prophet ﷺ never allowed it at all

Some Ahl ul-'Ilm have thought that the killing of women was allowed during the early period of Islām and then it was abrogated. This doubt has affected some people of knowledge due to the hadīth of as-Sa'b bin Jaththāmah:

> The Messenger of Allāh ﷺ was asked about: women and children of the Mushrikīn (polytheists) being harmed during a night-raid,

---

[1] *Sharh us-Sunnah*, vol.11, p.48.
[2] See *Mu'jam Maqāyīs il-Lughah*, vol.3, p.234 and *as-Sahhāh*, vol.1, p.425.
[3] Ahmad bin 'AbdulHalīm bin Taymiyyah al-Harrānī, *As-Sārim al-Maslūl 'alā Shātim ir-Rasūl* (Beirut: Dār ul-Kutub al-'Ilmiyyah, ed. Muhammad Muhiyyudīn 'AbdulHamīd, n.d.), p.104.

and the Messenger of Allāh ﷺ responded by saying *"They are from their fathers."*¹

Abū 'Ubayd bin Sallām ؎ – d. 224 AH – stated after transmitting the *hadīth*:
Then after that came the prohibition of killing women and children within many ahādīth.²

Shaykh ul-Islām Ibn Taymiyyah ؎ stated:
Killing a woman merely on account of kufr is not permissible and we do not know that it was allowed to kill any disbelieving woman at any time whatsoever. Rather, the Qur'ān and the sequence of its revelation prove that it is not allowed at all, due to the first verses revealed about fighting,

---

¹ Reported by al-Bukhārī, *Kitāb ul-Jihād*, chapter *'Ahl ud-Dār yabayitoon'*; also in *Sahīh Muslim* with the same wording in *Kitāb ul-Jihād wa's-Sīr*, chapter *'jawāz qatl in-Nisā' wa's-Sibyān'*, vol.3, p.1364, *hadīth* no.1745.

² *Al-Amwāl*, p.42

Translator's Note: Shaykh 'AbdulMālik ar-Ramadānī al-Jazā'irī highlights in *Takhlīs ul-'Ibād min Wahshiyyat Abī'l-Qatād* (Jeddah: Maktabah al-Asālah al-Athariyyah, 1422 AH), p.235, ftn.2:
As-San'ānī ؎ said in *Subul us-Salām*, vol.4, pp.101-02:
...attacking them at night time out of heedlessness while their women and children are mingled among them and then they get hurt during the attack unintentionally. The hadīth which is reported by Ibn Hibbān from as-Sa'b (and has the addition of "..and then he prohibited this on the Day of Hunayn"). In the Sunan of Abū Dāwūd there is another addition in the hadīth: Sufyān said: az-Zuhrī said: **"and then the Messenger of Allāh ﷺ prohibited the killing of women and children after that."** What supports the prohibition being after Hunayn is what is mentioned in Bukhārī, that the Prophet ﷺ said to one of them: *"Go to Khālid and tell him: do not kill children or hired-workers."* What indicates this is what was reported by Ibn Hibbān from as-Sa'b bin Jaththāmah who said: "I asked him about the children of the Mushrikīn and them getting killed among the enemy. He ﷺ said: *'yes (it's ok) they are from them'*, then he prohibited their killing on the Day of Hunayn." Al-Albānī authenticated this in *Sahīh Mawrārid ith-Thumān*, p.1380.

Chapter 11

﴿ أُذِنَ لِلَّذِينَ يُقَاتَلُونَ بِأَنَّهُمْ ظُلِمُوا ۚ وَإِنَّ ٱللَّهَ عَلَىٰ نَصْرِهِمْ لَقَدِيرٌ

ٱلَّذِينَ أُخْرِجُوا مِن دِيَٰرِهِم بِغَيْرِ حَقٍّ ﴾

"Permission [to fight] has been given to those who are being fought, because they were wronged. And indeed, Allāh is competent to give them victory. [They are] those who have been evicted from their homes without right..." *{al-Hajj (22): 39-40}*

So it was allowed for the believers to fight in defending themselves and to retaliate against those who evicted them from their homes and prevented them from the tawhīd of Allāh and His worship, and women are not included from those who do this. Then it was prescribed for them to fight absolutely and this is explained in His saying,

﴿ وَقَٰتِلُوا فِى سَبِيلِ ٱللَّهِ ٱلَّذِينَ يُقَٰتِلُونَكُمْ ﴾

"Fight in the way of Allāh against those who fight you...."
{Baqarah (2): 190}

So those people who are not people of combat are not permitted to be fought against.[1]

Likewise, those who try to prove that the killing of women was allowed during early Islām and then it was abrogated, refer to some positions taken by the Companions such as az-Zubayr bin al-Awwām's ﷺ objection to Abū Dujānah ﷺ when he let a woman go and did not kill her.[2] Abū Ja'far Muhammad bin Jarīr at-Tabarī (d. 310 AH) stated:

> Within this hadīth is also an exposition that killing the women of the Mushrikīn who are at war was permissible and then the Messenger of Allāh ﷺ prohibited it later, either around the conquest of Makkah, before it or just after it. This is because when az-Zubayr objected to Abū Dujānah leaving the women

---

[1] *As-Sārim al-Maslūl*, p.101
[2] *Tahdhīb ul-Āthār*, pp.560-61

and letting her go after raising his sword to her and az-Zubayr said to Abū Dujānah "I saw you raise your sword away from the woman after you had directed it to her."¹ When az-Zubayr said this to Abū Dujānah, Abū Dujānah did not say "The Messenger of Allāh forbade killing women", rather he said "I respect the sword of the Messenger of Allāh ﷺ too much to use it on a woman." Within this then is a clear evidence that killing women during warfare at the time of the Battle of Uhud and before that was allowed and then prohibited after.²

This does not show that there was a prior allowance to kill women rather the prohibition was possibly from the knowledge that escaped some of the Companions.³

---

¹ **Translator's Note:** the woman was Hind bint al-'Utbah.
² *Tahdhīb ul-Āthār*, pp.560-61
³ **Translator's Note:** Ibn ul-Munāsif stated that Ash-hab relayed that Mālik was asked about enemy women and their children who are on the turrets throwing rocks against the Muslims and assisting against the Muslims, "should they be killed?" Mālik responded: "The Messenger of Allāh ﷺ prohibited the killing of women and children". Ibn ul-Mundhir reported this saying from Mālik from a group of Mālik's companions (refer to *an-Nawādir wa'z-Ziyādāt*, vol.3, p.58 and *adh-Dhakīrah*, vol.3, pp.397-98). See Ibn ul-Munāsif, *op.cit.*, vol.1, pp.234-35.

Chapter 11

The use of manjanīq from Imām al-Mujtahid Ibn ul-Munāsif's (563-620 AH/1168-1223 AH) "Kitāb ul-Injād fi Abwāb il-Jihād"[1]

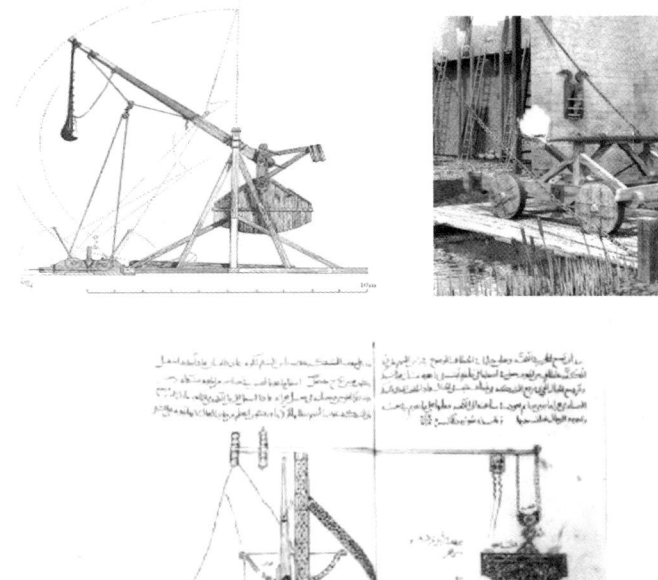

Awlakī states in his "explanation" of Ibn an-Nahhās' book *Mashāri' ul-Ashwāq ilā Masāri' il-'Ushshāq*, CD 11, Track 6:

---

[1] The translator's notes for this section are to the edit of Shaykh Muhammad bin Zakariyyā Abū Ghāzī and our Shaykh Mashhūr Hasan Āl Salmān to Imām al-Mujtahid Abū 'Abdullāh Muhammad bin 'Īsā bin Muhammad bin Asbagh al-Azdī al-Qurtubī (aka Ibn ul-Munāsif), *Kitāb ul-Injād fi Abwāb il-Jihād* (Beirut: Mu'assasah ar-Rayān, 1425 AH/2005 CE), vol.1, pp.225-235. any footnotes upon the words of Imām Ibn ul-Munāsif here are from Shaykh Mashhūr and Muhammad bin Zakariyyā Abū Ghāzī unless stated otherwise.

Chapter 11

By the way the use of al-Manjanīq (catapults) does not distinguish between male, female, young or old. A catapult is equivalent to a modern-day missile, in fact a modern-day missile is more accurate because at least it can be guided or aimed[1] but a catapult just hits somewhere. So since Rasoolullāh (salasalām) {sic} used that in Hisār (the siege) at-Tā'if and the Muslims after that used it every generation this is an evidence that even though Muslims should avoid the killing of women and children and the elderly but it does happen that some of them will die as collateral damage and this should not hinder the jihād fī sabeelillāh. If a town is placed under siege and there's no way to open it but by using al-Manjanīq then it can be used even if that might lead to the death of some innocent people because that's for the benefit of the whole. One would rather have a few innocent people die and then the rest of the people be saved from Hellfire than have them live and generation after generation they keep on entering into Jahannam.

Imām Ibn ul-Munāsif ﷺ however states in *Kitāb ul-Injād fī Abwāb il-Jihād*:

> They (the scholars) differed over the use of attacking the forts of the enemies with Manjanīq (catapults) and the likes of such destructive weapons when women, children[2] and Muslim prisoners are within the fortified enemy abodes. Mālik, ash-Shāfi'ī, Abū Hanīfah, al-Awzā'ī and others allowed them to be used which we will explain from them. It was also stated that: they are not to be used as mentioned by Fadl that Ibn ul-Qāsim, from the companions of Mālik, relayed from him that attacking them with catapults (Majānīq) is not permissible, neither is

---

[1] This is a naive view from Awlakī! As look at all of the cases in Afghanistan for example where families, people at weddings and other innocents have been killed via the use of modern-day missiles.

[2] What are called today: civilians.

Chapter 11

flooding them out with water in order to drown them, if women and children are among them.[1] As for Abū Ḥanīfah then he viewed that it was permissible to use catapults and to use fire even if there are Muslim prisoners and children (held by the enemy within their forts) and even if they use the Muslims as human-shields, as long as the intended targets are the kuffār

---

[1] See *Qudwat ul-Ghāzī*, pp.172-73; *adh-Dhakhīrah*, vol.3, p.409; *al-Kharashī*, vol.4, p.17; *al-Bayān wa't-Ta'sīl*, vol.3, pp.31-2 – wherein four statements are relayed:
1. It is permissible to throw fire at the enemy as a projectile via catapults, this is the view of Asbagh as Ibn Mazīn relayed from him.
2. It is not permissible at all to do any of this, this is the view of Ibn ul-Qāsim as relayed Fadl relayed from him.
3. It is permissible to use catapults against them and to use water to flood them out, but it is not permissible to use fire as projectiles against them, this is the view of Ibn Habīb as mentioned in *al-Wādihah*.
4. It is permissible to use catapults against them but it is neither permissible to drown them out with water nor burn them, this is the madhdhab of Mālik as mentioned in *al-Mudawwanah*. As for there being Muslim prisoners held by the enemy fighters then in such as instance they are not to be attacked with fire or drowned with water. There is difference of opinion with regards to attacking them with catapults, some of them said it was permissible such as Ibn ul-Qāsim and Asbagh from Sahnūn and it was also said that it is not permissible, which is the view of Ibn Habīb as mentioned in *al-Wādihah*, he relayed this view from Mālik and his companions in Madīnah and Egypt. See *al-Bayān wa't-Ta'sīl*, vol.2, pp.44, 52; also see *adh-Dhakhīrah* for this view from Mālik's companions in Egypt and Madīnah. See Ibn ul-Mundhir, *al-Iqnā'*, vol.2, pp.465-66.

Translator's Note: this is also the view of Shaykh 'Abdullāh bin 'AbdurRahmān al-Bassām in his explanation of the hadīth in Abū Dawūd regarding the use of catapults against the people of Tā'if, see *Tawdīh ul-Ahkām min Bulūgh il-Marām* (Makkah al-Mukarramah, KSA: Maktabah al-Asadī, 1424 AH/2003 CE, 5th Edn.), vol.6, p.385. Shaykh 'Abdullāh al-Bassām states:

> As for intending to attack those who are not fighting such as women, children, the elderly, those in monasteries, churches and the likes – then this is not permissible, as long as they neither provide a benefit (to the enemy troops) via their views or strategies nor have committed murder. For example, the Prophet ﷺ acknowledged the execution of Durayd bin as-Samah on the Day of Hunayn because he was a strategist, and just as the Qaradhiyyah woman was executed because she had murdered one of the Companions.

(fighters). If a Muslim is hit then there is no blood-money to be paid and no expiation to be made.[1] Ash-Shāfi'ī said: "there is no problem with hitting the fortified bases with catapults and fire and with whatever will affect the enemy, even if there are women and children present." But Abū Hanīfah did not view that it was permissible to use catapults if the enemies are using Muslims as human-shields except at times of compulsion.

Any Muslim that harms those who were not intended to be targeted then that Muslim has to free a slave and there is no blood-money to pay. If the Muslim saw him (a Muslim and yet still targeted the enemies with the Muslim being there) and saw where he was and then hurled (the projectile) due to being compelled to do that then he has to pay blood-money and make expiation. If he was not compelled into hurling the projectile and intended to strike the Muslim then qisās (retaliation against that Muslim attacker) has to be implemented.[2] Al-Awzā'ī stated: "forts can be attacked with catapults and fire even if there are Muslim captives therein. If any Muslim captives are harmed (due to being harmed from the projectiles from Muslim fighters) then this is an error which demands some form of expiation or blood-money to be paid." Al-Awzā'ī[3] viewed that the Muslim captives

---

[1] This is because they were not intended as the target and in this case to throw projectiles via catapults is permitted and does not necessitate any expiation to be made or any blood-money to be paid. See *al-Mabsūt*, vol.5, pp.64-5; *Tuhfat ul-Fuquhā*, vol.3, p.295; *Bidā'i' us-Sanā'i'*, vol.7, pp.100-01; *al-Lubāb*, vol.4, p.118; *ar-Radd 'alā Sīr al-Awzā'ī*, p.16; al-Jassās, *Ahkām ul-Qur'ān*, vol.3, pp.395-96; *al-Hidāyah Sharh Bidayāh al-Mubtadī*, vol.2, p.428; *al-Bināyah fī Sharh il-Hidāyah*, vol.5, p.656; *Fath ul-Qadīr*, vol.5, pp.447-48; *Majmā' ul-Anhar*, vol.2, p.413; *Radd al-Muhtār*, vol.3, p.179; *al-Bahr ur-Rā'iq*, vol.5, p.128 and *Tabyīn ul-Haqā'iq*, vol.3, p.243. This is the view of the majority of the Hanafīs like al-Hasan bin Ziyād, the companion of Abū Hanīfah, see *Bidā'i' us-Sanā'i'*, vol.7, p.101.

[2] *Al-Umm*, vol.4, p.257; *Rawdat ut-Tālibīn*, vol.10, pp.244-45; *Asnā ul-Matālib*, vol.4, p.191.

[3] See at-Tabarī, *Ikhtilāf ul-Fuquhā*, p.5 (with the edit of Yūsuf Sakht); *al-Umm*, vol.7, p.369; *al-Mughnī*, vol.13, p.142; *al-Istidhkār*, vol.14, p.66, no.19412; *Hāshiyat ul-*

not be put in danger if the enemy are using them as human-shields. From Mālik it is reported that he viewed it permissible to attack with catapults but that it was not permissible to use fire, except if there were none but fighters within the fortified bases. I do not know of any statement from Mālik with regards to the issue of the human-shields, what is apparent from the madhdhab is that it is not allowed (to attack when the enemies use the Muslims as human-shields).[1]

As for the evidence which permits to use catapults against a fortified base is what was reported by Muslim and Bukhārī from as-Sa'b bin Jathāmah who said:

> The Prophet ﷺ was asked about an abode wherein the Mushrikīn were staying the night (and was subsequently attacked) and they had women and children who were attacked there (unintentionally), he ﷺ said: *"They are from them."*

Qalīyūbī, vol.4, p.219. there is another narration from al-Awzā'ī about the impermissibility of throwing projectiles against the fortified bases of the Mushrikīn if there are Muslim prisoners therein or if the enemies are using the Muslim captives as human-shields. Ibn Rushd transmitted this from him in *Bidāyat ul-Mujtahid*, vol.1, p.416 (Egypt: Dār ul-Hamāmī), also see: *Fiqh ul-Imām al-Awzā'ī*, vol.2, p.400.

[1] See *'Aqd ul-Jawāhir ath-Thamīnah*, vol.1, p.469, al-Qarāfī transmitted this from him in *adh-Dhakhīrah*, vol.3, 408; *al-Bayān wa't-Tahsīl*, vol.3, p.44; *an-Nawādir wa'z-Ziyādāt*, vol.3, p.66; *Hāshiyat ud-Dusūqī 'ala'sh-Sharh al-Kabīr*, vol.2, p.178; *al-Kāfī*, vol.1, pp.466-67; *al-Qawānīn al-Fiqhiyyah*, p.98; Ibn ul-'Arabī, *Ahkām ul-Qur'ān*, vol.4, p.1696; *Tafsīr ul-Qurtubī*, vol.16, pp.286-87; *Hāshiyat ur-Rahūnī 'alā Sharh az-Zurqānī li-Mukhtasar Khalīl*, vol.3, p.146 and *Hāshiyat ul-'Adawī 'alā Sharh al-Kharashī*, vol.3, p.114. The avoidance of attacking when Muslims are being used as human-shields is the more correct view according to the Mālikī scholars and also with the *Hanābilah*. See *al-Mughnī*, vol.13, p.141; *al-Insāf*, vol.4, p.129; *al-Mabda'*, vol.3, p.324 and *Matālib Uola'n-Nahy*, vol.2, pp.518-19. This is also the view of al-Hasan bin Ziyād, the companion of Abī Hanīfah, as mentioned previously. Likewise, this is the view of al-Layth bin Sa'd as mentioned in *al-Mughnī*, vol.13, p.142.

The meaning of *"they are from them"* raises any blame from the Muslim fighters in them being compelled or forced to hurt them (i.e. collateral).[1]

Shaykh 'AbdulMālik ar-Ramadānī al-Jazā'irī on using the hadīth in Abū Dāwud regarding the indiscriminate attack on the people of Tā'if with manjanīq[2]

The story of the people of Tā'if being attacked with *manjanīq* is not relayed with an authentic *sanad*, it has only been reported by Abū Dāwūd in his *Marāsīl*[3]; al-Wāqidī[4] in his *Maghāzī*, vol.3, p.927 and Ibn

---

[1] Abridged from Ibn ul-Munāsif, *op.cit.*, vol.1, pp.236-39.

[2] Based on what the Shaykh mentioned in *Takhlīs ul-'Ibād min Wahshiyyat Abi'l-Qatād* (Jeddah: Maktabah al-Asālah al-Athariyyah, 1422 AH), pp.237-39.

[3] **Translator's Note:** If in the chain of a particular *hadīth*, the link between the successor *(tabi'ī)* and the Prophet is missing, the *hadīth* is *mursal* (hurried), e.g. when a *tabi'ī* says, *"The Prophet said..."* A *mursal hadīth* is the strongest type of weak *hadīth* and requires supporting narrations to strengthen it to the level of *"hasan due to supporting evidence"*, thereby removing doubt. For more on this see Dr. Mahmūd at-Tahhān, *Taysīr Mustalah al-Hadīth* (Riyadh: Maktabah Ma'ārif, 1425 AH/2004 CE, 10th Edn.), pp.87-91.

[4] **Translator's Note:** Al-Wāqidī died in 207 AH/823 CE. Shaykh Sālih Āli Shaykh states in *Dawābit fī Ma'rifat is-Sīrah* [Principles for Understanding the Sīrah] that:
> Likewise, those who gave importance in authoring works on the *sīrah* include al-Wāqidī, some scholars praise him for his *maghāzī* and yet some scholars say that **"his works on maghāzī should be regarded as his affair in hadīth, his hadīth are not accepted."**[4] The [original] *maghāzī* of al-Wāqidī does not exist with us today and many of the people of knowledge rely upon it and what is correct is that *al-Wāqidiyyah* is not totally verified in what has been transmitted and it is maybe the case that he obtained narrations and transmissions which are not known to the people of knowledge. Therefore, his *hadīth* of the *maghāzī* which the people of knowledge reject are not accepted, especially that which differs from the basis of *usūl* or opposes that which the speech of the people of knowledge indicates about *sīrah*.

See: http://www.salafimanhaj.com/pdf/SalafiManhaj_UnderstandingSeerah.pdf.

Hishām in his *Sīrah*, vol.2, p.483. Imām as-Ṣan'ānī ﷺ stated in *Subul us-Salām*, vol.4, p.111:
> Abū Dāwūd reported the hadīth in the *Marāsīl* and its men (i.e. the narrators) are *thiqāt* and al-'Uqaylī relayed the hadīth with a da'īf isnād from 'Ali ﷺ, at-Tirmidhī relayed the hadīth from Thawr from Makhūl, but he did not mention Makhūl. This type of hadīth is Mu'dal.[1]

This is a Mursal narration from Abū Dāwūd within his *Marāsīl* (az-Zahrānī's edition), as for Tirmidhī's narration, vol.5, p.94 which is *mu'dal* then it contains 'Umar bin Hārūn from Thawr and al-Hāfidh stated in *at-Taqrīb* about this 'Umar: **"matrūk, but he was a hāfidh"**. Ibn Sa'd also reports the story in *at-Tabaqāt*, vol.2, p.159 and so does Ibn al-Jawzī in *al-Muntadham*, vol.3, p.341 via ath-Thawrī from Thawr from Makhūl in a *mursal* form. Ibn ul-Mulaqqin raised the hadīth in *Khulāsat ul-Badr al-Munīr*, vol.2, p.345 and also az-Zayla'ī in *Nasb ur-Rāyah*, vol.4, p.104 and also al-Mubārakfūrī in *Tuhfat ul-Ahwadhī*, vol.8, p.37. As for the narration of al-'Uqaylī as reported in *ad-Du'afā'*, vol.2, p.243 from 'Ali in a *mawsūl* (connected) form then it contains 'Abdullāh bin Kharāsh from al-'Awwām bin Hawshab. Al-Bukhārī stated in *at-Tārīkh al-Kabeer*, vol.5, p.80: 'Abdullāh bin Kharāsh from al-'Awwām bin Hawshab is munkar hadīth (i.e. rejected).[2] According to al-Hasan ar-Rāmahurmuzī in *al-Muhaddith al-Fāsil*, pp.316-17, he said:
> Muhammad bin 'Uthmān bin Abī Shaybah narrated to me saying: "I heard 'Ali ibn al-Madīnī say: 'I sat with 'Abdullāh bin

---

Khalidi mentioned in his book *Arabic Historical Thought in the Classical Period* (Cambridge: Cambridge University Press, 1994), p.48 that: **"Waqidi was attacked for loose isnād usage by strict practitioners of Hadith…"**.

[1] A *mu'dal hadīth* is a *hadīth* whose reporter omits two or more consecutive reporters in the *isnād*.

[2] Also see Shaykh 'Abdullāh bin 'AbdurRahmān al-Bassām, *Tawdīh ul-Ahkām min Bulūgh il-Marām* (Makkah al-Mukarramah, KSA: Maktabah al-Asadī, 1424 AH/2003 CE, 5th Edn.), vol.6, p.384.

Kharāsh and while I was talking I heard him say: "Al-'Awwām narrated to us from Ibrāhīm at-Taymī from his father from 'Ali who said: 'The Prophet ﷺ attacked the people of Ṭā'if with manjaneeq', **then I realised that he was a liar!**"

In the *Sunan* of al-Bayhaqī *al-Kubrā*, vol.9, p.84 via Hishām bin Sa'd from Zayd bin Aslam from his father 'Ubaydah ؓ:

The Messenger of Allāh ﷺ attacked the people of Ṭā'if and used catapults against them for seventeen days.

Abū Qilābah said: "this *ḥadīth* was rejected from him," then al-Bayhaqī commented: "it is as if he rejected its *isnād* and it is possible that at the time he rejected them being attacked with catapults." Abū Dāwūd relays the *ḥadīth* in *al-Marāsīl* from Abū Ṣāliḥ from Abū Isḥāq al-Fazārī from al-Awzā'ī from Yaḥyā (who is Ibn Abī Kathīr) who said:

The Messenger of Allāh ﷺ attacked them for a month. I said: "has it reached you that he used catapults against them?" He rejected that saying: "this is not known." - This narration is in *Marāsīl Abī Dāwūd*, p.322 (az-Zahrānī's edition).

CHAPTER 12

'AWLAKI CLAIMS THAT IMAM MUHAMMAD BIN 'ABDULWAHHAB GAVE HIS BAY'AH TO THE OTTOMAN KHALIFAH IN ISTANBUL!?

'Awlakī states in his "explanation" of Ibn an-Nahhās' book *Mashāri' ul-Ashwāq ilā Masāri' il-'Ushshāq*, CD 2, Track 14:

> Muhammad ibn 'AbdulWahhāb, there are some letters that indicate his bay'ah was to the Khalīfah of Istanbul and he did not declare that Saudiyyah was an independent state. They used to rule it independently, they didn't want the Ottomans to interfere in their internal affairs, but they did not declare a Khilāfah and they considered themselves to be under the Khalīfah of Istanbul. And there's actually a letter written by Shaykh Muhammad bin 'AbdulWahhāb stating, where he's refuting the claims of people who say he has succeeded the Khilāfah, <u>and he's saying "our bay'ah is to you" and he was very straight forward</u>."

So here 'Awlakī regurgitates, like other Harakīs, the myth that the Ottomans ruled over the entire Muslim world. First of all, where is this 'letter' which Imām Muhammad bin 'AbdulWahhāb ﷺ wrote to the Ottomans saying **"our bay'ah is to you"**? Can 'Awlakī refer us to the sources and references for such a letter? Considering that 'Awlakī stated this as if he is an authority on the issue! Secondly, the Ottoman Empire did not rule of the entire Muslim world in the first place, 'Awlakī falls into the simplistic and romantic idea of the Ottomans ruling over the entire Muslim world, which is an incorrect assertion promoted in the West initially by *Hizb ut-Tahrīr* and their offshoots. Thus, *Hizb ut-Tahrīr*, with its roots in Shām where the Ottomans did rule over, began to praise the Ottoman Empire as if it was a *Khilāfah* in the sense that all Muslims had to obey it and blindly follow it. We also know that Imām 'Uthmān Dan Fodio (Ibn Fūdī) for example had his own Caliphate in the nineteenth century CE which was totally independent from Ottoman rule. The Mughal Empire was also independent from Ottoman rule, as were the *'Alawī* rulers of Morocco. While the Mughal Empire had relations with the Ottomans[1], the Moroccan dynasty of the Sa'dīs and 'Alawīs had no relations with the Ottomans whatsoever. Likewise, Najd in Arabia was independent from Ottoman rule. Thirdly, though it is true that Imām Muhammad ibn 'AbdulWahhāb held the same view of Ahl us-Sunnah that Muslims should not revolt against their leaders, the Ottomans were not his leaders to begin with. Let's look at the views of Imām Muhammad bin 'AbdulWahhāb in regards to revolting and rebelling against the Muslim rulers, which in fact 'Awlakī would benefit from reading himself! Imām Muhammad ibn 'AbdulWahhāb stated:

> **The Imāms from every Madhhab are agreed concerning the one who forcefully took over a region or regions that he has the ruling of "Imām" in all matters. If this had not been so then the affairs of the world would never have been established. This is because for a very long time, before the era of Imām Ahmad till this day of ours, the people have never gathered behind a single Imām. And they do not know anyone from the Scholars who has**

---

[1] An interesting book on this topic is by Naimur Rahman Farooqi, *Mughal-Ottoman Relations: A Study of the Political and Diplomatic Relations Between Mughal India and the Ottoman Empire, 1556-1748* (Delhi: Idarah-i Adabiyat-i Delhi, 1989). Francis Robinson has also conducted some research on Mughal-Ottoman relations in his paper *Ottomans-Safavids-Mughals: Shared Knowledge and Connective Systems*. All of this research indicates that the Mughals had relations with the Ottomans but were not under their authority whatsoever.

mentioned that any of the Sharī'ah rulings cannot be correct (effected, implemented) except by the overall Imām (the Khalīfah).[1]

Let's turn to what some Islāmic historians have concurred, as opposed to the mere diatribes of the unqualified![2] Shaykh 'Abdul'Azīz Āl-'AbdulLatīf said:

> Some opponents of the Salafi da'wah claim that Imam Muhammad ibn 'Abd al-Wahhāb rebelled against the Ottoman Caliphate, thus splitting the Jamā'ah (main body of the Muslims) and refusing to hear and obey (the ruler).[3]

Imām Muhammad ibn 'AbdulWahhāb said in his letter to the people of al-Qasīm:

> وأرى وجوب السمع والطاعة لأئمة المسلمين برّهم وفاجرهم ما لم يأمروا بمعصية الله ومن ولي الخلافة واجتمع عليه الناس ورضوا به وغلبهم بسيفه حتى صار خليفة وجبت طاعته وحرم الخروج عليه.
>
> I believe that it is obligatory to hear and obey the leaders of the Muslims, whether they are righteous or immoral, so long as they do not enjoin disobedience towards Allāh. Whoever has become Caliph and the people have given him their support and accepted him, even if he has gained the position of Caliph by force, is to be obeyed and it is harām to rebel against him.[4]

---

[1] *Ad-Durarus-Sunniyyah fil-Ajwibatun-Najdiyyah* vol.7, p.239.
[2] Refer to the book by Professor Sulaiman Bin Abdurrahman al-Huqail (Professor of Education at Imām Muhammad bin Saud University, Riyadh), *Muhammad Bin Abdulwahhāb – His Life and the Essence of his Call* (Riyadh: Ministry of Islamic Affairs, Endowments, Dawah and Guidance, KSA, First Edition, 1421 AH/2001 CE), with an introduction by Sheikh Saleh Bin Abdulazīz Al-Sheikh.
[3] Abdul'Azeīz ibn Muhammad Āl 'AbdulLatīf, *Da'āwa al-Munāwi'īn li Da'wat al-Shaykh Muhammad ibn 'Abd al-Wahāb* (Riyadh: Dār ul-Watan, 1412 AH), p. 233.
[4] *Majmū'at Mu'allafāt al-Shaykh*, vol.5, p.11.

And he also said:

الأصل الثالث : أن من تمام الاجتماع السمع والطاعة لمن تأمّر علينا ولو كان عبداً حبشيّاً...

One of the main principles of unity is to hear and obey whoever is appointed over us even if he is an Abyssinian slave...[1]

And Shaykh 'Abdul'Azīz Āl-'AbdulLatīf said:

وبعد هذا التقرير الموجز الذي أبان ما كان عليه الشيخ من وجوب السمع والطاعة لأئمة المسلمين برّهم وفاجرهم ما لم يأمروا بمعصية الله : فإننا نشير إلى مسألة مهمة جوابا عن تلك الشبهة فهناك سؤال مهم هو : هل كانت نجد موطن هذه الدعوة ومحل نشأتها تحت سيطرة دولة الخلافة العثمانية ؟

After stating these facts, which explain that the Shaykh believed it was obligatory to hear and obey the leaders of the Muslims whether they are righteous or immoral so long as they do not enjoin disobedience towards Allāh, we may refer to an important issue in response to that false accusation. There is an important question which is: was Najd, where this call originated and first developed, under the sovereignty of the Ottoman state?

Dr Sālih al-'Abūd answered this by saying:

لم تشهد " نجد " على العموم نفوذا للدولة العثمانية فما امتد إليها سلطانها ولا أتى إليها ولاة عثمانيون ولا جابت خلال ديارها حامية تركية في الزمان الذي سبق ظهور دعوة الشيخ محمد بن عبد الوهاب رحمه الله ومما يدل على هذه الحقيقة التاريخية استقرار تقسيمات الدولة العثمانية الإدارية

---

[1] *Majmū'ah Mu'allafāt al-Shaykh*, vol.1, p.394; quoted in *Da'āwa al-Munāwi'īn*, pp.233-234.

Chapter 12

فمن خلال رسالة تركية عنوانها : "قوانين آل عثمان مضامين دفتر الديوان"يعني : " قوانين آل عثمان في ما يتضمنه دفتر الديوان" ، ألّفها يمين علي أفندي الذي كان أمينا للدفتر الخاقاني سنة 1018 هجرية الموافقة لسنة 1609م من خلال هذه الرسالة يتبين أنه منذ أوائل القرن الحادي عشر الهجري كانت دولة آل عثمان تنقسم إلى اثنتين وثلاثين ايالة منها أربع عشرة ايالة عربية وبلاد نجد ليست منها ما عدا الإحساء إن اعتبرناه من نجد...

Najd never came under Ottoman rule, because the rule of the Ottoman state never reached that far, no Ottoman governor was appointed over that region and the Turkish soldiers never marched through its land during the period that preceded the emergence of the call of Shaykh Muhammad ibn 'AbdulWahhāb ﷺ. This fact is indicated by the fact that the Ottoman state was divided into administrative provinces. This is known from a Turkish document entitled Qawānīn Āl 'Uthmān Mudāmīn Daftar ad-Dīwān (Laws of the Ottomans Concerning what is Contained in the Legislation), which was written by Yamīn 'Ali Effendi who was in charge of the Constitution in 1018 AH/1609 CE. This document indicates that from the beginning of the eleventh century AH the Ottoman state was divided into 23 provinces, of which 14 were Arabic provinces, and the land of Najd was not one of them, with the exception of al-Ihsa', if we count al-Ihsa' as part of Najd.[1]

And Dr 'Abdullāh al-'Uthaymīn said:

---

[1] 'Aqīdat al-Shaykh Muhammad ibn 'Abd al-Wahhāb wa atharuha fi'l-'Ālam al-Islami (unpublished), vol.1, p.27.

ومهما يكن فإن " نجداً " لم تشهد نفوذاً مباشراً للعثمانيين عليها قبل ظهور دعوة الشيخ محمد بن عبد الوهاب كما أنها لم تشهد نفوذاً قويّاً يفرض وجوده على سير الحوادث داخلها لأية جهة كانت فلا نفوذ بني جبر أو بني خالد في بعض جهاتها ولا نفوذ الأشراف في بعض جهاتها الأخرى أحدث نوعاً من الاستقرار السياسي فالحروب بين البلدان النجدية ظلت قائمة والصراع بين قبائلها المختلفة استمر حادًّا عنيفاً.

Whatever the case, Najd never experienced direct Ottoman rule before the call of Shaykh Muhammad ibn 'AbdulWahhāb emerged, just as it never experienced any strong influence that could have an impact on events inside Najd. No one had any such influence, and the influence of Bani Jabr or Bani Khālid in some parts, or the Ashrāf in other parts, was limited. None of them were able to bring about political stability, so wars between the various regions of Najd continued and there were ongoing violent conflicts between its various tribes.[1]

Imām 'Abdul'Azīz ibn 'Abdullāh ibn Bāz ﷺ said in response to this false accusation:

لم يخرج الشيخ محمد بن عبد الوهاب على دولة الخلافة العثمانية فيما أعلم وأعتقد فلم يكن في نجد رئاسة ولا إمارة للأتراك بل كانت نجد إمارات صغيرة وقرى متناثرة وعلى كل بلدة أو قرية – مهما صغرت – أمير مستقل... وهي إمارات بينها قتال وحروب ومشاجرات والشيخ محمد بن عبد الوهاب لم يخرج على دولة الخلافة وإنما خرج على أوضاع فاسدة في

---

[1] 'Abdullāh ibn Sālih al-'Uthaymīn, *ash-Shaykh Muhammad ibn 'Abd al-Wahhāb Hayātuhu wa Fikruhu* (Riyadh: Dār ul-'Ulūm, 1412 AH) p.11; quoted in *Da'āwa al-Munāwi'īn*, pp.234-235.

> بلده فجاهد في الله حق جهاده وصابر وثابر حتى امتد نور هذه الدعوة إلى البلاد الأخرى...

> Shaykh Muhammad ibn 'AbdulWahhāb did not rebel against the Ottoman Caliphate as far as I know, because there was no area in Najd that was under Turkish rule. Rather Najd consisted of small emirates and scattered villages, and each town or village, no matter how small, was ruled by an independent emir. These were emirates between which there were fighting, wars and disputes. So Shaykh Muhammad ibn 'AbdulWahhāb did not rebel against the Ottoman state, rather he rebelled against the corrupt situation in his own land, and he strove in jihād for the sake of Allāh and persisted until the light of this call spread to other lands...[1]

Refer to these maps of the Ottoman Empire which clearly show that the Ottomans did not have authority in Najd, just as the Ottomans had no authority in West Africa, Morocco, Sudan, India and Persia. See:

---

[1] Conversation recorded on tape; quoted in *Da'āwa al-Munāwi'īn*, p. 237.

Chapter 12

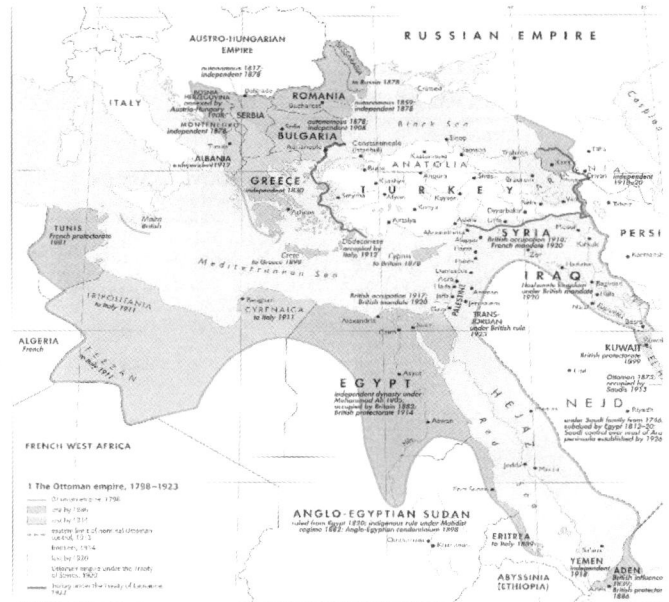

Ottoman Empire, 1798-1923:
See: http://ww1.huntingdon.edu/jlewis/syl/IRcomp/MapsOttoman.htm.

Chapter 12

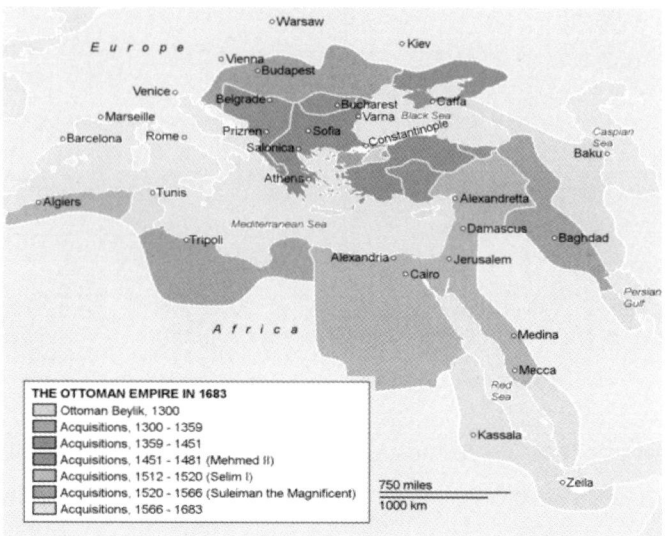

See: http://www.mideastweb.org/Middle-East-Encyclopedia/ottoman.htm.

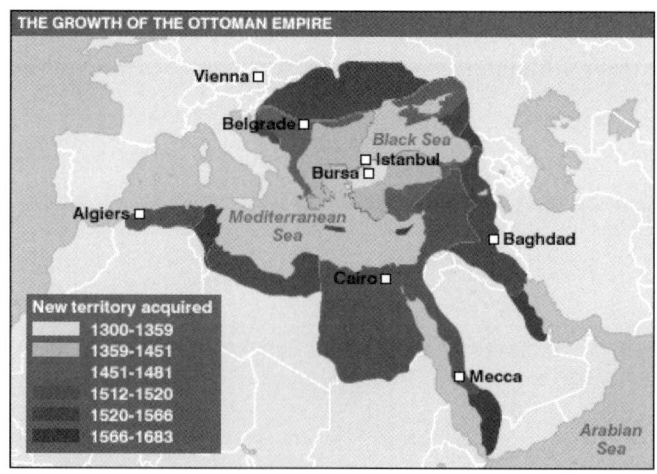

Chapter 12

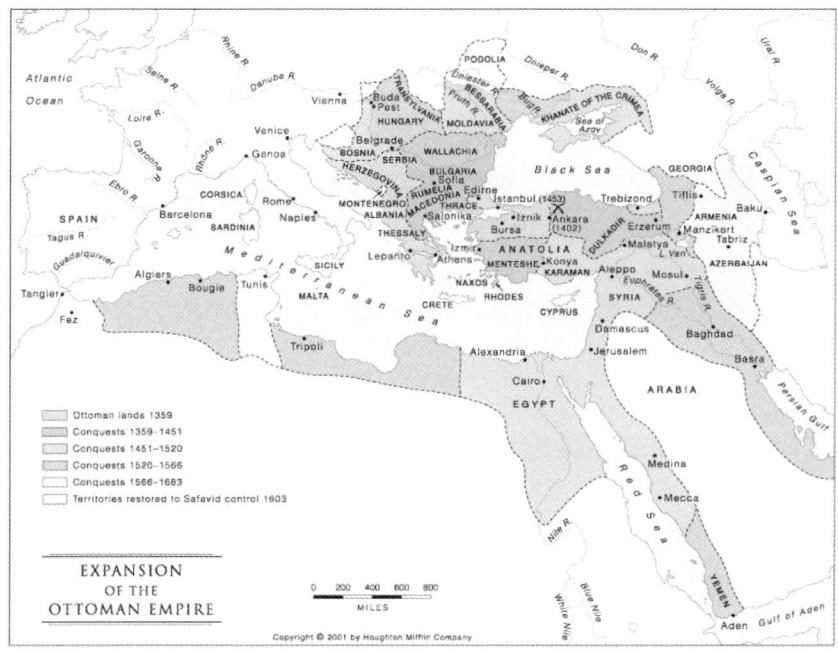

EXPANSION OF THE OTTOMAN EMPIRE

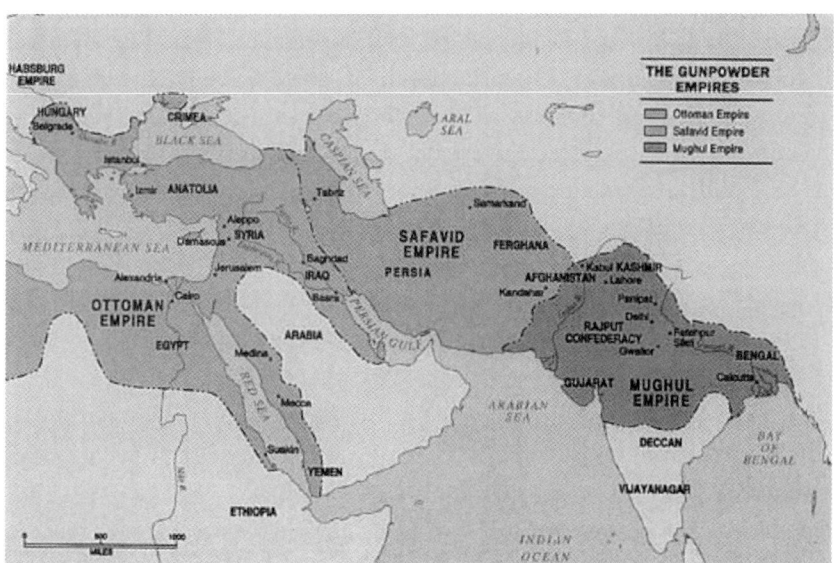

THE GUNPOWDER EMPIRES

Chapter 12

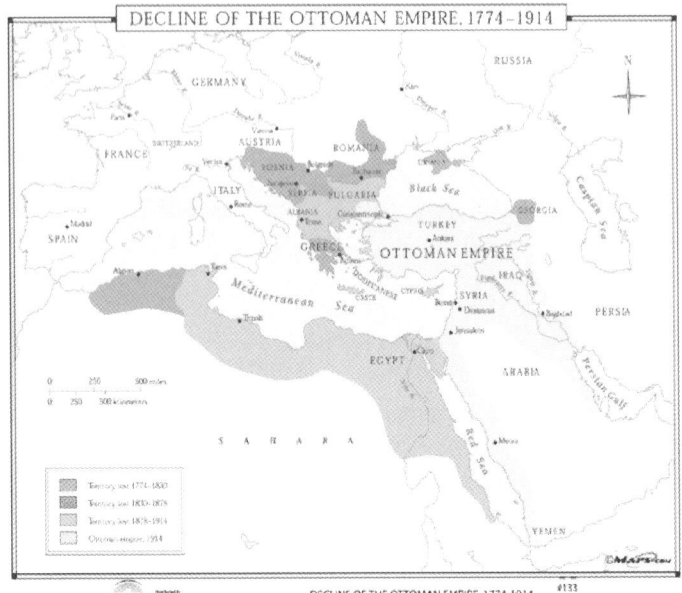

See: http://worldmapsonline.com/UnivHist/30335_6.gif.

Hence, 'Awlakī's odd claim, which was unsubstantiated, that there are letters wherein Imām Muhammad bin 'AbdulWahhāb stated to the Ottoman Khalīfah **"our bay'ah is to you"** is completely incorrect and it has no evidence therefore should not be said. Imām Muslim ؓ reports in his Sahīh on the authority of Abū Hurayrah ؓ that the Prophet ﷺ stated in a hadith:

$$((كفى بالمرء كذباً أن يحدث بكل ما سمع))$$

"It is sufficient a lie for a person to relay all he hears."

This trait of not authenticating or verifying reports and quotations is actually endemic within the method of Awlakī as we have seen in this study.

CHAPTER 13

MOCKERY OF USUL?
THE "MASLAHAH AND MAFSADAH" IN FIQH OF JIHAD ACCORDING TO 'AWLAKI

'Awlakī states in his "explanation" of Ibn an-Nahhās' book *Mashāri' ul-Ashwāq ilā Masāri' il-'Ushshāq*, CD 9, Track 3:

> Ya'nī, this Maslahah and Mafsadah thing {sic} is taken to the extreme and it's only limited to worldly calculations without getting the spiritual and Ākhirah calculations in it. You know you always mention "what's the Maslahah and Mafsadah in this" and it's always looked at from a worldly point of view in terms of numbers and physical loss. If that's the case then there's not gonna be any battle because the assumption is that you want to win a war without any losses and that will never happen...

'Awlakī also states in part 2 of his explanation of al-Qā'idah member Yūsuf al-'Ayrī's *Thawābit 'ala'd-Darb il-Jihād* [Constants on the Path of Jihād], after 41:30:

> So this completely defies the logic of people who always say "let's weigh the benefit and let's weigh the harm in everything" until everything is Sharī'ah becomes a vegetable soup, everything in Sharī'ah is lost. You don't have any constants in Sharī'ah any more, because they subjugate everything to this rule of benefit and harm: "Whats the benefit in doing this? It will cause a lot of harm." **SubhānAllāh! The whole issue of fighting fi sabeelillāh brings harm,** your putting your life and your wealth in danger!

Chapter 13

So when you look at it from this Maslahah and Mafsadah point of view – it is a Mafsadah! You are putting yourself and your wealth in danger, isn't this a harm? So using this in Jihād fī sabeelillāh doesn't work because Jihad in itself is something that will bring you harm, so you shouldn't subjugate it to this rule of benefit and "trying to outplay the benefit and harm of Jihād fee sabeelillāh" - it doesn't work that way.

First of all, we clearly see two things:
1. Al-'Awlakī demonstrates his ignorance of the Usūl and Qawā'id in fiqh hence his carte blanche dismissal of the role of taking into consideration the Maslahah and Mafsadah.
2. Al-'Awlakī's ignorance as to Jihād, wherein he says above that it is a "Mafsadah"!?

Secondly, both of these quotes are a clear example of 'Awlakī's negation of any Usūl in the Fiqh of Jihād and folly of attemting to jump straight into detailed books such as Ibn an-Nahhās' book *Mashāri' ul-Ashwāq ilā Masāri' il-'Ushshāq* which was authored during a particular context, which is not the case today. Indeed, today the enemies of Islām encroach into the Muslim lands in the first instance due to actions caused by the Khawārij of the era whom 'Awlakī now supports and says nothing against! The **"Maslahah and Mafsadah thing"**, as 'Awlakī refers to it, has a basis in the dīn and 'Awlakī throws doubt on it in order to try to show that it has no foundation in the fiqh of jihād. Shaykh ul-Islām Ibn Taymiyyah stated:

الشريعة جاءت لتحصيل المصالح وتكميلها وتحصيل أعظم المصلحتين وتقليلها ، وأنها ترجيح خير الخيرين وشر الشرين ، وتحصيل أعظم المصلحتين وتفويت ادناهما ، وتدفع أعظم المفسدتين باحتمال ادناهما.

The Sharī'ah came with obtaining benefits (Masālih) and completing them and averting harms (Mafāsid) and reducing them. (Opting for) the best of two good options and (averting) the most evil of two evils; so as to obtain the better of two benefits and averting the worst of two evils.[1]

Shaykh Sulaymān bin Sahmān ؓ stated in *ad-Durar as-Saniyyah*, vol.8, p.491:

وقد ذكر أهل العلم أن درء المفاسد مقدم على جلب المصالح، فدرء مفسدة قمع أهل الحق وعدم إظهار دينهم واجتماعهم عليه والدعوة إلى ذلك، وعدم تشتيتهم وتشريدهم في كل مكان؛ مقدم على جلب مصلحة الإنكار على ولاة الأمور، مع قوتهم وتغلبهم وقهرهم، وعجز أهل الحق عن منابذتهم وإظهار عداوتهم، والهجرة عن بلادهم.

Ahl ul-'Ilm say: "averying the harms (Mafāsid) takes precedence over achieving benefits (Masālih)." So averting the harms (Mafāsid) of the people of truth being suppressed, or them not being able to manifest their dīn and be gathered on it, and of calling to it, and them being scattered and vagrants all over the world – takes precedence over achieving the benefits of: rejecting what those in authority do... and manifesting enmity to them and making Hijrah from their lands.

As for Jihād then 'Awlakī boldly states **"it is a Mafsadah"** and this is a ridiculous statement as obviously Jihād is a Maslalah in the end. So for 'Awlakī to say, in an emotional outburst which characterises many of his lectures, about Jihād that **"the whole issue of fighting fi sabeelillāh brings harm"** demonstrates his lack of knowledge. As the harm within it is does not outweigh the actual manifest benefits in it in the long-term. Allāh says,

---

[1] Ibn Taymiyyah, *Majmū' al-Fatāwā* (Tartīb 'AbdurRahmān bin Qāsim and his son Muhammad, 1398 AH, 2nd Edn.) vol.20, pp.48, 52-53; *al-Fatāwā al-Kubrā* (Dār ul-Arqam bin Abi'l-Arqam, 1420 AH/1999 CE, ed. Shaykh Ahmad Kan'ān), vol.3, p.544.

Chapter 13

﴿ يَٰٓأَيُّهَا ٱلَّذِينَ ءَامَنُوا۟ هَلْ أَدُلُّكُمْ عَلَىٰ تِجَٰرَةٍ تُنجِيكُم مِّنْ عَذَابٍ أَلِيمٍ تُؤْمِنُونَ بِٱللَّهِ وَرَسُولِهِۦ وَتُجَٰهِدُونَ فِى سَبِيلِ ٱللَّهِ بِأَمْوَٰلِكُمْ وَأَنفُسِكُمْ ذَٰلِكُمْ خَيْرٌ لَّكُمْ إِن كُنتُمْ تَعْلَمُونَ ﴾

"O you who have believed, shall I guide you to a transaction that will save you from a painful punishment? [It is that] you believe in Allāh and His Messenger and strive in the cause of Allāh with your wealth and your lives. That is best for you, if you should know."
{as-Saff (61): 10-11}

So when one strives in that which is salvation from a painful torment, how on earth can it be described as being "a Mafsadah"?! Allāh also says:

﴿ وَقَٰتِلُوهُمْ حَتَّىٰ لَا تَكُونَ فِتْنَةٌ وَيَكُونَ ٱلدِّينُ لِلَّهِ ﴾

"Fight them until there is no [more] fitnah and [until] worship is [acknowledged to be] for Allāh." {Baqarah (2): 193}

'Awlakī's brazen intellectual denial of the importance of the Maslahah and Mafsadah is reflected in his views on suicide bombing. He views that in Palestine for example there are according to him **"huge benefits"** in them merely on account of a thousand or so Jewish-Zionist settlers staying away from Palestine due to such attacks. However, the falsity of such an equation is evident as these numbers who stay away are insignificant in comparison to the few thousands and more Palestinians who suffer as a whole in the reprisals that occur after such suicide bomb attacks. So it may be a benefit (Maslahah) that such Zionist settlers stay away however the huge amounts of Palestinian Muslims who are killed by the enemies of Allāh is a far greater harm (Mafsadah). And averting the harms (Mafāsid) takes precedence over achieveing benefits

(Masālih). Furthermore, many of the major suicide bombings over the last nine years have brought about more harms than good for the Muslims.

Even if there may be some insidious kuffār involvement in *some* of these examples, there are still ignorant expendable pawns that can be utilised due to their corrupted Takfīrī-Jihādī methodology which sanctions such actions in the first place and justifies them. 'Awlakī's disregard of the principle of averting the harms taking precedence over achieving the benefits is therefore manifest in his support of suicide bombings which itself is based on a total disregard of the principle. It also demonstrates 'Awlakī's corrupt Usūl which has led him to justify all sorts of contraventions of the Sharī'ah in the name of merely achieving a short term "benefit", as the Takfīrī-Jihādī would claim, in causing some grief to the Kuffār. Yet upon inspection it is evident that with such actions only harms (Mafāsid) increase as opposed to any benefits (Masālih) being achieved. The manifest harms involved in some of 'Awlakī's *fiqh* of Jihād as we have seen are many:

- *Killing oneself with one's own hands.*
- *Bringing about greater reprisals from the enemies of Islām.*
- *The killing of civilians.*
- *The killing of those non-Muslims who Muslims have agreements with, thus going against the Sharī'ah.*
- *Killing those with whom Muslims have covenants of security and safety.*
- *Use of stories, some of which are unauthentic to justify certain practices.*
- *Disregard of qualified scholarship in favour of the views of mere speakers and Khawārij.*
- *Lying, treachery and betrayal.*
- *Corrupting the image of Islām.*
- *Scaring people aware from the dīn.*

These are but a few of the harms (Mafāsid) involved in 'Awlakī's jihād fiqh. The assumed "benefits" in such attacks are minimal, if anything, in comparison to the manifest harms (Mafāsid) involved in them. 'Awlakī however, totally denies any Mafāsid that result from suicide bombings and carries on as if they are all praiseworthy. This shows us the importance of referring back to qualified scholarship when wanting to know the Islamic stance on such serious issues, as Allāh says:

﴿ وَإِذَا جَآءَهُمْ أَمْرٌ مِّنَ ٱلْأَمْنِ أَوِ ٱلْخَوْفِ أَذَاعُوا۟ بِهِۦ ۖ وَلَوْ رَدُّوهُ إِلَى ٱلرَّسُولِ وَإِلَىٰٓ أُو۟لِى ٱلْأَمْرِ مِنْهُمْ لَعَلِمَهُ ٱلَّذِينَ يَسْتَنۢبِطُونَهُۥ مِنْهُمْ ۗ وَلَوْلَا فَضْلُ ٱللَّهِ عَلَيْكُمْ وَرَحْمَتُهُۥ لَٱتَّبَعْتُمُ ٱلشَّيْطَٰنَ إِلَّا قَلِيلًا ﴾

"And when there comes to them something (i.e. information) about (public) security or fear, they spread it around. But if they had only referred it back to the Messenger or to those of authority among them, then the ones who (can) draw correct conclusions from it would have known about it. And if not for the favour of Allāh upon you and His mercy, you would have followed Shayṭān, except for a few of you."
{an-Nisā (4): 83}

Ibn Kathīr says about this noble ayah:
> This ayah refers to proper investigation, or extraction of matters from their proper resources.

In regards to this, Imām al-Albānī was asked, as documented and transmitted by his prolific student Shaykh 'Ali Hasan al-Halabī al-Atharī *(hafidhahullāh)*:
> Is it allowed to drive a booby-trapped car packed with explosives and drive it into the enemies? What is currently called "suicide bombings", with evidence.

Answer from Imām al-Albānī ﷺ:

We have said regularly and frequently about that these questions that: during these times they are not allowed[1] because they are either individual and personal actions wherein the individual is unable to be outweigh the benefits over the harms, or the harms over the benefits; or, if it is not an individual action it is from an organisation, Jamā'ah or (group) leader – and this leader is not Divinely Leigslated (Sharī'), and at this point such an action is considered suicide! As for the evidence: then this is well-known from the ahādīth in the Two Sahīhs,[2] that whoever commits suicide with any instrument will be punished with it (in the Hereafter).

The likes of these suicide operations, as they say today, are only when there is Islamic rule headed by a Muslim ruler who rules by what Allāh has revealed and applies Allāh's Sharī'ah in all aspects of life, such as the military and soldiers which are also to be in line with the restrictions of the Shar' (Divine Legislation). The higher leader, and then those who represent him such as the Army General – if they view that there is a Maslahah for the Muslims by performing these suicide operations in order to achieve a Divinely Legislated benefit, then they are permitted. The Muslim ruler is the one who estimates this via seeking advice from those whom he seeks counsel in his

---

[1] Shaykh 'Ali Hasan al-Halabī al-Atharī *(hafidhahullāh)* says about this:
This is a clear and frank text on this issue which shows the error of some of our noble brothers who understand from some words of our Shaykh that such actions are allowed with "a number of restricted and detailed conditions!"

[2] In Bukhārī (hadīth no.5442) and Muslim (hadīth no.109) from Abū Hurayrah ؓ from the Prophet ﷺ who said: *"Whoever throws himself off a mountain killing himself, will be in Hellfire throwing themselves off for ever and eternity. Whoever drinks poison to kill himself will drink poison in his hand eternally in the Hellfire for ever. Whoever kills himself with iron (a weapon) then this iron will be in his hand and he will be killing himself with it in Hellfire for ever and eternity."*

gatherings with them, only in these instances are they allowed and anything other than this is not allowed.¹

---

¹ From Shaykh 'Ali Hasan al-Halabī al-Atharī, *Su'alāt 'Ali bin Hasan bin 'AbdulHamīd al-Halabī al-Atharī li'sh-Shaykhihi Imām al-'Allāmah al-Muhaddith al-Faqīh Shaykh Muhammad Nāsiruddīn al-Albānī* ﷺ. Makkah al-Mukarramah, KSA: Dār 'Abdullāh Bū Bakr Barakāt, 1430 AH/2009 CE, First Edn. Vol.1, pp.389-390.

CHAPTER 14

'AWLAKI'S FLAGRANT DISREGARD OF THE COVENANTS OF SAFETY AND SECURITY IN ISLAM AND HIS PRAISE OF MAJOR NIDAL HASAN AND THE FORT HOOD SHOOTING

Trustworthiness and keeping to promises is from the characteristics of the *dīn*, Allāh says,

﴿ وَأَوْفُواْ بِٱلْعَهْدِ إِنَّ ٱلْعَهْدَ كَانَ مَسْـُٔولاً ﴾

"And fulfil (every) commitment. Indeed, the commitment is ever (that about which one will be) questioned." *{Al-Isrā' (17):34}*

And Allāh also says:

﴿ يَٰٓأَيُّهَا ٱلَّذِينَ ءَامَنُوٓاْ أَوْفُواْ بِٱلْعُقُودِ ﴾

"O you who have believed, fulfil all contracts (promises, covenants and oaths)" *{Al-Mā'idah (5): 1}*

In Sahīh Muslim from Hudhayfah ibn ul-Yamān ﷺ said: *"The only thing that prevented me from being at Badr was that I was out with my father Husayl when the kuffār of the Quraysh got us and said 'you want Muhammad?' We said 'we do not want him, we just want to get to Madīnah.' They took from us the promise of Allāh and His covenant that we would go to Madīnah and not fight with him. The Messenger of Allāh came to us and informed us saying 'Go! For you have made a promise with them and we seek Allāh's help against them.'"* They promised the *kuffār* that they would not fight and then the Prophet ﷺ came and informed them *"do not fight with us."* Contemplate, this is trustworthiness and honesty, this is from the characteristics and rules of trustworthiness which our beloved Prophet came with. The *dīn* of Islām is one of trustworthiness and fulfilling trusts. Allāh says:

﴿ إِنَّ ٱللَّهَ يَأْمُرُكُمْ أَن تُؤَدُّوا۟ ٱلْأَمَٰنَٰتِ إِلَىٰٓ أَهْلِهَا وَإِذَا حَكَمْتُم بَيْنَ ٱلنَّاسِ أَن تَحْكُمُوا۟ بِٱلْعَدْلِ ۚ إِنَّ ٱللَّهَ نِعِمَّا يَعِظُكُم بِهِۦٓ ۗ إِنَّ ٱللَّهَ كَانَ سَمِيعًۢا بَصِيرًا ﴾

"Indeed, Allāh commands you to render trusts to whom they are due and when you judge between people to judge with justice. Excellent is that which Allāh instructs you. Indeed, Allāh is ever Hearing and Seeing." *{An-Nisā (4): 58}*

﴿ وَٱلَّذِينَ هُمْ لِأَمَٰنَٰتِهِمْ وَعَهْدِهِمْ رَٰعُونَ ﴾

"And they who are to their trusts and their promises attentive" *{Al-Muminūn (23): 8}*

The Prophet ﷺ said: *"Fulfill the trust of one who makes a promise with you. Do not be like the one who is treacherous to you."*[1]

Continuing in his disregard of the Usūl ul-Fiqh, 'Awlakī has demonstrated that he has a problem with the issue of 'Ahd ul-Amān and in his talks has either glossed over it or talked as if it is non-existent in the religion, even though the 'Ulamā have discussed it at length. When discussing the fiqh of jihād it appears to be the main issue that he totally disregards and this is probably the clearest proof that he follows the beliefs of the Khawārij of the era. In this section we hope to shed light on this and bring what the classical scholars have stated about this very important matter in order to assess whether Awlakī is in conflict with Ahl us-Sunnah or not in this issue. We will also highlight what

---

[1] Hasan, recorded by Abū Dāwud.

Ibn an-Nahhās ؑ mentioned on this issue in his book *Mashāri' ul-Ashwāq ilā Masāri' il-'Ushshāq* which 'Awlakī purportedly has "explained"!?

A further example of 'Awlakī's notions of covenants can be seen in a reactionary article recently wherein he praised a shooting by a Muslim against his colleagues. The shooting was at an American military base called Fort Hood in Texas and the shooter was an American Major in the US army who turned on his colleagues in the US military. 'Awlakī's article praised the shooting which led to a storm in cyberspace with some, mainly Muslims in America, condemning Awlakī with others supporting what was stated by 'Awlakī, while others oddly claimed that Awlakī did not write the article, even though it was on his very own blog! In any case, the whole event revealed the machinations of the likes of 'Awlakī, as the blog was immediately taken down! As is the way of Ahl ul-Bida' in trying to cover their tracks.In the article entitled *'Nidal Hasan Did the Right Thing'* dated November 9 2009 CE on 'Awlakī's blog, 'Awlakī states:

> **Nidal Hassan is a hero.** He is a man of conscience who could not bear living the contradiction of being a Muslim and serving in an army that is fighting against his own people. This is a contradiction that many Muslims brush aside and just pretend that it doesn't exist. Any decent Muslim cannot live, understanding properly his duties towards his Creator and his fellow Muslims, and yet serve as a US soldier. The US is leading the war against terrorism which in reality is a war against Islam. Its army is directly invading two Muslim countries **and indirectly occupying the rest through its stooges.** Nidal opened fire on soldiers who were on their way to be deployed to Iraq and Afghanistan. How can there be any dispute about the virtue of what he has done? In fact the only way a Muslim could Islamically justify serving as a soldier in the US army is if his intention is to follow the footsteps of men like Nidal. **The heroic act** of brother Nidal also shows the dilemma of the Muslim

Chapter 14

American community. Increasingly they are being cornered into taking stances that would either make them betray Islam or betray their nation. Many amongst them are choosing the former. The Muslim organizations in America came out in a pitiful chorus condemning Nidal's operation. The fact that fighting against the US army is an Islamic duty today cannot be disputed. No scholar with a grain of Islamic knowledge can defy the clear cut proofs that Muslims today have the right - rather the duty - to fight against American tyranny. Nidal has killed soldiers who were about to be deployed to Iraq and Afghanistan in order to kill Muslims. **The American Muslims who condemned his actions have committed treason against the Muslim Ummah and have fallen into hypocrisy.** The inconsistency of being a Muslim today and living in America and the West in general reveals the wisdom behind the opinions that call for migration from the West. It is becoming more and more difficult to hold on to Islam in an environment that is becoming more hostile towards Muslims.

The above article was rapidly and hurriedly removed by 'Awlakī and his followers as is the way of Ahl ul-Bida' when they try to cover their tracks and after their distortions of the religion have been exposed. Awlakī also stated in an interview with Abdulelah Hider Shaea, a Yemeni journalist, as documented in *The Washington Post* in an article entitled *'Cleric Says he was Confindent to Hasan'* on Monday November 16 2009 CE:

I blessed the act because it was against a military target. And the soldiers who were killed were not normal soldiers, but those who were trained and prepared to go to Afghanistan and Iraq.

All of this is a far cry from what 'Awlakī stated (!!) after 10 minutes and 50 seconds into *The Life of Muhammad (The Medinan Period)*, track 23:

Akhlāq are important even with your enemy, even with your enemy the Muslim should deal with him in a good way with dignity. A Muslim is not cruel, a Muslim is not wicked, a Muslim is not deceptive, a Muslim is not a liar. A Muslim deals with everyone with honesty, dignity, straight-forwardness and kindness towards all of the creation of Allāh ﷻ except those who deserve to be dealt with cruelly...

And a far cry from what 'Awlakī himself stated (!!!) in a documentary on Ramadān in 2001/02:

I think that in general Islām is presented in a negative way, I mean there's always this association between Islām and terrorism when that is not true at all, **I mean Islām is a religion of peace**"[1]!?

'Awlakī in his "explanation" of Ibn an-Nahhās' book *Mashāri' ul-Ashwāq ilā Masāri' il-'Ushshāq*, CD 12, Track 11, himself quotes where Ibn an-Nahhās says (according to Awlakī's "explanation"):

If the Muslim is weak in the land of the disbelievers and is not able to publically show his religion then it is harām to live there. If he is unable to emigrate then he is excused, if the Muslim is strong and able to publically practice Islām then they can live in the disbelievers' land but it is still recommended to move to a Muslim land.

Indeed, Ibn an-Nahhās ؒ in the complete version of his book *Mashāri' ul-Ashwāq ilā Masāri' il-'Ushshāq* mentions more! All of which 'Awlakī conveniently neglects to mention in his "explanation". Ibn an-Nahhās states in *Mashāri' ul-Ashwāq ilā Masāri' ul-'Ushshāq* in the edit of Idrīs Muhammad 'Ali and Muhammad Khālid Istanbūlī, pp.1062-1063 that:

---

[1] See 2:45 here: http://www.youtube.com/watch?v=3BgG2ZLm2M8.

> Issue: ar-Rāfi'ī, an-Nawawī and others state that: if a Muslim is weak within Dār ul-Kufr and is unable to manifest his dīn it is prohibited for him to reside there and he must make Hijrah to Dār ul-Islām. If he is unable to make Hijrah then he is excused until he is able. If he is able to manifest his dīn out of him being obeyed by his people or because he has a family protecting him and he does not fear fitnah in his dīn – it is not obligatory on him to make Hijrah, however it is recommended. If he becomes of them and inclines towards them however it is obligatory to make Hijrah. The first view is Sahīh.[1]

Then Ibn an-Nahhās ؓ continues by commenting on all this by saying (p.1063):

> The Madhhab of Ahmad is in agreement with all that has preceded, an-Nawawī says: "the author of *al-Hāwī* said: 'if he manifests Islām there by his residing there then it is better that he resides there. If he is able to stay away (from fitnah in his dīn) while in Dār ul-Harb then he must reside there, as where he is (over there) is Dār ul-Islām and if he migrates it will become Dār ul-Harb and this is prohibited.'"[2]

Secondly, according to 'Awlakī and his minions, a Muslim within the US army is no longer a Muslim any more anyway and is in fact a kāfir! It was odd to see hardcore Takfirists and Jihādists suddenly extolling the virtues of the shooter Major Nidal Hasan as if he has redeemed himself by the act, according to them! This demonstrates their corrupt understanding of Islām and their weak basis, along with them following their own desires. How can a person who goes against the Sharī'ah, by breaking a covenant without notice or clarity, be deemed as a "hero" who has performed a "heroic act"? Not to mention the fact that the day

---

[1] Imām an-Nawawī, *Ar-Rawdat ut-Tālibīn* (al-Maktab al-Islāmī), vol.10, p.282.
[2] Ibid.

before he was happily mingling and associating with them with no sign of animosity towards them whatsoever!

Thirdly, to attack those who are not aware of any aggression, and after they have affirmed that they have safety and security from you, it is not allowed in Islām to then turn on them without manifesting the aggression. Ibn 'Abbās is also reported to have said, as recorded in *Kitāb ul-Jihād* of *al-Muwatta'* of Imām Mālik:

> Yahyā related to me from Mālik from Yahyā ibn Said that he had heard that 'Abdullāh ibn 'Abbās said, "Stealing from the spoils does not appear in a people but that terror is cast into their hearts. Fornication does not spread in a people but that there is much death among them. A people do not lessen the measure and weight but that provision is cut off from them. A people do not judge without right but that blood spreads among them. **A people do not betray the covenant except that Allāh gives their enemies power over them.**"

Furthermore, passports, visas and residency permits in the current era are taken as covenants of safety and security, as affirmed by scholars of the past. The *fuquhā* of the era have formed the view that these procedures which are implemented by states in this manner represent an *'Aqd ul-Amān* [Agreement of Safety and Security]. This is based on the principle of *al-'Ādatu Muhakkamatun* ['custom is the basis of judgement'][1] and the *fiqh* principle: 'the example is by motives and meanings not via words and deductions'. What is worth mentioning is that this is for a Muslim when he enters a disbelieving country, or for when a non-Muslim enters the Muslim abodes.[2] This is again where we

---

[1] Courts which are based on the *Sharī'ah* and the *fuqahā* base their judgements on customs which are not explicitly found within the sources of the Book and the Sunnah, this is as long as the custom is something which is contemporary and common among the people and is not in conflict with the *Sharī'ah*.

[2] For a detailed study of this refer to Shaykh Mashhūr's study of this here: http://www.salafimanhaj.com/pdf/SalafiManhaj_Covenant.

come across' Awlakī's selective perception of jihād, as the classical scholars of jihād such as Ibn ul-Munāsif (563-620 AH/1168-1223 CE) have noted that this is not allowed. Ibn ul-Munāsif states in *Kitāb ul-Injād fī Abwāb il-Jihād*:

> As for writing and the indications and the likes that it contains, then all of that are terms and understandings which are no different to spoken words.[1] The ruling of this takes into account meanings and understandings not mere words. What affirms this is that the Messenger of Allāh ﷺ wrote to the kings of *kufr* calling them to Islām and signalled to his Companions. Also the signal that was given in regards to the Jewish person who hit a girl with two stones. She signalled with her head (i.e. nodded) when she was asked as to who the culprit was and when the name of the culprit was mentioned a third time she said: "yes" and nodded with her head, then the Messenger of Allāh had the culprit executed for his crime via the use of two large stones. The hadīth was reported by Muslim in his Sahīh.[2] All of this is clear evidence and a lucid proof of the Divine Legislation fulfilling acting upon understandings. If a Muslim does not intend to grant the covenant of security that the (non-Muslim) combatant thinks he has due to what the Muslim done which appears to be a covenant, yet the combatant is assured (that he has a covenant of

---

[1] In the *Muwatta'* Imām Mālik ؓ, when asked whether safe conduct promised by gesture had the same status as that promised by speech, said:
> **Yes. I think that one can request an army not to kill someone by gesturing for safe conduct, because as far as I am concerned, gesture has the same status as speech.**

[2] In *Kitāb ul-Qasāmah wa'l-Mahāribīn wa'l-Qisās wa'd-Diyāt* [The Book of Oaths, Combatants, Retribution and Blood-Monies], (Bab Thabūt ul-Qisās fī Qatl bi'l-Hijārah wa Ghayruhu), vol.10, p.1672, on the authority of Anas bin Mālik ؓ. Al-Bukhārī also reported the hadīth in many instances within his Sahīh: hadīth nos. 2413, 2746, 5295, 6876, 6877, 6879, 6884 and 6885.

Translator's Note: The hadīth is also reported by Imām Bukhārī in his *Sahīh* (Kitāb ud-Diyāt) on the authority of Anas.

security) – then the sanctity of a covenant of security is granted to the combatant. As for fulfilling what the combatant thinks (is a covenant of security) or granting him safe passage without attacking him, after he thought that he has a covenant of assurance and security anyway which insured that he would not killed or imprisoned, then Allāh says,

﴿وَإِمَّا تَخَافَنَّ مِن قَوْمٍ خِيَانَةً فَانبِذْ إِلَيْهِمْ عَلَىٰ سَوَاءٍ﴾

"If you [have reason to] fear from a people betrayal, throw [their treaty] back to them, [putting you] on equal terms." *{al-Anfāl (8): 58}*

Allāh instructs to inform them of any rejection of what they thought they had agreed to which insured their security and trust. **It is not permissible to attack them until they know with insight what their affair is and they are warned, this was the origin for everything that the people of kufr felt was a covenant and a trust from the Muslims.**

As for the one who indicates in a way in which a covenant of security is sensed or does something which apparently establishes a covenant of security yet does not intend to give (a trust of covenant), then he falls into one of two conditions:

- Either he was inattentive and did not intend to grant a trust or covenant of security thus, he did not adhere to the assurance at all, then in which case he was still a cause for assuring (the combatant). As a result, the Muslim has to maintain this trust as he was the cause for (the combatant thinking) that he had a trust.
- Or he pretended to give a covenant and trust on purpose knowing that he does not intend to grant security whatsoever. All he wishes to do is delude the person in order to gain power over the person, **this is the basis of treachery and betrayal is harām according to the consensus.** For this reason 'Umar bin al-Khattāb ﷺ promised what he

did and there is no known difference among the Muslims in regards to the prohibition of treachery and betrayal. We will clarify *inshā'Allāh* the difference between the deception which is allowed during warfare and the treachery which is not allowed in regards to the trust and covenant of security.[1]

Then Ibn ul-Munāsif states, explaining the difference between *khuda'* (deception in warfare) and *khiyānah* (treachery) and *ghadr* (betrayal):

Deception and plotting during warfare via administrative planning is a well-known practice and an affirmed tradition. However, maybe some whom we see are confused over the conditions which they think permit the deception that is allowed during warfare. We thus viewed that we clarify the differences. We say: the obligation to fulfil (trusts and promises) is verified and so is the warning of betrayal, the restricted descriptions of covenants or security are also affirmed. Yet with this, the Prophet's statement allowing deception during warfare is also affirmed. It is clear however that the permitted deception is: **whatever is referred back to proficient consideration and administrations of obscure war plans and views which are unbeknown to the enemy or which the enemy are heedless of. Anything which resembles such plans in order to weaken the enemy fall into this type, as long as a trust of security is not presumed and does not include people feeling that they had such a trust at any given time.** Scheming (against those who think they have trust), dissolution (of the trust or covenant) and hatching plots (against those who think they have a trust or covenant) are all included within this. Digression at the time of fighting and seizing an opportunity to attack is likewise included (as impermissible actions towards those who think they have a trust or covenant). Also from what is not included (as being

---

[1] *Kitāb ul-Injād*, vol.2, pp.309-310.

legitimate and permissible deception during war) is for the Muslim to make it seem as if he is with the enemy or on the same religion as them or that he has come to advise them (when he really wants to attack them). If they (the enemy) are found to be inattentive then this is included as being a trust or covenant, because the enemy feels that they have mutual peace and harmony from the Muslim and they allow him to live among them, in such an instance it is not permissible for the Muslim to be treacherous. So the main difference (between deception during warfare and the treachery which is not allowed within granting covenants to non-Muslims) is that we have given him assurance that we have entered a covenant of security. He (the non-Muslim) goes with a sense of mutual peace and harmony (with the Muslim) and thinking that all of that will be fulfilled, trusting the Muslim due to what the Muslim manifested to him. He (the non-Muslim) was not taken in due to a change in the situation rather (this assurance) came from the Muslim's treacherous manifestation of friendship to him, hereby committing treachery. In the issue of plotting and deception his assurance (without clearly achieving it from the other) was only due to his own negligence and deficiency of the other... and the likes which reflects his irresponsibility without any ascribing treachery to the other (who gave no indication of there being any assurance of security). This is clear, *alhamdulillāh*.

The issue can at times apparently resemble the matter of Amān (security and safety) and at other times the matter of permissible plotting. There is no differentiation except in the different instances of the enemy's assurance based on the regulations that we have drawn up. For if a Muslim man observed a Harbī in a certain direction of enemy land or elsewhere and manifested to him that he has thrown down his weapon, and walked towards the direction of warfare, indicating that he has seen him, going towards him as if he is surrendering or making peace with him, and the likes, then the other (i.e. the Harbī) will be assured of this; until the Muslim achieves his goal (of killing the Harbī) - then this is deception which is not permissible, for it (what he has done) is a covenant (Amān).

Also, in another example, even if the Harbī, who is negligent, sees what he (the Muslim) is doing by putting down his weapon and walking towards the direction of the Harbī, as in the first example, the Muslim may just manifest that he is unaware of the Harbī so that the Harbī does not feel that the Muslim has seen him and is going towards him in peace. However, the Muslim deludes him into thinking that he is unaware of where the Harbī is. This action of his is the action of one who removes his weaponry so as to rest, if he is assured when doing that, until the enemy feels assured due to what he has been deluded as thinking is the Muslim's heedlessness, not out of feeling there is a trust from him – then this is permissible.[1] This is classed as *Tawriyah* (trickery) and *Makīdah* (plotting) both of which are neither connected to treachery nor Amān (sanctified safe-passage), and Allāh knows best.[2]

Ibn an-Nahhās ﷺ also states in *Mashāri' ul-Ashwāq ilā Masāri' il-'Ushshāq* (!!) in the edit of Idrīs Muhammad 'Ali and Muhammad Khālid Istanbūlī, pp.1060-1062:

Indicating a covenant of safety and security to a Mushrik is taken as an Amān (covenant of safety and security) according to Mālik and ash-Shāfi'ī.[3] The author of al-Mughnī states: "If he (i.e. the

---

[1] **Translator's note:** meaning that it is allowed to feign ignorance as a tactic, but it is not allowed to fake an agreement or trust. So for example, a tactic would be to play dead allowing one's enemy to get close after which one could harm the enemy. But it would not be allowed to claim surrender only to then kill the enemy when one is close to them, this is betrayal and treachery.

[2] *Kitāb ul-Injād*, pp.311-313.

[3] Muhammad ash-Shirbīnī al-Khatīb, *Mughnī ul-Muhtāj ilā Ma'rifat Ma'ānī Alfādh il-Minhāj* (Maktabah al-Islāmī), vol.4, p.238.

Muslim) indicates towards them with what they view as an Amān and then (the Muslim) says 'I did not intend an Amān' then this is just his word (the Amān remains)."[1]

Issue: an-Nawawī says in ar-Rawdah, in following ar-Rāfi'ī: "An Amān made with every word indicates a clear objective and is also made by ambiguous implication (kināyah). What is a clear objective is: 'I grant you protection' or 'you are protected' or 'I have granted you safety' or 'you are safe and secure' or 'you are in my safety so no harm will come to you' or 'do not fear' or 'do not be scared' or 'do not be frightened' or says it in a foreign language by saying 'Matars'.[2] By Kināyah (ambiguous implication) is to say: 'you are as you like' or 'be how you will'. An Amān is also established by writing or messaging, whether the Messenger is a Muslim or disbeliever. Or the Amān can be

---

[1] Ibn Qudāmah, *al-Mughnī*, vol.10, p.559.

[2] (مطرس أو مترس وهي كلمة فارسية تعريبها: لا تخف ومترس ومطرس بإبدال التاء طاء والعكس)
The word 'Mattars' is a Persian word relayed in some narrations in the Musannaf of Ibn Abī Shaybah in the Book of Jihād in the section on the definition and description of granting Amān. It has been relayed as being 'Matars', 'Mattars', 'Matras' and 'Mattaras' and it all means **'do not be scared, you are safe'**.

In this section there are seven narrations relayed on the issue of granting and accepting covenants of safety and security. The first narration in the section (no. 34082) is: 'Abbād bin al-'Awwām narrated to us from Husayn from Abū 'Atiyyah who said: 'Umar wrote to the people of Kūfa saying: *"It has been mentioned to me that the word 'Mattars' in the Persian language signifies assurance and safety so if you say it to those who do not speak your (Arabic) language then it signifies Amān."*

Another narration (no. 34085) is: Wakī' narrated to us: al-'A'mash narrated to us: from Abū Wā'il who said: "the letter of 'Umar reached us and we were in Khāniqīn (in eastern 'Irāq, south of the Kurdish regions and near the Irānian border): if a man says to another **'la tadhul (do not be scared)'** then he has granted him safety and security. If a man says to another: **'do not fear'** then he has granted him safety and security. If he says **'matras'** then he has granted him safety and security, because Allāh knows all languages."

See *al-Musannaf li Ibn Abī Shaybah: al-Imām Abū Bakr 'Abdullāh bin Muhammad bin Abī Shaybah al'Absī al-Kūfī* (159-235 AH) (Jeddah, KSA: Dār ul-Qiblah li'th-Thaqāfat il-Islāmiyyah, 1427 AH/2006 CE, ed. Muhammad 'Awwāmah), vol.18, pp.108-116.

Chapter 14

by a sign which is understood by one who is able to speak. This is a broad subject. As for the one who was assured (the Mu'amman), with a fatha on the mīm, then he must know about this and the news of the Amān must reach him. If this does not reach him then there is no Amān for him. If a Muslim was to then kill this (Harbī) then this is allowed and his (the Harbī) verbal acceptance it is not a condition (if the Amān does not reach him). Rather an indication and a sensed sign are sufficient as acceptance (from the Muslims), or the kāfir says 'I have accepted your covenant but I do not grant you trust so beware'. The Imām said: 'he has rejected the Amān' because the Amān is not confirmed by one side without the recognition of the other. If the Imām (Muslim leader) views there is a Maslahah (benefit) in allowing the entry of traders and says 'whoever enters for trade is safe and secure' - then this is allowed."[1]

Similar to this was also mentioned by Ibn ul-Juzayy ؓ in *al-Qawānīn ul-Fiqhiyyah* towards the end of *Kitāb ul-Jihād*. Ibn an-Nahhās above also referred to Ibn Qudāmah ؓ and what he said in *al-Mughnī*;[2] what Ibn Qudāmah stated was:

وأما خيانتهم فمحرمة، لأنهم إنما أعطوه الأمان مشروطاً بتركه خيانتهم، وأمنه إياهم من نفسه، وإن لم يكن ذلك مذكوراً في اللفظ، فهو معلوم في المعنى، ولذلك من جاءنا منهم بأمان فخاننا كان ناقضاً لعهده. فإذا ثبت هذا لم تحل خيانتهم لأنه غدر ولا يصلح في ديننا الغدر. وقد قال النبي ﷺ: ((المسلمون عند شروطهم)) فإن خانهم أو سرق منهم، أو اقترض شيئاً، وجب عليه رد ما أخذ.

---

[1] An-Nawawī, *ar-Rawdah*, vol.10, pp.279-280.
[2] In *Kitāb ul-Jihād, Mas'alat Man Dakhala Ard ul-'Aduw bi-Amān* [The Issue of Entering the Land of the Enemy with an Agreement/Covenant of Safety and Security].

...and as for betraying them, then it is harām (prohibited), because they gave him the covenant of safety and security on the condition that he will neither betray them nor harm them, and even if this was not written therein as it is known contextually. Thus, whoever gained a covenant of safety and security into our countries and betrayed us then it is as if he withdrew his covenant. And thus, if this was true, then it is prohibited to betray them, because our religion prohibits betrayal. In this respect, the Prophet ﷺ said:

((المسلمون عند شروطهم)).

"...the Muslims must stick to their conditions"[1]

Ibn Qudāmah here was himself commenting on what was stated by al-Khirqī al-Hanbalī ؓ when al-Khirqī said:

جاء في متن الخرقي الحنبلي (من دخل أرض العدو لم يخنهم).

It is found in the text of al-Khirqī al-Hanbalī: "Whoever enters the land of the enemy should not betray them (betray the covenant or agreement with them)."

Abu'l-Hasan 'Alī bin Abī Bakr bin 'AbdulJalīl al-Marghīyānī (511-593 AH/1118-1197 CE)[2] stated in *al-Hidāyah: Sharh ul-Bidāyah al-Mubtadi'*, p.134:

---

[1] *Hasan Sahīh*; reported by Abū Dāwud (3594) from Abū Hurayrah; at-Tirmidhī (1352) from 'Amr Ibn 'Awf al-Muzanī; and our sheikh classified Sahīh therein, while al-Bukhārī reported it *ta'līqan* (without a chain of narrators), and so in case one betrays them, steals from them, or borrows anything, then he should give back what he took. See *al-Mughnī*, vol.10, p.507.

[2] The great Hanafī jurist, was born at Marghiyān in the vicinity of Farghana in Present Day Uzbekistan. He studied with Najmuddīn Abū Hafs 'Umar an-Nasafī, his son Abu'l-Layth Ahmad bin 'Umar an-Nasafī and other eminent teachers, and excelled in Hadīth, Tafsīr, Fiqh and other studies.

وإذا دخل المسلم دار الحرب تاجرا فلا يحل له أن يتعرض لشيء من أموالهم ولا من دمائهم لأنه ضمن أن لا يتعرض لهم بالاستئمان , فالتعرض بعد ذلك يكون غدرا ، والغدر حرام.

> If a Muslim enters Dār ul-Harb as a trader, then he is like a Muslim who is Musta'min in Dār ul-Harb, and it is therefore not permissible for him to dishonour them in anything in terms of their wealth and blood as he is within Isti'mān which necessitates he does not dishonour them. If he dishonours them after this then this is betrayal and betrayal is harām.[1]

Our Shaykh, Mashhūr Hasan *(hafidhahullāh)* thus states:

> Based upon this it becomes clear to us the accuracy of what has been acknowledged by the 'Ulamā of our era in regards to the prohibition of wreaking havoc, hijacking airplanes and killing non-Muslims in their lands which is committed by some young Muslims who enter those lands with Amān (safe-passage and security),[2] in the form of entry-visas. For this is an example of betrayal and treachery, the prohibition is intensified when it is ascribed to the Sharī'ah and considered as being from "Jihād", as they claim![3]

It was mentioned in the acknowledgement of the *Council of Senior Scholars* stated in regards to the Riyadh bombings[4] of 1424 AH[5] that

---

[1] *Kitāb us-Siyar, Bāb ul-Musta'min.*
[2] And if they are Mu'āhadīn then the opposition to the *Sharī'ah* would be from two angles, like a person who steals pork and eats it!
[3] From the edit of Shaykh Muhammad bin Zakariyyā Abū Ghāzī and our Shaykh Mashhūr Hasan Āl Salmān to Imām al-Mujtahid Abū 'Abdullāh Muhammad bin 'Īsā bin Muhammad bin Asbagh al-Azdī al-Qurtubī (aka Ibn Munāsif), *Kitāb ul-Injād fī Abwāb il-Jihād* (Beirut: Mu'assasah ar-Rayān, 1425 AH/2005 CE), vol.1, pp.63-81.
[4] On the evening of 11/3/1424 AH.
[5] Reported in the paper al-Jazeerah, no.11186, Thursday 14 Rabī' al-Awwal 1424 AH.

which certifies the accuracy of our previous words. They state, after explaining the prohibition of transgressing against people such as Mu'āhadīn, Ahl udh-Dhimmah and Musta'manīn and relaying the texts in regards to this, that:

> The intent is that whoever enters with a covenant of security or an agreement from the leader based on a benefit that he sees fit then it is neither permitted to dishonour such a person nor transgress against him or his wealth. If this is clear then the bombing which occurred in the city of Riyadh is prohibited and not acknowledged by the religion of Islām whatsoever. The impermissibility of it is from a number of angles:
> 1. The action transgresses on the sanctity of the Muslim lands and breeds fear among those living in security within them.
> 2. The action involved killing souls which are sanctified within the Islamic Sharī'ah.
> 3. The action causes corruption on the earth.
> 4. The action includes taking sanctified wealth.

They also stated:

> The *Council of Senior Scholars* therefore clarifies the issue in order to caution the Muslims from falling into prohibited and destructive matters and so as to caution them from the plots of Shaytān. For Shaytān entices the servant until he makes him fall into destruction either via *ghulū fī'd-dīn* (religious extremism) or by turning away from the *dīn* and fighting against it, Allāh's refuge is sought. Shaytān does not care via which means he gains triumph over the servant as both the path to extremism and aversion are ways of Shaytān which both lead the person to gain the Anger of ar-Rahmān and His punishment.

They also stated:

> Also, all should know that the Islamic Ummah today is suffering from the incursion of the enemies from all sides and they are

pleased with any means which facilitate their control over the people of Islām, their humiliation and exploitation of their mineral wealth. So whoever helps them in their aims to conquer the Muslims and the Islamic lands has co-operated in helping the degradation of the Muslims and the dominance over their lands, and this is of the gravest crimes. It is thus obligatory to attach importance to *Shari'* knowledge based on the Book and Sunnah and in agreement with the Salaf of the Ummah as taught within the schools, universities, Masājid and media outlets. Likewise, it is important to attach concern to commanding the good and forbidding the evil and to mutually advise to good. For there is a need, or rather a necessity now because the time more than ever demands it, for the Muslim youth to have good opinion of their *'Ulamā* and take knowledge from them. The youth also have to know that the enemies of the dīn wish to cause a gulf between the Ummah's youth and their *'Ulamā* and leaders so that their power will be weakened so as to facilitate their control over them all - so it is obligatory to pay concern to this. May Allāh protect all from the plots of the enemies and it is upon the Muslims to have *taqwā* of Allāh secretly and publically, and to make a sincere truthful repentance unto Allāh from all sins for no calamity descends except due to sins and the calamity is not lifted except by *tawbah*. We ask Allāh to rectify the condition of the Muslims and to avert all evil and harm from the Muslims' lands. And may prayers and peace be upon our Prophet Muhammad, his family and his companions.

Al-'Allāmah Shaykh 'Abdul'Azīz bin Bāz was asked: **"What is the ruling of transgressing against foreign tourists and visitors in Islamic lands?"**

Answer:

This is impermissible, transgression against anyone is not allowed whether against tourists or workers because they are Musta'minūn (non-Muslims who have agreements of safe-passage in a Muslim land) and they have entered with an agreement ('Ahd) hence it is impermissible to transgress against them. Rather, the state should be advised so as to prevent them from that which should not manifest. As for transgression against them then this is impermissible, as for an individual then it is not upon him to kill, beat or harm them. Rather it is upon him to raise the matter to those in authority as transgression against them is transgression against a people who have entered a land with an agreement ('Ahd) and it is impermissible to transgress against them. Rather their situation is to be raised with those who are able to prevent their entry or is able to prevent their apparent evil. If they are Muslims then it is sought-after to advise them and call them to Islām or advise them to leave evil via referring to the *Shari'* proofs, *Allāhu Musta'ān, wa la hawla wa la quwwata ila billāh.* May prayers and peace be upon our Prophet Muhammad, his family and his Companions.[1]

Imam Bin Bāz was also asked:
Some youth think that harming the kuffār, including citizens within an Islamic country or those who travel to the Islamic country, is from the *Shar'.* For this reason, they make it permissible to kill them if they see that which they dislike.

Answer:
It is neither allowed to kill the disbelieving citizen or the Musta'min who is a visitor who the state grant entry and safe-passage to, nor to kill sinners or transgress against them. Rather whatever evil occurs from them is to be referred back to the

---

[1] Imām Bin Bāz, *Majmū' al-Fatāwā wa'l-Maqālāt*, vol.8, p.239.

Chapter 14

Divine Legislation and what the Sharī'ah Courts view as being applicable.

The questioner then asks: **"What if there are no Sharī'ah courts?"**

Answer from the Shaykh ﷺ:

If there are no Sharī'ah courts then advice only, advice to those in authority, guiding them to good and co-operating with them so that they judge by Allāh's *Shar'*. As for the one commanding the good and forbidding the evil raising his hand to kill or hit anyone then this is not allowed. However, one should co-operate with those in authority in a way which is closer to righteousness so that they judge by Allāh's *Shar'* in regards to Allāh's servants. If not then it is wājib to give advice and guide towards good and reject evil in a way which is closer to goodness. This is obligatory, Allāh says:

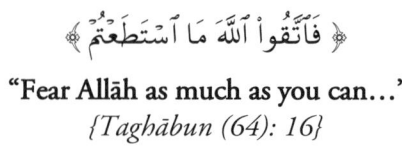

"Fear Allāh as much as you can…"
{Taghābun (64): 16}

For his forbidding the evil with his hand via killing or beating will no doubt result in more evil and corruption.[1]

Shaykh al-'Allāmah al-Faqeeh Muhammad bin Sālih al-'Uthaymīn ﷺ stated in a Jumu'ah Khutbah in regards to the Khobar bombings, wherein he relayed many texts in regards to Amān (agreements of safe-passage and security)[2]:

---

[1] Imām Bin Bāz, *Majmū al-Fatāwā wa'l-Maqālāt*, vol.8, p.207; also see vol.1, pp.276-280 in his *fatwa* on 'Hijacking Planes and Terrorising People who have safe-passage.'

[2] Which are also relayed by Ibn ul-Munāsif in the first section of Chapter Six of *Kitāb ul-Injād fī Abwāb il-Jihād*.

Based on this, the kuffār here have an Amān which is sanctified and their blood is sanctified, hence you see the error of the bombing which took place in Khobar¹ at the compound which housed those whose blood and wealth is inviolable. Eighteen people were left for dead and 386 people were injured including Muslims, children, women, elderly and the youth. Wealth and property was destroyed in that attack and there is no doubt that this incident is neither acknowledged at all in the *Shar'* [Divine Legislation of Islām] nor by the intellect or natural disposition. As for the *Shar'* then you have heard the Qur'anic and Prophetic texts which indicate the obligation of respecting Muslims in regards to their blood and property, and likewise respect for the kuffār who have contracts of protection or promises or contracts of Amān (safe-passage and security). Respect for those Mu'āhadīn, Musta'manīn and Dhimmiyīn is from the good qualities of the Islamic religion and this respect for them depends on the agreements with them and this does not necessitate love, (religious) allegiance or (religious) support for them, rather it is fulfilment of trusts, Allāh says:

﴿ إِنَّ ٱلۡعَهۡدَ كَانَ مَسۡـُٔولٗا ﴾

"Indeed, the commitment is ever [that about which one will be] questioned." *{al-Isrā' (17): 34}*

As for the intellect then the intelligent person does not deal with anything prohibited because he knows the evil consequence of that and the punishment, and he does not deal with anything permitted until its consequence and what it involves has become clear to him. The Prophet ﷺ said:

*"Whoever believes in Allāh and the Last Day then let him say good or keep quiet."*²

---

¹ On Wednesday 10th Safar 1417 AH/26 June 1996 CE.
² Reported by al-Bukhārī (hadīth no.6018) and Muslim (hadīth no. 74) from Abū Hurayrah ؓ.

Chapter 14

He ﷺ made īmān's perfection that a person only say that which is good or otherwise keep quiet, likewise it can be said: from īmān's perfection is for a person to do good or otherwise restrain themselves. There is no doubt that this evil (terrorist bombing) operation is based on a number of corrupt aspects which we will mention according to what Allāh facilitates. As for this evil action (i.e. bombing) opposing the *fitrah* (natural disposition) then all who have a natural sound disposition hates transgression towards others and views that as being evil, for what was the sin of those Muslims who were injured in the attack? What was the sin of those who were safe in their beds in their homes that led to them being injured in this painful incident? What was the sin of those Mu'āhadīn and Musta'manīn? What was the sin of those children, old people and frail people? This was an unjustified atrocity!! Its corrupt aspects are the following:

FIRST: It contains disobedience to Allāh and His Messenger, and it contains transgressing Allāh's prohibitions. It also leads to the curse of Allāh, the angels and all the people[1] and nothing will be accepted from the one who committed the atrocity.

SECOND: It distorts the image and reputation of Islām for the enemies of Islām will exploit such atrocities to further their distortion of the image and reputation of Islām and make people flee from Islām. This is even though Islām is innocent from these actions as the manners of Islam inculcate: truthfulness, piety and trust, and the Islamic religion sternly warns against such (evil terrorist actions).

THIRD: Fingers, from inside and outside, will point to this atrocity and brand it as being an action of those committed to Islām. Even though we know for sure that those who are committed to the Sharī'ah of Allāh in reality would neither do

---

[1] **Translator's note:** hence, the advocates of such terrorist actions end up being thrown into the jails of the kuffār with neither constructive repercussions of their beliefs nor positive outcomes resulting from their methods.

such actions nor be happy with such actions at all. Rather they (those truly committed to the Sharī'ah) free themselves from such actions and denounce them unequivocally because the one who is truly committed to the Allāh's dīn is the one who establishes Allāh's dīn according to how Allāh wants and not according to his own desires which are based on emotion and a deviant methodology. Committal to the dīn in accordance with the Sharī'ah is abundant with our youth and all praise is due to Allāh.

FOURTH: Many of the common people who are ignorant of the reality of committal to Allāh's dīn will look at many of those who are committed to the dīn and distance themselves from them.[1] They will have enmity, fear, caution and warning vis-a-vis those who are committed to the religion, as we hear from some of the ignorant common people who warn their children from being committed to the religion especially after they witnessed the Riyadh bombings.

FIFTH: It causes chaos in this country which should actually have the most security and safety of all lands of the earth because it includes Allāh's House which He made a sanctuary for the people as it contains the Ka'bah which Allāh gave a standing to people with which their dīn and dunyā is rectified. Allāh says,

﴿ وَإِذْ جَعَلْنَا ٱلْبَيْتَ مَثَابَةً لِّلنَّاسِ وَأَمْنًا ﴾

"And [mention] when We made the House a place of return for the people and [a place of] security." *{Baqarah (2): 125}*

And Allāh says,

﴿ جَعَلَ ٱللَّهُ ٱلْكَعْبَةَ ٱلْبَيْتَ ٱلْحَرَامَ قِيَٰمًا لِّلنَّاسِ ﴾

---

[1] **Translator's note:** This is a common manifestation in Muslim countries in particular, such as in Morocco and other countries.

Chapter 14

"Allāh has made the Ka'bah, the Sacred House, standing for the people..." *{al-Mā'idah (5): 97}*

And it is well-known that people do not pray towards this Sacred House except via passing through this land from one of its directions.

SIXTH: The taking of life and wealth and the harms that have come to lives and wealth as people see in the media. Hearts blown up, livers disintegrated and tears flowing when one sees children on hospital beds injured in their eyes, ears, hands, legs or other parts of their bodies. Is there anyone who condones or is pleased with such (terrorist) actions? I do not know what they want with these attacks, do they want rectification? Rectification does not come about by such actions for evil does not bring about good and evil means are not a route to rectification whatsoever.[1]

The respected Shaykh Sālih al-Fawzān was asked:

Some have given rulings permitting the killing of Americans all over the world saying that they (the Americans) are "warring" (against Islām and Muslims), what do you say about this respected Shaykh?

Answer:

This Muftī is an ignoramus! Because there is some detail (that needs to be acknowledged) in this issue. So those whom we have made agreements with and they have entered our lands with agreements ('Ahd) and safe-passage (Amān), or whom we have employed to do work which we are in need of – they are under our agreement and protection and it is neither permissible to betray (the trust) with them nor kill them. The states with which

---

[1] *At-Tahdhīr min at-Tasarru' fi't-Takfīr*, pp.53-65

there is an agreement between us and them, along with diplomatic representation, it is impermissible to betray them. The kuffār (non-Muslims) who enter our countries with our permission it is not permissible to betray them. Allāh says:

﴿ وَإِنْ أَحَدٌ مِّنَ ٱلْمُشْرِكِينَ ٱسْتَجَارَكَ فَأَجِرْهُ حَتَّىٰ يَسْمَعَ كَلَٰمَ ٱللَّهِ ثُمَّ أَبْلِغْهُ مَأْمَنَهُۥ ﴾

"And if any one of the polytheists seeks your protection, then grant him protection so that he may hear the words of Allāh. Then deliver him to his place of safety." *{at-Tawbah (9): 6}*

It is not permissible to betray those who enter Muslim countries with the permission of the Muslims, or those who the Muslims employ, it is not permissible to make such pronouncements. The Harbī is the one whom we have no agreement or covenant of security and safety with – this is the Harbī.[1]

Shaykh Sālih al-Fawzān was also asked:
Are there any kuffār (disbelievers) in these (Muslim) countries whom it is permitted to kill or assassinate? Especially because there are those who permit this action based on the hadīth of the Prophet ﷺ: "Expel the Mushrikīn from the Arabian Peninsula."

Answer:
If a disbeliever enters (the country) with an agreement from the one in authority or he came in order to fulfil something of importance and then leave – then it is not permissible to transgress against him. Islām is a religion of honouring trusts and it is not a religion of betrayal or treachery, it is impermissible to transgress against the disbeliever who we have an agreement with

---

[1] From the audio *Fatāwā al-'Ulama fī'l-Ahdāth ir-Rāhinah allatī Hadathat bi-Madīnat ir-Riyādh*, in the book *al-Fatāwā ash-Shar'iyyah fī'l-Qadāyā al-'Asriyyah*, p.124.

Chapter 14

and is under our safety. The world should not speak about Islām being a religion of betrayal and of reneging on agreements, this is not from Islām. As for the saying of the Prophet ﷺ: "Expel the Mushrikīn from the Arabian Peninsula"[1] this hadīth is Sahīh. However, it does not mean kill those who are Mu'āhad and Musta'min and under our covenant. Rather, this is for the Yahūd and Nasārā who do not have agreements and covenants with the Muslims.[2]

Yet, for 'Awlakī and his minions, all of this is irrelevant as he makes takfīr of all of the Muslim countries today including Saudi Arabia.[3] 'Awlakī says in his "explanation" of Ibn an-Nahhās' book *Mashāri' ul-Ashwāq ilā Masāri ul-'Ushshāq*, CD 12, Track 10:

> If enemy soldiers enter the land of Islām without an agreement then it is allowed to kill them and take their property. **Or if they enter with an agreement that is signed by a Murtad government.**

Clear proof of 'Awlakī following his desires! Ibn an-Nahhās does not mention the quote above from 'Awlakī, which we have underlined, about **"Murtad governments"**. Why did 'Awlakī therefore add it in? Why did he make out as if it was Ibn an-Nahhās' words when Ibn an-Nahhās does not mention that in *Mashāri' ul-Ashwāq ilā Masāri ul-'Ushshāq*? Why did he tamper with the words of Ibn an-Nahhās and add what Ibn an-Nahhās did not say? Ibn an-Nahhās in *Mashāri' ul-Ashwāq ilā Masāri ul-'Ushshāq* in the edit of Idrīs Muhammad 'Alī and Muhammad Khālid Istanbūlī, pp.1054-1056 does discuss the issue of

---

[1] Reported by al-Bukhārī (hadīth nos. 3168 and 3053) and Muslim (hadīth no. 1637) from the hadīth of Ibn 'Abbās ﷺ.
[2] From the audio recording entitled *Mu'āmalat ul-Kuffār* [Dealing with the Disbelievers].
[3] In an article in October 2009 CE which was on his now defunct blog, 'Awlakī stated:
> The rulers in the Arabian Peninsula are playing a central role in the fight against Islam especially the al Saud family. The al Saud of today is the Abdullah bin Ubay of yesterday.

not allowing entry to enemy troops into the Muslim territories and abodes. Ibn an-Nahhās also refers to the words of Ibn Qudāmah, Ibn 'AbdisSalām, Ibn Wahb, Imām Mālik, As-hab, Ibn Rushd and others. Yet what is clear from their evidences firstly is that the leader of the Muslims gives his view on these enemy troops who enter without Amān. Yet as 'Awlakī does not recognise any of the Muslim leaders of the world today as being in authority he bypasses them by thus branding them as being apostates!

Furthermore, scholars of the past also allowed the use of non-Muslim, kuffār and *mushrik* forces to be drafted upon for Muslims, if there is a benefit *(maslahah)* in that for the Muslims. Such as:
- Imām ash-Shāfi'ī
- Imām Ahmad ibn Hanbal
- Imām Abu'l-Qāsim al-Khirqī
- Imām Abu'l-Hasan as-Sindī
- Imām Bin Bāz
- Imām Ibn 'Uthaymīn ﷺ.

Therefore, this shows that the issue of drafting *kuffār* forces is something which was said by scholars in the past and the scholars who also ruled this in the present era were thus preceded in their rulings. Ibn Qudāmah al-Maqdisī ﷺ stated in *al-Mugnī* (vol.13, p.98):

> Help is not to be sought from a mushrik, this is what Ibn al-Mundhir, al-Jūzajānī and a group of the people of knowledge. There is present from Ahmad what indicates the permissibility of gaining assistance from them (i.e. mushrikīn) and the statements of al-Khirqī also indicate that, if there is a need and this is the school of thought of Shāfi'ī.

Imām an-Nawawī stated in his explanation, vol.11-12, p.403, under *hadīth* no.4677:

> His saying ﷺ: "Go back, for I do not seek help from a mushrik;" and it is mentioned in another hadīth that the Prophet ﷺ sought

help from Safwān bin Umayyah before his Islām, as a result some scholars give the first hadīth precedence over the second one. Imām Shāfi'ī and others said: "If the disbeliever has good opinion of the Muslims and the need has come to utilize him, if not then it is disliked." So these two hadīths are taken in light of two circumstances.

Shaykh as-Sindī stated in his explanation of the *hadīth "I do not gain assistance from a mushrik"*, from the *Sunan Ibn Mājah* (vol.3, p.376, under *hadīth* no.2832):

> It shows that gaining assistance from a mushrik is harām without a need. But if there is a need then it can be done as an exception and this is not opposed.[1]

---

[1] Bandar bin Nā'if bin Sanahāt al-'Utaybī, *Wa Jādilhum Bilatī Hiya Ahsan, Munāqishatun 'Ilmiyyatun Hādiyyatun li-19 Mas'alatin Muta'alaqatin bi-Hukkām il-Muslimīn* (Riyadh: Maktabah 'AbdulMusawwir bin Muhammad bin 'Abdullāh, 1427AH/2006 CE, Fourth Edition), pp.38-42.

CHAPTER 15

'AWLAKI'S PRAISE OF THE NIGERIAN YOUTH UMAR FAROUK ABDULMUTALLAB AND THE NORTHWEST AIRLINES FLIGHT 253 ATTEMPTED PLANE BOMBING

Umar Farouk AbdulMutallab was a young Nigerian man who attempted to detonate plastic explosives hidden in his underwear on board Northwest Airlines Flight 253 from Amsterdam to Detroit on December 25 2009. Umar Farouk was subsequently charged on six criminal counts, including attempted use of a weapon of mass destruction and attempted murder of 289 people. He is currently, at the time of writing this, in U.S. custody, awaiting further legal proceedings.

Umar Farouk was the youngest of sixteen children born to one of the richest men in Nigeria, Alhaji Umaru Mutallab, the former Chariman of First Bank of Nigeria and the former Nigerian Federal Commissioner for Economic Development. His family comes from Funtua in Katsina State but he was raised in an affluent area in Kaduna. From 2004-2005 Umar Farouk went to Yemen to study Arabic in San'a and he also attended lectures at Iman University. He began his studies at University College London in September 2005 where he studied Engineering and Business Finance and gained his BA degree in mechanical engineering in June 2008. During his time at UCL he was the president of the university's Islamic Society. In August 2009 Umar Farouk Abdul-Mutallab returned to Yemen to study in San'a again at the San'a Institute for the Arabic Language but dropped the course in September 2009 while remaining in Yemen, overstaying his student

Chapter 15

visa, to the concern of his family. One of the text messages Umar Farouk sent to his father was the following:

"I've found a new religion, the real Islam"; "You should just forget about me, I'm never coming back"; "Please forgive me. I will no longer be in touch with you"; and "Forgive me for any wrongdoing, I am no longer your child."

There are many ayat of Allāh wherein Allāh says:

﴿ وَٱتَّقُوا۟ ٱللَّهَ ٱلَّذِى تَسَآءَلُونَ بِهِۦ وَٱلْأَرْحَامَ إِنَّ ٱللَّهَ كَانَ عَلَيْكُمْ رَقِيبًا ﴾

"... And fear Allāh, through whom you ask one another and the wombs.[1] Indeed, Allāh is ever, over you, an Observer." {an-Nisā (4): 1}

﴿ وَوَصَّيْنَا ٱلْإِنسَٰنَ بِوَٰلِدَيْهِ حَمَلَتْهُ أُمُّهُۥ وَهْنًا عَلَىٰ وَهْنٍ وَفِصَٰلُهُۥ فِى عَامَيْنِ أَنِ ٱشْكُرْ لِى وَلِوَٰلِدَيْكَ إِلَىَّ ٱلْمَصِيرُ ﴾

"And We have enjoined upon man (to care) for his parents. His mother carried him, (increasing her) in weakness upon weakness, and his weaning is in two years. Be grateful to Me and to your parents; to Me is the (final) destination." {Luqmān (31): 14}

Allāh says in a verse which is particularly pertinent to this study:

﴿ فَهَلْ عَسَيْتُمْ إِن تَوَلَّيْتُمْ أَن تُفْسِدُوا۟ فِى ٱلْأَرْضِ وَتُقَطِّعُوٓا۟ أَرْحَامَكُمْ ﴾

"So would you perhaps, if you turned away, cause corruption on earth and sever your ties of relationship?" {Muhammad (47): 22}

---

[1] i.e. fear Allāh in regards to ties of kinship.

It is reported in *Kitāb ul-Jihād* of the Sahīh of Imām al-Bukhārī; *Kitāb ul-Birr wa's-Silah wa'l-Ādab* in the Sahīh of Imām Muslim; *Kitāb ul-Jihād* in the Sunan of Imām at-Tirmidhī; *Kitāb ul-Jihād* in the Sunan of Imām an-Nasā'ī; *Kitāb ul-Jihād* in the Sunan of Imām Abū Dāwud and in the Musnad of Imām Ahmad that:

'Abdullāh Ibn 'Amr said: "A man came to the Prophet and asked for his permission to go for jihād. He said,

((أحيٌّ والداك؟))

'Are your parents alive?'
The man replied, 'Yes.' The Prophet said:

((ففيهما فجاهد))

'Then your jihād is with them.'"

Imāms Ahmad and Abū Dāwud include the additional narrations, authenticated by Ibn Hibbān, from the Prophet:

((ارجع فاستأذنهما فإن أذنا لك فجاهد وإلا فبرهما))

Go back and seek their permission and if they grant you permission (then wage armed jihād) and if they do not (grant you permission) then be dutiful to them (and their wishes).

Hence, Ibn Hajar al-'Asqalānī stated in his magnum opus *Fath ul-Bārī*:

قال جمهور العلماء يحرم الجهاد إذا منع الأبوان أو أحدهما بشرط أن يكونا مسلمين لأن برهما فرض عين والجهاد فرض كفاية. أهـ.

The majority of the scholars say that it is prohibited to wage (armed) jihād if the parents, or one of them, prevent it. With the condition that they are Muslims because being dutiful to them is an individual responsibility while (armed) jihād is a collective responsibility.¹

The hadīth of the Prophet Muhammad ﷺ from Abū 'Amru ash-Shaybānī who said, *"The owner of this house narrated to us,"* and he indicated with his hand to the house of 'Abdullāh Ibn Mas'ūd ؓ, that he said ؓ:

I asked the Prophet ﷺ: "Which action is the most beloved to Allāh?" He said:

((الصلاة لوقتها))

"Prayer at its correct time."

I said, *"then which action?"* He said:

((ثم بر الوالدين))

"Birr (good treatment, kindness) to the parents."

I said, "Then which?" He said:

((ثم الجهاد في سبيل الله))

*"then Jihād in the way of Allāh."*²

So before *jihād*, the Prophet ﷺ mentioned being good and dutiful to parents.

A man asked *"O Messenger of Allāh who is most deserving of my birr?"* He said, **"Your mother."** The man asked, *"Then who?"* He said, **"Your**

---

¹ Al-Imām, al-Hāfidh Ahmad bin 'Ali bin Hajar al-'Asqalānī, *Fath ul-Bārī: Sharh Sahīh ul-Bukhārī* (Beirut: Dār ul-Kutub al-'Ilmiyyah, 1421 AH/2000 CE, 3ʳᵈ Edn., ed. Muhammad Fu'ād 'AbdulBāqī), *Kitāb ul-Jihād wa's-Sīr* [The Book of Jihād and Prisoners of War], vol.7, p.173.

² Mentioned in *Sahīh Adab al-Mufrad;* the hadīth is agreed upon and to be found in Sahīh ul-Bukhārī, *Kitāb ul-Mawāqīt us-Salāh* and Sahīh Muslim, *Kitāb ul-Īmān*.

mother." The man asked, *"Then who?"* He said, **"Your mother."** The man asked again, *"Then who?"* He said, **"Then your father."**¹

From Taysala bin Mayyās who said Ibn 'Umar ؓ said to me, *"Do you fear the fire and wish to enter the Paradise?"* I said, *"Of course, by Allāh!"* He said, *"Are your parents alive?"* I said, *"I have a mother."* He said, *"Then by Allāh! If you were to speak gently to her and feed her, you would certainly enter paradise, as long as you stay away from the Major sins."*²

From Abdullāh bin 'Umar ؓ who said, a man came to the Prophet ﷺ to give him the *bay'ah* for *hijrah*, and he left his parents crying. So the Prophet said:

((ارجع فأضحكهما كما أبكيتهما))

*"Return to your parents and make them laugh as you have made them cry."*³

In a *sahīh hadīth*, the Prophet ﷺ was informed by Asmā bint Abī Bakr as-Siddīq ؓ that her disbelieving mother was about to visit her saying:

قدمت عليّ أمي وهي مشركة في عهد رسول الله ﷺ، فاستفتيت رسول الله صلى الله عليه وسلم، قلت: إن أمّي قدمت وهي راغبة، أفأصل أمي؟

My mother came to me, and she was a *mushrik* at the time of the Prophet ﷺ. I asked the Prophet ﷺ: *"My mother has come to me and needs my help, so should I help her?"* He ﷺ said:

((نعم، صلي أمك))

*"Yes, keep in touch with your mother and treat her well."*¹

---

¹ Sahīh ul-Bukhārī and Muslim.
² Mentioned in *Sahīh Adab al-Mufrad;* See Imām al-Albānī, *as-Sahīhah,* no.2898.
³ Mentioned in *Sahīh Adab al-Mufrad;* Sunan, Imām an-Nasā'ī, *Kitāb ul-Bay'ah;* Sunan, Imām Abū Dāwud, *Kitāb ul-Jihād;* Sunan, Ibn Mājah, *Kitāb ul-Jihād;* Ibn Hibbān. See Imām al-Albānī, *at-Ta'līq ar-Raghīb,* vol.3, p.213.

Chapter 15

The Yemeni government suggest that Umar Farouk travelled to the Shabwah Province of Yemen where he met al-Qā'idah elements before leaving the country. Al-'Awlakī stated in an Arabic interview,[2] with Yemeni al-Qā'idah members, regarding the young Nigerian man Umar Farouk AbdulMutallab and his attempted suicide bombing of an American plane on December 25 2009:

> This operation achieved goals for the Mujāhideen and it is an operation considered a reaction to the Americans. This operation clarified the deficiency within the American security apparatus, be it in intelligence or security. American airports spend more than forty million dollars yet the Mujāhid 'Umar Farouk was able to surpass these security systems. - Then 'Awlakī states:-
> So the operation achieved tremendous goals even though not one person was killed... in regards to the brother 'Umar Farouk then he is also of my students and I am honoured that the likes of 'Umar Farouk are of my students and I support what he did.

It appears that al-'Awlakī from this instance began to believe his own hype, considering himself as one who has "students" and the like. Then 'Awlakī states, in feigning scholarship:

> As for the combatant then he is the one who brandishes weapons even if it is a woman, while the non-combatants are those who do not participate in warfare. As for the American people then collectively they are participants because they are the ones who selected this administration and fund this war. In these elections, and the last one, there were other choices for the American

---

[1] Bukhārī, *hadīth* no.2620 and Muslim, *hadīth* no.1003; See *Sharh us-Sunnah*, vol.13, p.13, *Kitāb al-Birr wa's-Silah, Bāb Silat al-Wālid al-Mushrik*.
[2] The interview conducted in Arabic, and available on Youtube, was accessed by us on Thursday 4th November 2010. At this time, 'Awlakī's lectures are still accessible on Youtube despite there being talk in early November 2010 about 'Awlakī's lectures being removed from Youtube as per the request of certain elements with the American and British governments.

public who did not want war yet such candidates only gained a very few votes. But before we speak about anything we have to look at the issue from the Sharī'ah viewpoint as this is what decides the issue and whether it is permissible or not.

Let us deal with this suggestion of 'Awlakī that the: **"American people collectively are participants because they are the ones who selected the US administration and fund this war."** Here 'Awlakī suggests that American citizens become enemy combatants on the mere basis of voting for a new administration, yet Islām teaches that it is not permitted to kill non-Muslims who are non-hostile, let alone Muslims! How does casting a vote, largely on acount of issues related to education, health care, economics etc, render a person a combatant? Also, how many of these 'voting-combatants of war' were women or old people? Many of the people voting have no idea where their monies are going let alone be deemed as complicit in a war wherein they also become combatants of war?! Is al-'Awlakī not aware that if most people had the choice whether to pay taxes or not that many, if not most, would refuse to pay taxes? It's actually only the threat of severe penalties that persuade many U.S citizens to pay taxes. Therefore, if many, many Americans wish not to pay taxes, how on this earth can one be considered a combatant of war? Is al-'Awlakī even aware that there that has been a pending bill for many years in the U.S Congress called the 'Peace Tax Fund Bill'?[1] Is it the tax-paying American's fault that this bill has not been passed?

Moreover, what about the Muslims who have to pay taxes in America? Are they also fair game for target according to 'Awlakī? Furthermore, if one is "funding" a war does this mean that one is equivalent to one who is giving direct strategic support in Islamic fiqh? Should we forsake the rules of engagement, which were laid down by Allāh's Messenger and resort to 'Awlakī's new-age definition of

---

[1] See www.peacetaxfund.org and also: http://www.cpti.ws/.

'combatant'? Now who's ruling by other than what Allāh has revealed?! Refer to the chapter on the prohibition on killing civilians. Then 'Awlakī states:

> If the heroic brother 'Umar Farouk was able to target hundreds of soldiers then this would be terrific, however we are speaking about the realities of the battlefield. If Allāh's Messenger was able to fight in the daytime he would of, but there were some instances wherein he sent squadrons to fight at night and due to the dark, women and children were killed. The Companions returned and sought explanation about this from the Prophet and he replied: "they are from them". Meaning: they take the same hukm as their fathers, so the Prophet permitted this operation. Also we can justify this via reference to the event mentioned in the Sīrah when Thaqīf fortified behind Tā'if and Allāh's Messenger attacked them with catapults and these catapults do not differentiate between men, women or children, so this is the reality of the battlefield. America today is the one who has weapons which are able to differentiate, specific weapons, and if they wanted to distinguish targets they would do that, yet with this they target weddings, funerals, families and kill many women and children... this shows that the Americans deliberately intend to kill women and children.

The justifications that al-'Awlakī mentions here have been addressed prior within this study and the fact that he has regurgitated them again is a further clear demonstration of what we have noted beforehand regarding his weak basis of deduction and inference and his lack of requisite Islamic knowledge.

CHAPTER 16

'AWLAKI INSINUATES THAT THE UK AND US IS DAR UL-HARB AND THEREFORE MUSLIMS CAN EXTRACT AL-FAY' FROM THESE LANDS, BUT NOT GHANIMAH!!?

The Prophet ﷺ rented some armour from Safwān ibn 'Umayyah, who was a disbeliever, and then returned the armour back to Safwān after the fighting. Safwān ibn 'Umayyah narrated from the Messenger of Allāh ﷺ that he loaned some armour from Safwān on the Day of the battle of Hunayn. Safwān said *"Are you taking them by force O Muhammad?"* meaning: do you take this armour from me by force without thinking to return to me? The Prophet Muhammad ﷺ said: *"No, this is a loan with a guarantee of their return."* Meaning: I have borrowed these things from you and it is guaranteed that I will return them to you. The Messenger of Allāh ﷺ then fought in the battle of Hunayn. When the mushrikīn were defeated, the armour of Safwān was collected. Some of the armour was lost. The Messenger of Allāh ﷺ said to Safwān: *"We have lost some armour from the armour we loaned from you. Should we pay compensation to you?"* What did Safwān, who was not even Muslim, say about this? He said *"No. For I have in my heart today what I did not have that day. Today O Messenger of Allāh I want to accept Islām!"*[1]

Contemplate. This is what encourages people to accept Islām, this was during the end of the Battle of Hunayn, the Prophet ﷺ borrowed

---

[1] Sahīh, reported by Ahmad and Abu Dāwud.

something from Safwān and then returned it to him; the Prophet ﷺ did not say: **"This is permissible for me for me to take now!"** Rather, he returned the things to Safwān. So when Safwān said *"Are you taking them by force O Muhammad?"* the Prophet ﷺ did not say: **"Yes, by force, I use force over you now!"** Rather, he said: *"this is a loan with a guarantee of their return,"* and when the Prophet ﷺ lost something from it he guaranteed its compensation. Shaykh AbdulMālik ar-Ramadānī al-Jazā'irī stated about this:

> This is being conscious of Allāh with regards to the people's rights and their money and this made the man enter into the *dīn* of Allāh and be assured of it. Firstly, the Messenger of Allāh ﷺ loaned some armour as a trust and then later gave Safwān some of the spoils of Hunayn as has been authenticated in the narration from Imām Muslim. Secondly, Safwān was a disbeliever when the Messenger of Allāh ﷺ loaned the armour from him. Abū Dāwud said **"It was loaned before he became Muslim, and then he became Muslim."** Thirdly, there is no doubt that this was after the legislated fighting, as he was in the battle of Hunayn before the victory over Makkah. Therefore, it is incumbent on the Muslims to warn against all those who steal and take (without right) money from other people in that country (Britain). It is harām and such a person who consumes it has consumed nothing but fire for which he/she will be asked about on the Day of Judgement. People's wealth is respected and it is not permissible for anyone to take it, just as you warn against bombings, being associated with them and rejoicing when they happen. None of this is permissible at all in any shape whatsoever! How can a person unjustly take the money of those who have made good his residence? All of that is not permissible. How can they bomb illegally and indiscriminately? Allāh says,

﴿ وَلَا تَزِرُ وَازِرَةٌ وِزْرَ أُخْرَىٰ ﴾

Chapter 16

"And no bearer of burdens will bear the burden of another…"
{Fātir (35): 18}

How can you punish for a crime of some of them, it is mentioned in the *Sahīhayn* that an ant bit one of the Prophets of Allāh, so the Prophet punished the ant by burning the entire ants nest. Allāh admonished this Prophet for the burning of a whole ant's nest due to one ant. Contemplate! This is with ants and it is not permissible to transgress except against one who transgresses you.[1]

We seek refuge in Allāh from oppression and from the darkness of this uncouth innovation that those people have fallen into and this is not from jihād in the path of Allah at all! If you want to do jihad, guide the people to the *dīn* in that country (Britain), may Allāh bless you. The people are in need to know this *dīn* so that they will enter into it in multitudes because this *dīn* is the truth and is perfect, ensuring people a righteous worldly life and ensuring them the Hereafter. The Prophet ﷺ advised 'Alī ibn Abī Tālib during a battle at Khaybar: *"Do not fight them, advance with ease and gentleness until you have informed them of what Allāh has obligated upon them from the obligations of Islām. I swear by He in Whose Hand is my soul, if Allāh guides a person by you it is better for you than the red she-camel"* (meaning: a great reward). Contemplate upon this! Narrated in Bukhārī and Muslim. The foundation of jihād is to guide the people, this is jihād. Its foundation is *da'wah* and guiding the people and as for fighting, as has been mentioned beforehand, it has an importance in the *dīn* for defending the weak and oppressed in the face of those who stand in the face of the *da'wah*.[2]

---

[1] In the version of Bukhārī, it is mentioned that Allāh rebuked this particular Prophet ﷺ by saying: *"Why did you burn the entire ants nest when only one ant bit you, and when these ants glorify Allāh?"*

[2] The quote from Shaykh AbdulMālik ar-Ramadānī is from a lecture given at Masjid Ibn Taymiyyah (Brixton Mosque, London) on Sunday 21 August 2005 CE. The

'Awlakī in his "explanation" of Ibn an-Nahhās' book *Mashāri' ul-Ashwāq ilā Masāri' il-'Ushshāq*, CD 13, Track 3, states when answering a question from someone in the audience about whether this country (UK) is Dār ul-Harb and if Ghanīmah can therefore be taken from it:

> The second issue: taking Ghanīmah from Dār ul-Harb and whether these areas would be classified as Dār ul-Harb. I think that for us the issue should be beyond having second thoughts on whether this is Dār ul-Harb or not. I don't think there's even time for us to discuss the evidences for that. It's an issue which is beyond discussion, it should be clear and it should be common knowledge and the straw that broke the camel's back is 'Irāq, but that's just a straw. **So from a fiqh point of view, from a fiqh point of view, there is no issue here with the legality of taking Ghanā'im, from a strictly Sharī'ah point of view.** However, that statement needs to be studied from a fiqh point of view and a strategic point of view.

So here 'Awlakī has given a ruling about the UK and US being Dār ul-Harb, albeit by allusion, and that according to him: **"there is no issue here with the legality of taking Ghanā'im, from a strictly Sharī'ah point of view"**. Then 'Awlakī continues by saying however that: **"…only a Jama'ah can take a decision in these areas."** Hereby negating any role of the Muslim leaders at all and then deferring the rules and regulations on this to takfīrī-jihādī ideologues!? Then 'Awlakī says:

> **All of such money needs to be dealt with as Fay' and not Ghanīmah**,[1] it should be dealt as if it is Fay' and not Ghanīmah. Therefore, none of it goes to the individual, the entire amount goes to the Jamā'ah, and that's also a safety-valve to make sure

---

lecture was based on Shaykh AbdulMālik's book *Takhlīs al-'Ibād min Wahshiyyati Abi'l-Qatād* (Jeddah: Maktabah al-Asālah al-Athāriyyah, 1422 AH).

[1] Meaning: the money which is "taken", by whatever means however insinuating criminal means while in the West.

that people are not gonna start doing things for their own personal gain and benefit![1] And that is fasad! And also from a fiqh point of view it looks like Fay'! **There's no fighting involved so how can it be Ghanīmah?**[2] How can a person take from a fifth of it or a half of it or whatever **if there's no fighting involved**? So it should be dealt with as Fay' and not Ghanīmah. And when it is Fay' all of it goes to the Jamā'ah and then it's up to the discretion of the 'Amīr to give the concerned individuals part of it as a pay for their effort, if they have gone through some risk because there could be some risk and they could end up paying a hefty price for it so they need to be compensated for that – but that's up to the discretion of the 'Amīr.

Mashā'Allāh! 'Awlakī wraps up his *bātil* by making out that it is a mere fiqh ruling! Due to this "fiqh ruling" of al-'Awlakī some of the Muslim youth in South London have performed armed robberies of security vans which transport money and these brothers have narrated to us that they justified these robberies based on what Anwar al-'Awlakī said! Firstly, *al-Fay'* (common booty for all Muslims to benefit from) is, as stated by Imām Ibn Kathīr ؆ in his *Tafsīr*,

...all wealth and property taken from the kuffār without fighting (them to assume ownership of it).[3]

Hence, it is only extracted when the Muslims have successfully conquered a land and the conquered peoples have accepted the arrangement! This can definitely not be applied to the UK as there is no conquest whatsoever by any armies and no recognition that *al-Fay'* can be taken by any Muslim army. Imām Abū 'Ubayd al-Qāsim ibn as-

---

[1] This Robin Hood type of attitude is supposed to give some sort of nobility to "taking" such monies.
[2] Meaning then: that the money can just be taken in any which way, and without fighting the owners of such money, just merely take it!
[3] Ibn Katheer, *Tafsīr*, vol.4, p.396 – tafsīr of the seventh *ayah* of *Sūrat ul-Hashr*.

Chapter 16

Sallām, 162-224 AH/774-836 CE ﷺ, stated in *Kitāb ul-Amwāl* [The Book of Revenue], with the translation of Professor Nyazee, that:

أول ما نبدأ به من ذكر الأموال ما كان منها لرسول الله ﷺ خالصاً دون الناس. وذلك ثلاثة أموال.

(أولها) ما أفاء الله على رسوله من المشركين، مما لم يوجف المسلمون عليه بخيل ولا ركاب. وهي فدك، وأموال بني النضير، فإنهم صالحوا رسول الله ﷺ على أموالهم وأرضيهم، بلا قتال كان منهم، ولا سفر تجشمه المسلمون إليهم.

> The first types of wealth (amwāl) we begin with are those that are exclusively for the Messenger of God (pbuh) and not for the community. These amwāl are of three types:
> First is fay' that God has granted to His Messenger from the (wealth of) idolaters, and for the acquisition of which the Muslim army has not been mobilized. It includes Fadak and the wealth of Banū al-Nadīr as they made a peace settlement with the Messenger of God (pbuh), upon their wealth and lands, without engaging in combat and without (military) manoeuvres that would necessitate the mobilization of the Muslim army against them.[1]

Imām Abū 'Ubayd ﷺ also stated:

> The wealth of fay' is that which includes all kinds of wealth of the dhimmīs **that they have agreed upon by way of settlement.**[2]

---

[1] Abū 'Ubayd al-Qāsim ibn Sallām, *Kitāb al-Amwāl* [The Book of Revenue] (Reading, UK: Garnet Publishing, 2003, translated by Professor Imran Ahsan Khan Nyazee), p.7; see also Arabic text critically edited and studied by Dr Muhammad 'Ammārah (Cairo: Dār ush-Shurūq, 1409 AH/1989 CE) p.75.
[2] Ibid., p.15

So even with *al-Fay'* there has to be an agreement and acknowledgement of this from the kuffār! Then Imām Abū 'Ubayd ؓ also relays, as per the translation of Professor Nyazee:

> Isḥāq ibn 'Īsā related to me from Sufyān ibn 'Uyayna from Ibn Abī Nujayh from Mujāhid, who said:
>
> 369_عن مجاهد قال: أيما مدينة افتتحت عنوة فأسلم أهلها قبل أن يقسموا فهم أحرار، وأموالهم فيء للمسلمين.
>
> **Whenever a city is conquered by the force of arms, and its residents embrace Islām before the decision for division, they are free persons, but their wealth is fay' for the Muslims.**[1]

These statements from Imām Abū 'Ubayd were fully relayed and corroborated by his student Humayd ibn Zanjawayh (d. 251 AH/865 CE) in his *Kitāb ul-Amwāl* which has been critically edited and studied by Dr Shākir Zayb Fayyāḍh (Riyadh: King Faisal Complex, 1306 AH/1986 CE), vol.1, p.90.

Therefore, it is established that *al-Fay'* is taken when Muslims successfully conquer a place, not that it can be "taken", as 'Awlakī would have us think, by Muslims residing in non-Muslim lands?! Secondly, 'Awlakī appears to have a romantic notion of the fiqh of jihād and his hasty manhaj has shaped his reading of the fiqh. Hence al-'Awlakī, due to his emotive reading of Sīrah, transmits this onto the current situation and as a result he actually thinks that the Muslims today are in the same situation as the *Salaf* when they conquered lands and extracted *Ghanīmah* and *al-Fay'*.

Thirdly, even if we say that these lands are Dār ul-Harb, al-'Awlakī has totally bypassed what classical scholars such as Ibn Qudāmah al-Maqdisī ؓ stated in *al-Mughnī* regarding Muslims who enter Dār ul-Harb. Ibn an-Nahhās in his book *Mashāri' ul-Ashwāq ilā Masāri' il-'Ushshāq* (!!!) - in the edit of Idrīs Muhammad 'Ali and Muhammad

---

[1] Ibid., p.138, no.369; see Arabic version of text critically edited and studied by Dr Muhammad 'Ammārah (Cairo: Dār ush-Shurūq, 1409 AH/1989 CE), p.223.

Chapter 16

Khālid Istanbūlī, pp.1060-1062 - made reference to Ibn Qudāmah ؒ and what he said in *al-Mughnī* as follows: [1]

وأما خيانتهم فمحرمة؛ لأنهم إنما أعطوه الأمان مشروطاً بتركه خيانتهم، وأمنه إياهم من نفسه، وإن لم يكن ذلك مذكوراً في اللفظ، فهو معلوم في المعنى، ولذلك من جاءنا منهم بأمان فخاننا كان ناقضاً لعهده. فإذا ثبت هذا لم تحل خيانتهم لأنه غدر ولا يصلح في ديننا الغدر. وقد قال النبي ﷺ: «المسلمون عند شروطهم» فإن خانهم أو سرق منهم، أو اقترض شيئاً، وجب عليه رد ما أخذ.

...and as for betraying them, then it is harām (prohibited), because they gave him the covenant of safety and security on the condition that he will neither betray them nor harm them, and even if this was not written therein as it is known contextually. Thus, whoever gained a covenant of safety and security into our countries and betrayed us then it is as if he withdrew his covenant. And thus, if this was true, then it is prohibited to betray them, because our religion prohibits betrayal. In this respect, the Prophet ﷺ said:

((المسلمون عند شروطهم))

"...the Muslims must stick to their conditions."[2]

Ibn Qudāmah here was himself commenting on what was stated by al-Khirqī al-Hanbalī ؒ when al-Khirqī said:

---

[1] In *Kitāb ul-Jihād, Mas'alat Man Dakhala Ard ul-'Aduw bi-Amān* [The Issue of Entering the Land of the Enemy with an Agreement/Covenant of Safety and Security].

[2] *Hasan Sahīh*; reported by Abū Dāwūd (3594) from Abū Hurayrah; at-Tirmidhī (1352) from 'Amr Ibn 'Awf al-Muzanī; while al-Bukhārī reported it *ta'līqan* (without a chain of narrators), and so in case one betrays them, steals from them, or borrows anything, then he should give back what he took. See *al-Mughnī*, vol.10, p.507.

جاء في متن الخرقي الحنبلي (من دخل أرض العدو لم يخنهم).

It is found in the text of al-Khirqī al-Hanbalī: "Whoever enters the land of the enemy should not betray them (betray the covenant or agreement with them)."

In Sahīh ul-Bukhārī the long hadīth of the treaty of Hudaybiyah mentions that al-Mughīrah ibn Shu'bah ﷺ knew some people during Jāhilliyah that used to make alcohol and get drunk, and Mughīrah killed them and took their money. Mughīrah was thinking about accepting Islām after he had taken the money from these people, then he went to the Messenger of Allāh informing him that he wanted to be a Muslim and that he had with him the money from those people. What did the Messenger of Allāh ﷺ say to him? He said ﷺ:

((أما الإسلام فأقبل، وأما المال فلست منه في شيء)).

"As for your Islām, I accept it and as for the money then I have nothing to do with it."

Meaning: I accept your Islām but as for the money that you acquired from the people without right I have nothing to do with it. Also there was no jihād at that time so what do those people who make permissible robbing and stealing other people's money say? This was after the jihād and Allāh's Messenger ﷺ is not a Messenger of treachery. If such wealth was allowed to keep then Allāh's Messenger ﷺ would have accepted it with no problem. Ibn Hajar stated in regards to this hadīth in *Fath ul-Bārī*:

قوله: (وأما المال فلست منه في شيء) أي لا أتعرض له لكونه أخذه غدرا. ويستفاد منه: أنه لا يحل أخذ أموال الكفار في حال الأمن غدراً؛ لأن الرفقة يصطحبون على الأمانة، والأمانة تؤدى إلى أهلها مسلما كان أو كافرا، وأن أموال الكفار إنما تحل بالمحاربة والمغالبة، ولعل النبي ﷺ ترك المال في يده، لإمكان أن يسلم قومه فيرد إليهم أموالهم.

Chapter 16

His saying (ﷺ): *"As for the wealth then I have nothing to do with it whatsoever"* it means: I have no part of it as it was taken via betrayal and treachery.

The benefit from this is that it is not permissible to take wealth and property (Amwāl) from the kuffār treacherously when they have trusted you during a period of safety and security, and trusts should be fulfilled whether the person is a Muslim or a disbeliever. The wealth and property (Amwāl) of the kuffār is only permissible to take through warfare or combat. Maybe the Prophet ﷺ left the wealth that was in his (Mughīrah's hand) because of the possibility of his people embracing Islām and then their wealth would have to be returned to them.[1]

Imām Abū Bakr Muhammad bin Ibrāheem Ibn ul-Mundhir an-Naysābūrī (d. 318 AH) stated in *al-Awsat fi's-Sunan wa'l-Ijmā' wa'l-Ikhtilāf* that Imāms ash-Shāfi'ī, al-Awzā'ī and Ahmad viewed it impermissible for a Muslim to betray the people of Dār ul-Harb when the Muslim enters their land with a covenant of safety and security.[2] Al-Awzā'ī used the hadīth of al-Mughīrah as a proof for this view. Ibn ul-Mundhir stated:

إذا دخل الرجل دار الحرب بأمان فهو آمن بأمانهم، وهم آمنون بأمانة، ولا يجوز له أن يغدر بهم، ولا يخوفهم، ولا يغتالهم، فإن أخذ منهم شيئاً، فعليه رده إليهم، فإن أخرج منه شيء إلى دار الإسلام وجب رد ذلك إليهم، وليس لمسلم أن يشتري ذلك ولا يتلفه، لأنه مال له أمان.

---

[1] Ibn Hajar al-'Asqalānī, *Fath ul-Bārī: Sharh Sahīh ul-Bukhārī* (Beirut: Dār ul-Kutub al-'Ilmiyyah, 3rd Edn., 1421 AH/2000 CE, ed. Muhammad Fu'ād 'AbdulBāqī), *Kitāb ush-Shurūt* [The Book of Conditions], vol.6, p.428.

[2] Ibn ul-Mundhir however relays, as does Ibn ul-Munāsif in *Kitāb ul-Injād fī Abwāb il-Jihād*, that Imām Abū Hanīfah allowed betrayal, yet we have not come across this view within Hanafī fiqh books.

If a (Muslim) man enters Dār ul-Harb with a covenant of security then he is safe from them based on their agreement of security and they are also safe from him. Thus, it is not allowed for him to betray them, cause fear to them or kill them. If he takes anything from them he has to return it back to them and if he takes anything with him back to Dār ul-Islām he has to give it back. A Muslim should neither purchase such (taken) property nor destroy it because the wealth and property has a trust.[1]

Abū Yahyā Zakariyyah bin Muhammad al-Ansārī ash-Shāfi'ī (823-926 AH/1420-1520 CE) stated in *al-Asnā ul-Matālib*:

The wealth of the people of Harb (war) are prohibited to whoever from us has granted them safety and security. If a Muslim enters their abodes with a covenant of safety and security and borrows anything from them, or steals anything from them, and then returns to our land he has to return what he took; as he cannot dishonour them if he entered their lands with an agreement of safety and security.

As-Sarkhasī ؒ states in his *Sharh* of *Kitāb as-Siyar al-Kabīr* of Muhammad bin al-Hasan ؒ:

Muhammad said: "Chapter: what is classified as an Amān for those who enter Dār ul-Harb wa'l-Asrā and what is not an Amān:

If a group of Muslims go to the gate-keepers of Ahl ul-Harb and say to them 'we are Messengers of the Khalīfah' and produce a document which resembles an official document from the Khalīfah, or if they do not even produce any documentation, then this is them deceiving the Mushrikīn. If Ahl ul-Harb say to this Muslim group: 'Enter' and they enter Dār ul-Harb then it is

---

[1] Imām Abū Bakr Muhammad bin Ibrāhīm Ibn ul-Mundhir an-Naysābūrī, *al-Awsat fi's-Sunan wa'l-Ijmā' wa'l-Ikhtilāf* (Riyadh, KSA: Dār Tayyibah, 1420 AH/1999 CE, ed. Dr Abū Hammād Sagheer Ahmad bin Muhammad Hanīf), vol.11, p.292.

not permissible for them to kill any Ahl ul-Harb or take any wealth from them so long as they are within their land."

(As-Sarkhasī says): Because what they (the Muslims) have manifested to them (Ahl ul-Harb) if it is true then they have an Amān from Ahl ul-Harb and Ahl ul-Harb also have an Amān from them so it is not permitted to dishonour them in anything. This is the ruling for Messengers (of the Khalīfah) if they enter their lands as we have explained.[1]

Abu'l-Hasan 'Ali bin Abī Bakr bin 'AbdulJalīl al-Marghīyānī (511-593 AH/1118-1197 CE)[2] stated in *al-Hidāyah: Sharh ul-Bidāyah al-Mubtadi'*, p.134:

وإذا دخل المسلم دار الحرب تاجرا فلا يحل له أن يتعرض لشيء من أموالهم ولا من دمائهم لأنه ضمن أن لا يتعرض لهم بالاستئمان فالتعرض بعد ذلك يكون غدرا، والغدر حرام.

If a Muslim enters Dār ul-Harb as a trader, then he is like a Muslim who is Musta'min in Dār ul-Harb, and it is therefore not permissible for him to dishonour them in anything in terms of their wealth and blood as he is within Isti'mān which necessitates he does not dishonour them. If he dishonours them after this then this is betrayal and betrayal is harām.[3]

Our Shaykh, Mashhūr Hasan *(hafidhahullāh)* thus states:

---

[1] See Shaykh Faisal Jāsim, *Kashf ush-Shubuhāt fī Masā'il al-'Ahd wa'l-Jihād* (Kuwait: Jam'iyyah Ihyā at-Turāth al-Islāmī, 1425 AH/2004 CE, 4th Edn.), pp.54- 55. The book has intros by Shaykh Sālih bin 'Abdullāh bin Humayd (Head of the Saudi Shūrā Council and Imām of Masjid ul-Haram in Makkah), Shaykh, Dr Sālih as-Sadlān and Shaykh, Dr Fayhān bin Shālī al-Mutayrī.

[2] The great Hanafī jurist, was born at Marghiyān in the vicinity of Farghana in Present Day Uzbekistan. He studied with Najmuddīn Abū Hafs 'Umar an-Nasafī, his son Abu'l-Layth Ahmad bin 'Umar an-Nasafī and other eminent teachers, and excelled in Hadīth, Tafsīr, Fiqh and other studies.

[3] *Kitāb us-Siyar, Bāb ul-Musta'min.*

Based upon this it becomes clear to us the accuracy of what has been acknowledged by the *'Ulamā* of our era in regards to the prohibition of wreaking havoc, hijacking airplanes and killing non-Muslims in their lands which is committed by some young Muslims who enter those lands with Amān (safe-passage and security),[1] in the form of entry-visas. For this is an example of betrayal and treachery, the prohibition is intensified when it is ascribed to the Sharī'ah and considered as being from "Jihād", as they claim![2]

What ever happened to 'Awlakī's views (!!!) aired in a documentary on Ramadān in 2001/02:

I think that in general Islām is presented in a negative way, I mean there's always this association between Islām and terrorism when that is not true at all, **I mean Islām is a religion of peace**[3]!?

---

[1] And if they are Mu'āhadīn then the opposition to the *Sharī'ah* would be from two angles, like a person who steals pork and eats it!
[2] From the edit of Shaykh Muhammad bin Zakariyyā Abū Ghāzī and our Shaykh Mashhūr Hasan Āl Salmān to Imām al-Mujtahid Abū 'Abdullāh Muhammad bin 'Īsā bin Muhammad bin Asbagh al-Azdī al-Qurtubī (aka Ibn Munāsif), *Kitāb ul-Injād fī Abwāb il-Jihād* (Beirut: Mu'assasah ar-Rayān, 1425 AH/2005 CE), vol.1, pp.63-81.
[3] See 2:45 here: http://www.youtube.com/watch?v=3BgG2ZLm2M8.

CHAPTER 17

CRITIQUE OF AWLAKI'S 2011 'FATWA' ON 'THE RULING ON DISPOSSESSING THE DISBELIEVER'S WEALTH IN DAR UL-HARB'

The 'fatwa' is dated 12 Safar 1432 AH corresponding to Monday 17 January 2011 CE and is available online from a variety of websites. It was originally published in the English language al-Qā'idah magazine *'Inspire'*.[1] It is interesting as al-'Awlakī has risen to the occasion to give his own "ruling" hereby delving into a realm which is strictly for scholars, furthermore 'Awlakī is giving a "ruling" on a very serious issue which no doubt needs qualified scholarship to discuss. Within the 'fatwa' it is hard to decipher whether al-'Awlakī actually authored it due to the amount of spelling mistakes and so forth yet if the fatwa is not Awlakī's he has neither renounced nor rejected the "ruling". If the "ruling" was actually written by Samir bin Zafar Khan or others and then was subsequently "approved" by Anwar al-'Awlakī then this is also not made clear. Yet as the "ruling" carries the name of "Shaykh Anwar al-'Awlakī" on it we will regard 'Awlakī as the author and refer to him as such.

---

[1] This professionally designed and colourful Online magazine is the work of the former moderator of the old 'InshAllāh Shaheed' Jihādi website, Samir bin Zafar Khan, a US citizen from Charlotte, North Carolina and New York who is now present in Yemen. The moderator himself is a classic example of an armchair Jihādi activist and IT geek who has not participated in even adequately defending himself on Western streets let alone on any sort of battlefield. He is a partisan follower of Anwar al-'Awlakī.

Chapter 17

One of the main errors in citation that can be observed in 'Awlakī's "ruling" is that when he makes reference to Arabic sources he provides neither page numbers nor volume numbers within the entire 16 page English "ruling". This would be understandable if 'Awlakī was quoting from mere booklets but 'Awlakī is quoting from voluminous works which number into tens of volumes! So for example, 'Awlakī's "ruling" refers to:

- *Fath ul-Qadīr* – by Imām Kamāluddīn Muhammad bin 'AbdulWāhid as-Sīwāsī as-Sikandarī aka "Ibn ul-Hamām" (d. 861 AH) which is in 10 volumes, ed. 'AbdurRazzāq Ghālib al-Mahdī (Beirut: Dār ul-Kutub al-'Ilmiyyah, 1424 AH/2003 CE).
- *Tuhfat ul-Muhtāj fī Sharh il-Minhāj* – by Ibn Hajar al-Haytamī which is 10 volumes (Dār Ihyā ut-Turāth al-'Arabī Print, n.d.).
- *Al-Minhāj* – by Imām an-Nawawī which is 12 volumes.
- *Fatāwā al-Subkī fī Furū' Fiqh ish-Shāfi'ī* – by Taqiuddīn Abu'l-Hasan 'Ali bin 'AbdulKāfī as-Subkī which is 2 volumes, ed. Muhammad 'AbduSalām Shahīn (Dār ul-Kutub al-'Ilmiyyah Print). Also printed by Dār ul-Jīl and Dār ul-Ma'rifah.
- *Al-Furū'* – by Abū 'Abdullāh Muhammad bin Muflih bin Muhammad bin Muflih al-Maqdisī ar-Rāmīnī as-Sālihī (d. 763 AH) which is 12 volumes, ed. Dr 'Abdullāh bin 'AbdulMuhsin at-Turkī (Beirut: Mu'assasat ur-Risālah, 1424 AH/2003 CE, First Edn.).

The titles of the above works are given and rulings are claimed to be deduced from what is found in these books yet there is no adequate citation of the sources, no page or volume numbers whatsoever!

Furthermore, it is interesting to see how 'Awlakī's "ruling" makes no reference whatsoever to Ibn an-Nahhās ﷺ and his magnum opus on jihād fiqh *Mashāri' ul-Ashwāq ilā Masāri ul-'Ushshāq (fī'l-Jihād wa*

Faḍā'ilihi). After 'Awlakī attained notoriety for partially "explaining" the abridged version of Ibn an-Nahhās' book in the form of 'Awlakī's audio series entitled '*The Story of Ibn al-Akwa (aka Book of Jihād by Ibn an-Nahhās)*' it now appears that for expediency 'Awlakī has now put that book back on the shelf. 'Awlakī has now opted for other sources due to the reality that Ibn an-Nahhās' book neither supports nor condones 'Awlakī's contorted and corrupt fiqh. We mentioned prior that Ibn an-Nahhās' complete book mentions for example on page 1023 of the Idrīs and Istanbūlī edit that:

> **It is prohibited to kill women and children if they do not fight according to ash-Shāfi'ī, Mālik, Ahmad and Abū Hanīfah. If they fight (against the Muslim armies however) then they are to be killed (as they are combatants).**

Also Ibn an-Nahhās states on p.558 (of Idrīs and Istanbūlī edit) that Abū 'Abdullāh al-Qurtubī said in his Tafsīr:

> The 'Ulamā have differed over a man making iqtihām during warfare against the enemy ranks by himself. Al-Qāsim bin Mukhaymarah, al-Qāsim bin Muhammad and 'AbdulMalik from our 'Ulamā say: "there is no problem in a man by himself going against a large army if he has strength and a pure intention for Allāh. **If he does not have strength then that is from throwing oneself into destruction.**"

Then Ibn an-Nahhās relays (p.559) that Ibn Khuwayzmindād ؓ[1] said:

> As for a man going against a hundred or against a grouping of soldiers or a group of thieves, bandits (Muhāribīn) **or Khawārij** then that is in two cases: if he knows and thinks that it is likely that he will kill those he is facing and will be saved (from death) then that is good; likewise if he knows and thinks that it is likely

---

[1] Abū 'Abdullāh Muhammad bin Ahmad bin 'Abdullāh bin Khuwayzmindād, the Imām and scholar, his Shaykh was al-Abharī who died in 395 AH.

Chapter 17

he will be killed yet be able to harm or affect them so as to benefit the Muslims – then that is allowed also.[1]

Ibn an-Nahhās relays (p.560) that Muhammad bin al-Hasan said:
If a lone man goes against a thousand men from the Mushrikīn and he is by himself there is no problem in that if he is assured of escape or harming the enemy. **If this is not the case then that is disliked (Makrūh) because he has placed himself into destruction without any benefit for the Muslims.**[2]

Hence we find throughout this recent "ruling" 'Awlakī makes not a single reference to Ibn Nahhās' book whatsoever, most likely due to the fact that our online version of our critique of 'Awlakī in 2009-2010 exposed this *tadlīs* on the part of al-'Awlakī and his utter misuse of Ibn Nahhās.

Going back to the core of this "ruling" then 'Awlakī defines al-Fay as being merely **"...what is taken from the disbelievers without fighting"**. Yet al-Fay' is much more than this as we mentioned prior:

The first types of wealth (amwāl) we begin with are those that are exclusively for the Messenger of God (pbuh) and not for the community. These amwāl are of three types:

First is fay' that God has granted to His Messenger from the (wealth of) idolaters, and for the acquisition of which the Muslim army has not been mobilized. It includes Fadak and the wealth of Banū al-Nadīr as they made a peace settlement with the Messenger of God (pbuh), upon their wealth and lands, without engaging in combat and without (military) manoeuvres that would necessitate the mobilization of the Muslim army against them.[3]

---

[1] Tafsīr Qurtubī, vol.2, p.363-364.
[2] *Al-Jāmi' li-Ahkām wa'l-Hikam*, vol.2, p.364.
[3] Abū 'Ubayd al-Qāsim ibn Sallām, *Kitāb al-Amwāl* [The Book of Revenue] (Reading, UK: Garnet Publishing, 2003, translated by Professor Imran Ahsan Khan Nyazee), p.7;

Imām Abū 'Ubayd ﷺ also stated:
> The wealth of fay' is that which includes all kinds of wealth of the dhimmīs **that they have agreed upon by way of settlement.**[1]

So even with *al-Fay'* there has to be an agreement and acknowledgement of this from the kuffār! Then Imām Abū 'Ubayd ﷺ also relays, as per the translation of Professor Nyazee:
> **Ishāq ibn 'Īsā related to me from Sufyān ibn 'Uyayna from Ibn Abī Nujayh from Mujāhid, who said: "Whenever a city is conquered by the force of arms, and its residents embrace Islām before the decision for division, they are free persons, but their wealth is fay' for the Muslims."**[2]

So *al-Fay'* is only taken after a successful Muslim conquest of a land. Again, these statements from Imām Abū 'Ubayd were fully relayed and corroborated by his student Humayd ibn Zanjawayh (d. 251 AH/865 CE) in his *Kitāb ul-Amwāl*. Yet 'Awlakī within his quaint "ruling" poses a rhetorical question: **"Can ghanīmah and fai' be taken from the disbelievers in the West today?"** *Masha'Allāh,* nice question, but surely such a question is to be posed to scholars and not to the likes of "speakers" and "sermonizers" such as 'Awlakī. 'Awlakī then proceeds to deem all Muslim countries today as being under non-Islamic rule when he states:
> **First of all there is no Islamic leadership authorized to enter into covenants with the nations of disbelief in the present day. This is because the governments of the Muslim world have lost their legitimacy for many reasons, among them:**

---

see also Arabic text critically edited and studied by Dr Muhammad 'Ammārah (Cairo: Dār ush-Shurūq, 1409 AH/1989 CE) p.75.

[1] Ibid., p.15.

[2] Ibid., p.138, no.369; see Arabic version of text critically edited and studied by Dr Muhammad 'Ammārah (Cairo: Dār ush-Shurūq, 1409 AH/1989 CE), p.223.

- governance according to manmade laws
- taking the disbelievers as allies
- fighting the awliyā' of Allāh.

Therefore any agreements or treatise *{sic}* between the governments of the Muslim world and other parties are considered to be bātil (illegitimate).

'Awlakī then states:
> However, my conclusion on this matter is that Muslims are not bound by the covenants of citizenship and visa that exist between them and nations of dār al-harb. It is the consensus of our scholars that the property of the disbelievers in dār al-harb is halal for the Muslims and is a legitimate target for the mujahidin.

This is a recurring feature of Awlakī's jihād fiqh, that there is no Amān with disbelievers and this is another one of 'Awlakī's fragrant denials of what is mentioned in the works on the fiqh of jihād. Also, where is the "consensus" that al-'Awlakī is talking about and where have "our scholars" suggested such a stance? This view is clearly erroneous and totally opposes all of what has been stated on this issue by the classical scholars who 'Awlakī, in this latest "ruling", claims to utilise as a proof for his stance. 'Awlakī states:

> In the past, Muslim armies would march into the lands of the disbelievers and would then confiscate their wealth and distribute it according to the rules of shariah...

Wait a minute though, 'Awlakī has missed something out here: that the "Muslim armies" only did this when they successfully conquered a land! 'Awlakī continues: **"Today jihād is more clandestine and is performed by underground networks"**. Is it? Spoken like a true armchair activist! Please remind us upon which battlefield 'Awlakī has actually fought? 'Awlakī then states:

Chapter 17

> To the credit of our scholars, even these issues have been answered by them and are covered in our books of fiqh. So all praise is due to Allāh, we do not have to refer to many of the present day scholars who are either trying to appease the apostate governments of the Muslim world or are trying to appease the Jews and the Christians.

If this is the case why does 'Awlakī refuse to refer to these sources and books of fiqh? Who are the scholars that 'Awlakī is referring to? Why such insinuations? Why not just mention the names of the "present day scholars who are either trying to appease the apostate governments of the Muslim world" – in order to make it clear to the readers who to be aware of? 'Awlakī then gives his reasons as to why in this "ruling" he will be relying on scholars from the Hanafi madhhab:

> ...the Hanafi School was the official state madhab for the longest period in our history compared to other schools. It therefore covers issues relating to jihād in more detail because the foreign policy of the Islamic state was jihād in the path of Allāh.

What happened to Ibn an-Nahhās then?! Why has his work been dumped and trashed by 'Awlakī all of a sudden?! Moreover, this is a romantic account of the Ottoman Empire, who said that its foreign policy was "jihād in the path of Allāh"? Does this account for their promotion of Sufism within the Arab lands and fighting against the people of tawhīd and sunnah? Was this also from their "foreign policy"? This is a naive view.

'Awlakīs' Tadlīs

Now we come to the major example of tadlīs which 'Awlakī pulls within his so-called "ruling". 'Awlakī states:

> In al-Hidāyah by Imam al-Mirghanani it states: "If one or two individuals enter dar al-harb without the permission of the Imam and they take something, then it is not subjected to the one-fifth

rule." Here the author is stating that whatever is taken from the land of war by individuals and not by an army is not subjected to the regular rules of ghanīmah.

This is a clear misrepresentation of what al-Marghīnānī states in *al-Hidāyah*. Al-Marghīnānī actually states immediately after this, which 'Awlakī and his co-authors conveniently failed to mention:

> **The reason is that spoils are taken after conquest and overpowering and not through pilferage and theft, and the setting aside of a fifth is from the spoils.**[1]

'Awlakī consequently jumps the gun, as it were, and asserts that this means that because the wealth taken is not subject to the regulations of Ghanā'im it must therefore be something else. However, 'Awlakī neglects giving the full quote where 'sariqah' is explicitly mentioned. Also, because the individuals have 'taken' something this does not mean therefore that it was halāl for them to have done that. Lastly, 'Awlakī within his paper has skipped over the most important matter which is that the regulations of *al-Fay'* and Ghanā'im are only after a successful Muslim conquest of a land! Not for Muslim minorities living in non-Muslim countries while openly displaying peace with the non-Muslims. 'Awlakī then states:

> So if an individual takes wealth from the disbelievers in the land of war and he does not use force but takes it by means of theft or embezzlement, it is not considered ghanīmah according to the Hanafi School. So then what is it?

---

[1] See Burhān al-Dīn al-Farghānī al-Marghīnānī, *al-Hidāyah: The Guidance – A Translation of al-Hidāyah fī Sharh Bidāyat al-Mubtadi'*, A Classical Manual of Hanafi law, vol.2. Bristol, England: Amal Press, 2008, p.313. trans Imran Ahsan Nyazee. Also see the Arabic version printed by Maktabah al-Bushrā in Karachi, Pakistan, vol.4, p.244.

Chapter 17

This however insinuates that the Hanafi scholars have not deemed such wealth as "theft" and this is a blatant deception as we have seen from 'Awlakī's selective quoting from al-Marghīnānī. Furthermore, Imām Muhammad ash-Shaybānī, of the main students of Imām Abū Haneefah ﷺ, stated:

> If a Muslim enters Dār ul-Harb with an Amān then there is no problem in him taking from them **with their consent** in any shape or form.[1]

As for the Muslim who is Musta'min taking from the wealth of Ahl ul-Harb without their consent then Muhammad ash-Shaybānī ruled that such wealth should be returned back to their rightful owners as he has betrayed them and broke the right of the agreement/covenant and thus has to make tawbah.[2] Ibn ul-Hamām stated:

> **If a Muslim (in Dār ul-Harb) sells carrion or swine or gambles with the people in Dār ul-Harb and takes wealth as a result of these dealings then all of this is permissible according to Abū Hanīfah and Muhammad (ash-Shaybānī), Abū Yūsuf disagreed with them on this issue.**[3]

The Shāfi'ī scholars stated:

---

[1] Muhammad bin Ahmad bin Abī Sahl as-Sarakhsī (d. 390 AH), *Sharh us-Siyar al-Kabīr* (ash-Sharqiyyah: Matba'ah Sharikah al-I'lāmāt, 1972 CE), vol.4, p.1410.

[2] Ibid., vol.4, pp.1276, 1285, 1287, vol.5, p.1880; Imām 'Alāuddīn Abī Bakr bin Mas'ood al-Kāsānī al-Hanafī (d. 587 AH), *al-Bidā'i as-Sanāi' fī Tartīb ish-Sharā'i* (Beirut: Dār ul-Kitāb al-'Arabī), vol.7, p.133; 'AbdulGhani al-Ghunaymī ad-Dimishqī al-Maydānī al-Hanafī (d. 1298 AH), *al-Lubāb fī Sharh il-Kitāb* (Beirut: Dār ul-Hadīth Hims, 1399 AH, 4th Edition, ed. Shaykh Muhyuddīn 'AbdulHamīd), vol.4, p.135; Imām Kamāluddīn Muhammad bin 'AbdulWāhid bin 'AbdulHamīd bin Mas'ūd as-Sīwāsī as-Sikandarī, aka "Ibn ul-Hamām" (d. 681 AH), *Sharh Fath ul-Qadīr al-Hidāyah* (Dār Ihyāt ut-Turāth al-'Arabī, n.d.), vol.5, p.267.

[3] *Fath ul-Qadīr*, vol.6, p.177; *Sharh as-Siyar al-Kabīr*, vol.4, p.1493; Abū Bakr Muhammad as-Sarakhsī, *al-Mabsūt* (Beirut: Dār ul-Ma'rifah, 2nd Print, n.d.), vol.14, p.56.

If a Muslim enters Dār ul-Harb with an Amān and steals wealth and property form them (the people of Dār ul-Harb) or borrows money from them and returns back to Dār ul-Islām and then the one who owns the wealth comes to Dār ul-Islām with an Amān – it is obligatory for the Muslim to return back what he stole or borrowed [wajaba ala'l-Muslim radda mā sariqa aw iqtarida] because the Amān necessitates guaranteeing wealth on both sides; so he has to return it.[1]

Dr Ismā'īl Lutfī Fatānī stated in his Phd thesis *Ikhtilāf ud-Dārayn wa Atharahu fī Ahkām il-Munākahāt wa Mu'āmalāt*:

> The most accurate view is that of the majority of the jurists who say that it is not permissible for a Muslim or a Dhimmī who enters Dār ul-Harb with an Amān to deal with Ahl ul-Harb in a way which would be impermissible if conducted in Dār ul-Islām. If a Muslim does anything of this he has to give what he has taken back to its rightful owner...

Then Dr Ismā'īl Luftī highlights that whatever is halāl in Dār ul-Islām is likewise halāl in Dār ul-Harb; and whatever is harām in Dār ul-Islām is harām in Dār ul-Harb.[2] 'Awlakī then states in his "ruling":

> The Hanafi's {sic} stated that a Muslim is "permitted" to steal money from the disbelievers in dār al-harb but they didn't state that there is a reward in doing so.

Did they?! There is no text from the Hanafī jurists to this effect whatsoever, and in fact the opposite is found yet 'Awlakī purposefully left that out from the quote! The only thing which the Hanafī scholars have permitted is:

---

[1] Imām an-Nawawī, *al-Majmū': Sharh Muhadhhab ash-Shirāzī* (Jeddah, KSA: Maktabat ul-Irshad, n.d., ed Shaykh Muhammad Najīb al-Mutī'ī), vol.18, pp.326, 328.
[2] Dr Ismā'eel Lutfi Fatānī, *Ikhtilāf ud-Dārayn wa Atharahu fī Ahkām il-Munākahāt wa'l-Mu'āmalāt* (Cairo: Dār us-Salām, 1418 AH/1998 CE), p.394.

Chapter 17

- selling carrion to Ahl ul-Harb.
- selling swine to Ahl ul-Harb.
- gambling with Ahl ul-Harb.

And just because the Hanafīs allowed it does not mean that this is the sound, valid and accurate view in light of the evidences which have been discussed by the scholars. There is absolutely nothing about permitting stealing from Ahl ul-Harb within their lands, so why the games from 'Awlakī and his blind followers? 'Awlakī then states in his conclusion:

All of our scholars agree on the permissibility of taking away the wealth of the disbelievers in dār al-harb whether by means of force or by means of theft or deception.

Have they?! If 'Awlakī means by "our scholars" the scholars of the Takfīrī mavericks and Khawārij bandits then he is right in this. But if by "our scholars" 'Awlakī means the classical scholars and the Hanafī jurists of the past then he has clearly lied against the Imāms and *'Ulamā* of the Sunnah throughout history, none of whom have sanctioned such theft and robbery. 'Awlakī has not even relayed the views of the scholars from the other Madhāhib. Furthermore, 'Awlakī has blatantly left out important details which specifically mentioned theft within the books of the Hanafī jurists. He has not even adequately relayed the correct view from the Hanafī Madhhab let alone the views of the scholars. 'Awlakī then gives a suggested list of potential targets for robbery (!!):

Even though it is allowed to seize the property of individuals in dār al-harb, we suggest that Muslims avoid targeting citizens of countries where the public opinion is supportive of some of the Muslim causes. We therefore suggest that the following should be targeted:
- **government owned property.**
- **Banks.**
- **global corporations.**

- wealth belonging to disbelievers with known animosity towards Muslims.

It is odd that 'Awlakī, who has already deemed it permissible to kill civilians anyway, now for some reason rules that individual citizens or civilians not be targeted for theft?! This makes no sense whatsoever and is one of the factors that indicates 'Awlakī merely "approved" this "ruling" rather than penned it himself. Moreover, the frequency of typo errors also indicate that 'Awlakī may not have actually penned the "ruling" himself. With regards to "countries where the public opinion is supportive of some of the Muslim causes" – then again this is rather vague. Yet 'Awlakī has already stated in audio and video interviews that the populaces of the US and UK selected their respective governments and hence are to blame for what is occurring from these governments and thus also to be deemed as targets for attack. The logical step from this therefore is that this "ruling" is to be applied within the UK and US. Then 'Awlakī states:

> For Muslims who are associated with groups that work for jihād, we recommend that the decision to involve oneself in any illegal activity to acquire money be taken by the Amīr and the Shūrā of the Jamā'ah.

Who is this "Amīr" though? How is he to be chosen and what are his credentials? Then he says:

> It is recommended that Muslims who are not associated with groups that work for jihād and who acquire wealth from the disbelievers by illegal means to donate all that money to the cause of jihād unless if they are in need then the can take from it accordingly but not to exceed 80%, Islamic work cannot depend on volunteers.

In attempting to deflect criticisms of the "ruling" 'Awlakī presents some responses yet he merely responds to straw man arguments about "tarnishing the image of Islam" etc. The issue and challenge to 'Awlakī and his blind followers on this issue is clear: where is the documented, uncut, unedited statements from the Hanafī jurists wherein they permit Muslims stealing the wealth and property from Ahl ul-Harb within their lands which the Muslims have entered with documentation attesting to their covenant with Ahl ul-Harb? As we have seen, 'Awlakī, and those with him who helped prepare this void "ruling", has already blatantly left out a very important piece of information regarding "sariqah" [theft/stealing] so how can he be trusted in relaying anything else now when it comes to Islām?

Let's recap on some details which were mentioned prior but would be of benefit to relay them again here:

In Sahīh ul-Bukhārī the long hadīth of the treaty of Hudaybiyah mentions that al-Mughīrah ibn Shu'bah ﷺ knew some people during Jāhilliyah whom he killed them and took their money. Mugheerah later went to the Messenger of Allāh informing him that he wanted to be a Muslim and that he had with him the money from those people. What did the Messenger of Allāh ﷺ say to him? He said ﷺ:

((أما الإسلام فأقبل، وأما المال فلست منه في شيء))

As for your Islām, I accept it and as for the money then I have nothing to do with it.

Meaning: I accept your Islām but as for the money that you acquired from the people without right I have nothing to do with it. Also there was no jihād at that time so what do those people who make permissible robbing and stealing other people's money say?

Imām Abū Bakr Muhammad bin Ibrāhīm Ibn ul-Mundhir an-Naysābūrī (d. 318 AH) stated in *al-Awsat fi's-Sunan wa'l-Ijmā' wa'l-Ikhtilāf* that Imāms ash-Shāfi'ī, al-Awzā'ī and Ahmad viewed it impermissible for a Muslim to betray the people of Dār ul-Harb when the Muslim enters their land with a covenant of safety and security.[1] Al-Awzā'ī used the hadīth of al-Mughīrah as a proof for this view. Ibn ul-Mundhir stated:

> If a (Muslim) man enters Dār ul-Harb with a covenant of security then he is safe from them based on their agreement of security and they are also safe from him. Thus, it is not allowed for him to betray them, cause fear to them or kill them. If he takes anything from them he has to return it back to them and if he takes anything with him back to Dār ul-Islām he has to give it back. A Muslim should neither purchase such (taken) property nor destroy it because the wealth and property has a trust.[2]

Abū Yahyā Zakariyyah bin Muhammad al-Ansārī ash-Shāfi'ī (823-926 AH/1420-1520 CE) stated in *al-Asnā ul-Matālib*:

> The wealth of the people of Harb (war) are prohibited to whoever from us has granted them safety and security. If a Muslim enters their abodes with a covenant of safety and security and borrows anything from them, or steals anything from them, and then returns to our land he has to return what he took; as he cannot dishonour them if he entered their lands with an agreement of safety and security.

As-Sarkhasī ؒ states in his *Sharh* of *Kitāb as-Siyar al-Kabīr* of Muhammad bin al-Hasan ؒ:

> Muhammad said: "Chapter: what is classified as an Amān for those who enter Dār ul-Harb wa'l-Asrā and what is not an Amān: If a group of Muslims go to the gate-keepers of Ahl ul-

---

[1] Ibn ul-Mundhir however relays, as does Ibn ul-Munāsif in *Kitāb ul-Injād fī Abwāb il-Jihād*, that Imām Abū Hanīfah allowed betrayal, yet we have not come across this view within Hanafī fiqh books.

[2] Imām Abū Bakr Muhammad bin Ibrāheem Ibn ul-Mundhir an-Naysābūrī, *al-Awsat fī's-Sunan wa'l-Ijmā' wa'l-Ikhtilāf* (Riyadh, KSA: Dār Tayyibah, 1420 AH/1999 CE, ed. Dr Abū Hammād Sagheer Ahmad bin Muhammad Hanīf), vol.11, p.292.

Harb and say to them 'we are Messengers of the Khalīfah' and produce a document which resembles an official document from the Khalīfah, or if they do not even produce any documentation, then this is them deceiving the Mushrikeen. If Ahl ul-Harb say to this Muslim group: 'Enter' and they enter Dār ul-Harb - then it is not permissible for them to kill any Ahl ul-Harb or take any wealth from them so long as they are within their land."

(As-Sarkhasī says): Because what they (the Muslims) have manifested to them (Ahl ul-Harb) if it is true then they have an Amān from Ahl ul-Harb and Ahl ul-Harb also have an Amān from them so it is not permitted to dishonour them in anything. This is the ruling for Messengers (of the Khalīfah) if they enter their lands as we have explained.

CHAPTER 18

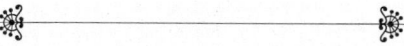

CONCLUSIONS REGARDING ANWAR AL-'AWLAKI

There are a number of points to conclude about al-'Awlakī:

1. When one listens to the earlier lectures and khutab of 'Awlakī it is immediately noticeable that he was Ikhwānī in his manhaj, appealing to the Middle-Class Muslim professionals in the US. Indeed, 'Awlakī during this stage sounded not much different to Hamza Yūsuf and in fact one could even be mistaken into thinking that it was actually Hamza Yūsuf speaking! 'Awlakī during this stage was nothing but a carbon-copy of Hamza Yūsuf but with more Ikhwānī sentiments within his speech.
Just one lecture which is evidence of this is the lecture entitled *Tolerance: The Hallmark of a Muslim* which can be heard here: http://www.halaltube.com/tolerance-a-hallmark-of-a-muslim.
Much of Awlakī's discourse was around themes such as **"we need to put aside our differences and unite for the greater good"** and similar Ikhwānī-type sound-bites, along with making reference to Sayyid Qutb and the likes. For example, 'Awlakī can be seen in this video from the PBS documentary *Muhammad: Legacy of a Prophet* (2003)[1] giving a *khutbah* at a MusAllāh in an American Congress building at Capitol Hill (!!!?). Hence, there has been a clear transition and methodological shift in the procedure of 'Awlakī from an

---

[1] Refer to 2:09- 3:27 of Part 5 of the documentary as it has been placed in *Youtube*.

Chapter 18

Ikhwānī to then full-blown Takfīrī, which in fact is the logical step for a dedicated Qutbī-Ikhwānī.

2. The reasons for this shift in the manhaj of al-'Awlakī was apparently due to a number of important factors: firstly, 'Awlakī was originally an adherent of the Ikhwānī-Qutbī methodology which not only has an outlined political program but is also based on whipping up emotions for populism and increasing audiences as part of **"collective work"**. Secondly, the injustices which were meted out to sections of the Muslim community in the US during the post-9/11 "war on terror" atmosphere served to inflame the already emotive outlook of 'Awlakī cultivated during his Qutbī phase which would soon after even manifest itself in support for the Khawārij of the era. Thirdly, at the same time 'Awlakī no doubt witnessed many of the youth being attracted to some of the Khawārij of the era and thus, in keeping with the Ikhwānī-Qutbī emphasis on populism and generating youthful audiences, apparently appears to have made a decision to also jump on this bandwagon and incline to the "hero" image, from whence in the US he rarely - if ever - discussed Jihād. Fourthly, 'Awlakī's Hijrah to Yemen gave him more freedom and autonomy to speak and antagonize America and continue his vendetta against the US. This vendetta was borne out of the events which occurred in the US during the post-9/11 environment and also on account of 'Awlakī being implicated and linked to individuals of interest to the US government. It is possible that at this point 'Awlakī reviewed his methodology to regain credibility after the likes of 'Abdullah Faisal al-Jamaykī in the late 1990s had actually condemned 'Awlakī for spreading **"CIA Islam"** and being a **"Murji'"**, **"spy"**, **"a plant of the government"**, **"an enemy of Islām"** etc. See Faisal's lecture here wherein he quotes from a *Jumu'ah Khutbah* given by al-'Awlakī

at Masjid ur-Ribāt in San Diego and condemns 'Awlakī for being a CIA agent[1] and after 25 minutes into the lecture Faisal asks the audience what should be done with 'Awlakī over one of his statements in the khutbah to which a person in the audience replies **"kill him brother, kill him"**. As a result therefore of a review of methodology primarily and of such aspersions cast by the likes of Faisal al-Jamaykī secondly, 'Awlakī then had to promote a radical image and this led 'Awlakī himself to go more extreme in order to bolster his credibility, thus jumping on the bandwagon of the Takfīrī mavericks and Khawārij bandits and ditching the wishy-washy Ikhwānī methodology. In this way then, 'Awlakī, already a well-known popular Ikhwānī speaker, shifted his methodology to that of the Takfīrī movement. More importantly, all of this also shows that al-'Awlakī was devoid of sound knowledge-based guidance and evidently took his knowledge via merely reading books, *Siyar* and *Tārīkh* and then subsequently cutting and pasting parts which helped to fashion his manhaj. This approach of "self-study" is borne out of the Ikhwānī approach of **"fiqh of priorities"** which is a euphemism for disregarding the patience which is demanding, yet highly necessary, in the da'wah to Tawhīd and the Sunnah.

3. Al-'Awlakī makes these statements within his lectures as if he is somehow qualified. His in-depth Islamic study however is negligible, yet he does have a B.S. in Civil Engineering from *Colorado State University*; an M.A. in Education Leadership from *San Diego State University* and was working on a Doctorate in Human Resource Development at *George Washington University*!!? So all of his education has not even been on anything to do with Islām! Indeed, he has mainly

---

[1] http://www.archive.org/details/CiaIslam-SheikhFaisalsTakfeerOfAnwarAwlaki.

studied within the US, hardly a huge endorsement of his Islamic educational background and study for him to be promoted to the level of a "Shaykh" and "Imām"?!

4. After we produced the original draft of this study in 2007, we found that some time after it was then presented that 'Awlakī has now obtained "ijāzāt" to relate: the Six Books of hadīth, *al-Muwatta', al-Adhkār, Bulūgh ul-Marām, Umdat ul-Ahkām, al-Minhāj, al-Waraqāt* and other books!? *Masha'Allāh.* So we are supposed to blindly follow him now? This reminds us of the 'ijāzah' game that some of the Sufis and 'Ash'arīs utilise in order to bolster their credibility. Therefore, the mere fact that 'Awlakī is now presenting his 'ijāzāt' then this is no way indicates that he has understanding of these texts let alone that the youth are supposed to refer to him for serious matters related to jihād, *takfīr* and the *hukkām*.

5. Al-'Awlakī has a clear problem with the issue of the 'Ahd ul-Amān (Covenant of Safety and Security) and especially where it has been discussed by the 'Ulamā in regards to this 'Ahd being extended to enemy forces. 'Awlakī denies this issue within his lectures on jihād even though it has been discussed clearly by the classical scholars in their books of jihād, such as Ibn ul-Munāsif and Ibn an-Nahhās. 'Awlakī's denial and lack of referring to this in detail shows that he has his own agenda and that the wrath that he has towards his own country, the US, has led him to disregard this issue. Furthermore, 'Awlakī himself is an American citizen which according to some of the Khawārij of the era is sufficient reason to kill a person! Indeed, some al-Qā'idah members have held that *anyone* who holds US citizenship is fair-game for murder. So it is as if al-'Awlakī has a kind of inferiority complex over his citizenship which has led

him to turn on the US even more in a kind of contorted notion of redemption.

6. Al-'Awlakī's ignorance in regards to the *da'wah* of Imām Muhammad ibn 'AbdulWahhāb ﷺ whereby 'Awlakī stated that Imām Muhammad ibn 'AbdulWahhāb gave his *bay'ah* to the Ottoman Khalīfah in Istanbul and that there are letters attesting to this wherein the Imām stated to the Ottoman Caliph: **"my bay'ah is to you"**? This demonstrates that: either 'Awlakī's verification of information is weak, or that he just made this up for his own agenda; in any case it demonstrates that he knows little about the *da'wah* of Imām Muhammad ibn 'AbdulWahhāb ﷺ.

7. Al-'Awlakī seems to forget about the well known Islamic principle that has been mentioned by scholars such as Ibn Taymiyyah and Ibn ul-Qayyim about abstaining from fighting during periods of weakness and inability, it is rather odd that 'Awlakī conveniently neglects all of this, which we have made reference to in this study.

8. Al-'Awlakī is not known for having participated in any "jihād" whatsoever and this is what has to be highlighted. For he calls to it and hypes up his audiences with it, yet the question has to be asked: upon which battlefield has he fought on and where has he fought? This is important as while the Salafis are accused by the Takfīrī movement of non-involvement in jihād, even though many Salafis have participated in a number of theatres of war which were endorsed by the 'Ulamā of Ahl us-Sunnah, these so-called "Jihādī Shaykhs" have practically done nothing! The sum total of their "contribution to jihād" is getting themselves arrested and imprisoned over their own foolish statements, or in the case of some, by gaining thrills by watching "Jihādī" videos! Hence, being thrown into prison

over one's own irresponsible and Khawārij statements, or one's links to the Khawārij of the era, or being imprisoned for plotting to intentionally kill or blow up innocent women and children in stores, planes or other civilian quarters, does not qualify as **"armed jihād in the Path of Allāh"**! No matter how hard these particular individuals may delude themselves into thinking they are the vanguard "Mujāhidīn" of the world.

And Allāh knows best. May He send *salah* and *salam* on His final Messenger Muhammad, his family and Companions.

Jamiah Media Publications

Previous Publications:

1. *Before Nicea*, by AbdurRahman Bowes and AbdulHaq al-Ashanti (2005).

2. *The Impact of Man-Made Laws in the Ruling of an Abode as Being One of Kufr or Islam,* by Shaykh Khālid al-'Anbarī (2006).

3. *Who's in for Iraq?* by Shaykh Abdul'Azīz bin Rayyis ar-Rayyis (2007).

4. *A Warning Against Extremism,* by Shaykh Sālih Āli Shaykh (2008).

5. *A Critical Study of the Multiple Identities and Disguises of 'al-Muhajiroun',* by Abu Ameenah AbdurRahman as-Salafī and AbdulHaq al-Ashantī (2009).

6. *The Noble Women Scholars of Hadīth*, by Shaykh Mashhūr Hasan Āl Salmān. (2010).

7. *The 'Aqīdah of Imām an-Nawawī,* by Shaykh Mashhūr Hasan Āl Salmān (2010).

8. *The Beautiful Advice to the Noble Salafīs of the West,* by Shaykh 'Abdul-Azīz ar-Rayyis (2010).

9. *Shirk According to the 4 Madhhabs*, by Shaykh, Dr Muhammad al-Khumayyis. (2011).

10. *What the Notables Have Narrated About not Going to the Rulers*, by Imām Jalāluddīn as-Suyūtī (2011).

11. *'Abdullah el-Faisal al-Jamayki' - A Critical Study of his Statements, Errors and Extremism in Takfīr*, by Abu Ameenah AbdurRahman as-Salafī and AbdulHaq al-Ashantī (2011).

12. *The Fiqh Madhhab of Ahl ul-Hadīth*, by Shaykh Mashhūr Hasan Āl Salmān (2011).

13. *7 Reasons Why Al-Muhajiroun Are Deviants*, by Abu Ameenah AbdurRahman Sloan and AbdulHaq al-Ashantī (2011).

14. *A Critique of the Methodology of Anwar al-'Awlaki and his Errors in the Fiqh of Jihad*, by Abu Ameenah AbdurRahman Sloan and AbdulHaq al-Ashantī (2011).